Sibshops

Workshops for Siblings of Children With Support Needs

THIRD EDITION

by

Don Meyer, M.Ed.
Founder, Sibling Support Project
Seattle, Washington

Emily Holl, LMSW
Director, Sibling Support Project
Bellevue, Washington

and

Patricia Vadasy, Ph.D.
Oregon Research Institute
Eugene, Oregon

·P A U L·H·
BROOKES
PUBLISHING C⁰ ®

Baltimore • London • Sydney

Paul H. Brookes Publishing Co.
Post Office Box 10624
Baltimore, Maryland 21285-0624
USA

www.brookespublishing.com

Typeset by Absolute Service, Inc., Towson, Maryland.
Manufactured in the United States of America by
Integrated Books International, Inc., Dulles, Virginia.

The illustrations appearing inside this book are the original work of Cary Pillo Lassen.

Library of Congress Cataloging-in-Publication Data

Names: Meyer, Donald J. (Donald Joseph), 1951- | Holl, Emily, author. |
  Vadasy, Patricia F., author.
Title: Sibshops : workshops for siblings of children with support needs /
  by Don Meyer, M.ED., Founder, Sibling Support Project, Seattle,
  Washington, Emily Holl, Director, Sibling Support Project, Bellevue,
  Washington, and Patricia Vadasy, Ph.D., Oregon Research Institute,
  Eugene, Oregon.
Description: Third edition. | Baltimore, Maryland : Paul H. Brookes
  Publishing Co., Inc., [2024] | Includes bibliographical references and
  index.
Identifiers: LCCN 2023043029 (print) | LCCN 2023043030 (ebook) | ISBN
  9781681255965 (paperback) | ISBN 9781681255989 (epub) | ISBN
  9781681255972 (adobe pdf)
Subjects: LCSH: Children with disabilities--Family relationships. |
  Children with disabilities--Home care. | Siblings. | BISAC: FAMILY &
  RELATIONSHIPS / Siblings | FAMILY & RELATIONSHIPS / Children with
  Special Needs
Classification: LCC HV888 .M495 2024 (print) | LCC HV888 (ebook) | DDC
  649/.151--dc23/eng/20231025
LC record available at https://lccn.loc.gov/2023043029
LC ebook record available at https://lccn.loc.gov/2023043030

British Library Cataloguing in Publication data are available from the British Library.

2027   2026   2025   2024   2023

10   9   8   7   6   5   4   3   2   1

Contents

About the Downloads

Purchasers of this book may download, print, and/or photocopy the forms, worksheets, and activities for professional and/or educational use.

To access the materials that come with this book:

1. Go to the Brookes Download Hub: http://downloads.brookespublishing.com

2. Register to create an account (or log in with an existing account).

3. Filter or search for the book title *Sibshops, Third Edition*.

About the Authors

Don Meyer, M.Ed., Founder, Sibling Support Project; Creator, Sibshops

Don Meyer is the founder of the Sibling Support Project and creator of Sibshops. He created the Sibling Support Project, a Washington State–based international program dedicated to the lifelong concerns of brothers and sisters of people with health, developmental, and mental health concerns. Don was the director of the Sibling Support Project from 1990 to 2019 and has conducted workshops on sibling issues and trainings on the Sibshop model in all 50 states and in 11 countries. He is the editor of *The Sibling Slam Book: What It's Really Like to Have a Brother or Sister With Special Needs* (Woodbine House, 2005), *Views From Our Shoes: Growing Up With a Brother or Sister With Special Needs* (Woodbine House, 1997), and *Uncommon Fathers: Reflections on Raising a Child With a Disability* (Woodbine House, 1995). With Patricia Vadasy, Don wrote *Living With a Brother or Sister With Special Needs* (University of Washington Press, 1996). With Emily Holl, he co-edited *The Sibling Survival Guide: Indispensable Information for Brothers and Sisters of Adults With Disabilities* (Woodbine House, 2014).

Don's work has been featured on ABC News and National Public Radio and in *Newsweek, The New York Times,* and *The Washington Post.* He is married to Terry DeLeonardis, a special education preschool teacher and consultant. They have four children and two grandchildren.

Emily Holl, MFA, LMSW, Director, Sibling Support Project

Emily Holl is the director of the Sibling Support Project at Kindering, the first national program dedicated to the lifelong and ever-changing concerns of millions of siblings of people with developmental and health concerns. Emily is a sibling, social worker, author, and trainer who has provided workshops and groups for siblings and families, and presented extensively on sibling issues. She has conducted and published sibling research. A board member of the national Sibling Leadership Network, Emily has written about her experiences in blogs, magazines, and books such as *Thicker Than Water* (Woodbine House, 2009). She was a co-editor of *The Sibling Survival Guide: Indispensable Information for Adult Brothers and Sisters of People With Disabilities,* published by Woodbine House in 2014. Emily earned a bachelor of arts degree from the University of Massachusetts, a master of fine arts degree from Columbia University, and a master of social work degree from Hunter College at the City University of New York. Emily and her family reside near Seattle, Washington.

Patricia Vadasy, Ph.D., Senior Research Scientist, Oregon Research Institute, Influents Innovations

Patricia Vadasy is a senior research scientist at Oregon Research and Influents Innovations in Eugene, Oregon, where she conducts research on early reading instruction. She is most interested in research to help children at risk for reading disabilities and children who are dual language learners. Patricia and her colleagues have developed programs that paraeducator tutors can effectively use to supplement instruction for beginning readers. Patricia also works with colleagues at Influents Innovations in Eugene to translate educational research findings into technology-based interventions for underserved students and families.

Foreword

It was 1992. Our son was 5 months old and not hitting the typical developmental milestones. We took him for evaluation and testing. Hearing the doctor say that part of his brain was missing and that his chromosomes were abnormal was devastating. My husband and I were told that he may never walk, talk, or be able to learn. Further, only 10 other cases in the world were similar to his genetic makeup, so his future would be unclear. The doctors had no answers, no advice.

As a young mom and a family educator, I knew this news would impact our family, especially his 3-year-old sister as she grew up. I felt unprepared as a parent, yet I expected that there must be research, information, and perhaps programs to help parents and siblings as they grow up with children with disabilities. After all, there had to be other families who had faced this before. There had to be information to help me, as a parent, navigate this new world of disability and family dynamics and answer my questions about what to tell my daughter and how to anticipate her needs.

I found all kinds of books and articles, even programs and organizations, that focused on the needs of *parents* raising a child with disabilities. But I searched and searched to find anything that talked about *siblings*. There were a few mentions of siblings here and there, but I was looking for solid information, research, and practical advice to help my very young daughter immediately and as she grew. I was looking for insight into her experiences and something that would help me prepare her for challenges and enable her to find joy with her brother, regardless of how his future would play out.

One evening, my husband and I were browsing in a bookstore, something we often did on "date nights." We'd get a babysitter and head to Barnes and Noble to spend a couple peaceful hours looking at books and reading home improvement magazines for ideas and to dream a little. Sometimes we made a purchase, but more often, we didn't. It was 1994, our son was 2, and our daughter was 5. I remember thinking that I should look through the small "Special Needs" bookshelf again, as I had done so many times before, to see if there was anything new that could help me with my questions regarding how to support my daughter.

And this time, there it was, right in the middle of the shelf of familiar book titles about disabilities: a book cover of colorful artwork with the words *Sibshops: Workshops for Siblings of Children with Special Needs* by Don Meyer and Pat Vadasy. I'll never forget grabbing it and immediately sitting down on the floor and reading as fast as I could. After a couple of hours, my husband said it was time to go. This time, I was making a purchase that would change not only the lives of me and my daughter, but the lives of siblings all over the state of Wisconsin and beyond.

Decades later, I enjoy a wonderful relationship with my daughter. We regularly discuss her concerns as a sibling, and I witness her loving relationship with her brother. Because of that evening in Barnes and Noble, I've had the privilege of introducing

Sibshops to thousands of children in Wisconsin and creating opportunities for siblings of all ages to discuss their unique joys and concerns with others who truly understand. I wish you much luck as you reach out to the young sibs in your community!

Harriet Redman, M.S.Ed., *is the founder and retired executive director of WisconSibs, a nonprofit organization dedicated to children and adults who have siblings with disabilities. She has been a classroom teacher, a family program developer, a marketing director for a Fortune 500 company, and a nonprofit organization manager. In 2021, Harriet became the first recipient of the Don Meyer Award from the Sibling Leadership Network for her outstanding contributions to sibling support throughout her career. She has an adult son with developmental disabilities whose sister is her inspiration and most honest critic.*

Preface

The fact that you are holding this book suggests that you already have an interest in the well-being of siblings of children with health, mental health, and developmental needs. Perhaps you are a parent of a child with support needs who wants to create peer support and educational programs for siblings in your community. Or, maybe you are an adult sib who wishes that there had been programs like Sibshops when you were younger and would like to share your experiences as a Sibshop facilitator. Or, perhaps you are a human services professional who realizes that there is much more to serving families of children with support needs than just meeting with parents. Congratulations! This book is for you.

It is our hope that this book will be different from other books you have read. Our goals for Sibshops are as follows:

1. To increase the number of programs, services, and considerations for siblings of individuals with health, mental health, and developmental needs. With this book, we hope to give you the rationale, tools, inspiration, permission, and encouragement to make community-based programs for siblings as available as Parent-to-Parent programs for parents of children with support needs. As important as these programs are, we know that they are not enough. We hope to provide you with information that will empower you to challenge current family support practices to expand to include siblings. We seek fundamental change in the way schools, disability service providers, and other community-based organizations "do business" with respect to brothers and sisters to ensure that siblings' issues are addressed.

2. To increase the reader's understanding of specific issues experienced by siblings of individuals with support needs. To be an effective Sibshop facilitator, and a resource for others in your community who are interested in learning about and supporting siblings, you will need to be conversant about sibs' lifelong and ever-changing issues. The first part of the book provides an overview of the unique concerns and opportunities experienced by siblings as reported in the clinical and research literature and by siblings themselves.

3. To provide specific information for local agencies and parent groups to create programs for siblings of individuals with support needs. The second part of this book is devoted to the Sibshop model, a lively peer support, educational, and recreational program for school-age brothers and sisters. In this section, we present activities that can be adapted for siblings of children with different disabilities and illnesses, as well as for different ages.

Throughout this book, we have tried to write in a style that is accessible and even enjoyable to read. We know that most people who wish to create services and programs for brothers and sisters are not academicians. We also know that most readers, even academicians, seem to enjoy and learn more from books that do not appear to be designed to induce sleep. And we know that there is much good news to share about siblings of people with support needs.

We have also been mindful of the importance of language, especially when it comes to describing people and the spectrum of ability they experience. Throughout the following pages, you will see the term *support needs* as shorthand for a wide array of developmental, health, and mental health needs. We acknowledge that this is an imperfect term and agree with advocates with and without disabilities who say that all human beings have needs that are met in unique ways. In this book, you will also see person-first language (e.g., *person with a disability*). We recognize and respect that some people prefer identity-first language (e.g., *disabled*). We also understand that some people prefer the more gender-neutral term *sibling* to *brother* and *sister*. Whenever possible, we defer to the person to decide what terminology they prefer. Our intent is to present the information that follows with the grace, vitality, respect, and insight we frequently see in siblings of people with support needs.

We hope you will let us know if we have accomplished our goals.

Acknowledgments

We are fortunate to have many friends who share our commitment to providing services for siblings of people with support needs. Many of the people listed here have pioneered programs for siblings in their communities; others have provided us with support, advice, and encouragement over the years and as we prepared this volume. Although their contributions are varied, each shares the belief that brothers and sisters deserve our time, effort, and consideration. We are grateful to them all: Yasuko Arima, Katie Arnold, Bobbi Beck, Lorena Beitia, Tamara Besser, Hanna Bjornsdottir, Meghan Burke, Rosanne Carter, Raphielle Chynoweth, Tara Conley, Terry DeLeonardis, Tom Fish, Cassandra Flores, María Girado, Carolyn Graff, Anne Guthrie, Nora Fox Handler, Donna Heim, Tom Holl, Traci Hopper, Amanda Johnson, Jessica Kruger, Mo Langley, Michelle Ellison McDaniel, Hayley Menges, Nancy Micca, Beth Mix, Suzanne Muench, Jessica Nix, Michelle O'Connor-Teklinski, Debbie Parkman, Tina Prochaska, Harriet Redman, Carol Robbins, Margaret Roberts, Diana Rovetti, Suzanne Salmo, Barbara Sapharas, Greg Schell, Ursala Schwenn, Sheila Swann-Guerrero, Maryjane Westra, and Christiana Yablonowski.

We would also like to thank Mimi Siegel, Lisa Greenwald, and the staff of Kindering, the Sibling Support Project's parent organization. Having offered Sibshops and programs for fathers of children with support needs for more than 20 years, the staff of the Kindering Center have been pioneers in providing family-centered services that acknowledge the contributions of all family members.

Finally, a special acknowledgment is reserved for the George A. and Marion M. Wilson Foundation and in loving memory of Mrs. Marion "Mickey" Wilson. Without the Wilson family's commitment to our work, you would not be holding this book and there would be far, far fewer Sibshops worldwide.

Sibshop facilitators are amazing people.

*They invariably offer Sibshops in addition to a million other things
they are supposed to be doing for their "day jobs."*

*They somehow find time in their busy schedules and give up weekends and evenings
because they care deeply about young siblings and their concerns.*

It is with gratitude that we dedicate this book to them.

1

What Are Sibshops?

For the adults who plan them and the agencies that sponsor them, Sibshops[SM] are best described as opportunities for siblings of children with health, mental health, and developmental needs to obtain peer support and education within a recreational context. They can reflect an agency's commitment to the well-being of the family member most likely to have the longest-lasting relationship with the person who has support needs.

However, for the young people who attend them and the energetic people who run them, Sibshops are better described as *events*. Sibshops are designed to provide siblings with opportunities for peer support. Because Sibshops are intended for school-age children, peer support is provided within a recreational context that emphasizes kids' perspectives.

Sibshops are lively, pedal-to-the-metal celebrations of the many contributions made by siblings of kids with support needs. Sibshops acknowledge that being the sibling of a person with support needs is a good thing for some, a not-so-good thing for others, and, for many, something in between. Sibshops reflect a belief that siblings have much to offer one another—if they are given a chance. The Sibshop model intersperses information and discussion activities with games (designed to be unique, upbeat, and appealing to a wide ability range), cooking and craft activities, and special guests who may teach participants how to mime, how to juggle, or, in the case of one guest artist who has cerebral palsy, how to paint by holding a toothbrush in your mouth. Sibshops are as fun and rewarding for the people who host them as they are for the participants.

Sibshops are not therapy, group or otherwise, although their effect may be therapeutic for some children. Sibshops acknowledge that most siblings of people with support needs, like their parents, are doing well despite the challenges posed by a family member's illness or disability. Consequently, although Sibshop facilitators always keep an eye open for participants who may need additional services, the Sibshop model takes a wellness approach that encourages children to recognize and build on their skills, talents, and strengths.

WHO ATTENDS SIBSHOPS?

Originally developed for 8- to 13-year-old siblings of children with developmental disabilities, the Sibshop model is easily adapted for slightly younger sibs and teens. It has been adapted for siblings of children with other disabilities and illnesses, including cancer and other health impairments, hearing loss, and mental health concerns. It has even been adapted for children of parents who have health, mental health, or developmental concerns. Children who attend Sibshops come from diverse backgrounds including suburban communities (e.g., Bellevue, Washington; Northbrook, Illinois), urban communities (e.g., New York City, St. Louis, Tokyo), rural areas (e.g., Wyoming, Wisconsin), and areas with unique cultural heritages (e.g., Alaska, Hawaii, South Central Los Angeles).

How Sibshops Address Different Needs

At Sibshops, kids are encouraged to talk about the good and not-so-good parts of being a sibling. We recognize that no two sibling experiences are exactly alike and that some siblings struggle more than others. We know there are siblings who have concerns for their physical and/or emotional safety for a variety of reasons, including challenging or even violent behaviors of their siblings with disabilities. Not every sibling has experienced trauma, but we believe that the basic principles of trauma-informed practices, as described by the U.S. Substance Abuse and Mental Health Services Administration, reflect the values of Sibshops: safety; trustworthiness and transparency; peer support; collaboration and mutuality; empowerment, voice, and choice; and recognizing cultural, historical, and gender issues. Applying these principles can benefit all Sibshop participants and facilitators alike (see Appendix F).

Creating Environments of Belonging

Across the United States and in countries around the world, Sibshops bring together young siblings and facilitators from a diverse array of cultural, ethnic, gender, racial, religious, and other identities. Because they bring all of these identities to Sibshops, we are committed to ensuring that Sibshops are inclusive, equitable spaces in which all participants and facilitators feel a genuine sense of belonging. We are dedicated to eradicating racial and other oppressive barriers to create a positive, safe, supportive, and comfortable Sibshop environment in which all children and adults can thrive in ways that are helpful and meaningful to them.

WHO SPONSORS SIBSHOPS?

Any agency serving families of children with support needs can sponsor a Sibshop, provided it can offer financial support, properly staff the program, and attract sufficient numbers of participants. We strongly recommend, however, that agencies consider working together to cosponsor a local Sibshop for all the siblings in a given community. (We discuss this important topic in greater detail in Chapter 5.) Among the organizations collaborating to host Sibshops in their communities are autism societies, chapters of The Arc, United Cerebral Palsy affiliates, children's hospitals, developmental disabilities councils, early intervention programs, Parent-to-Parent programs, parks and recreation programs, Ronald McDonald Houses, school districts, schools for the Deaf, and University Centers on Disabilities. We have found that Sibshops are well within the reach and abilities of most communities. They are not expensive to run and logistically are no more difficult to coordinate than other community-based programs for children, such as Scouts or Camp Fire USA.

WHO RUNS SIBSHOPS?

We believe that Sibshops are best facilitated by a team that includes service providers (e.g., social workers; special education teachers; physical, occupational, and speech therapists; nurses; child life specialists) and adult siblings of people with support needs. At the very least, the team of facilitators will need to be knowledgeable about the disability or illness

represented, possess a sense of humor and play, enjoy the company of children, and respect the young participants' expertise on the topic of life with a sibling with support needs. We discuss qualifications for Sibshop facilitators in Chapter 5.

Planning a Sibshops Experience

Since the first Sibshop launched in 1982, organizations across the United States and around the world have adapted the model to meet the needs of siblings in their local areas. Over the years, these Sibshops have grown into a community of dedicated facilitators and best practices that may serve as helpful guidelines for new Sibshops.

Group Size

Sibshops have been held for as few as five children and as many as 45. Smaller groups can provide fun and meaningful experiences for siblings, and larger groups can be unforgettable events for the kids who attend, as long as there is an adequate number of facilitators. We recommend a group size of about 12 children, with at least two facilitators. A group of this size is manageable for facilitators, and there are enough kids to increase chances that participants will connect with someone who laughs at the same jokes or enjoys the same sports or video games.

Scheduling

Sibshops are often held on or near weekends; for example, Fridays from 4:30 to 7:30 p.m., or Saturdays from 10:00 a.m. until 1:00 or 2:00 p.m. For in-person Sibshops, this allows ample time for games, discussion, and information activities and for making and eating lunch. For online Sibshops, which are typically 60–90 minutes in duration, weekdays may be an easier option. Of course, there is no day and time that will work perfectly for every family. We suggest surveying the families you wish to support to find a day and time that works for most. Each community will need to determine the best day and length for its Sibshop, as discussed further in Chapter 5.

When determining the frequency of Sibshops events, it is important to consider the needs and resources of the community. Sibshops may be offered as frequently as weekly (as with a 1.5-hour after-school program) or as infrequently as yearly (as with an all-day Sibshop that is a part of an annual conference for families from around a state or the nation). Generally, however, Sibshops are presented monthly or bimonthly. Set a schedule that is manageable for facilitators and that makes Sibshops feel like special occasions for participants.

Sibshops may also be offered like a class—that is, five Sibshops meeting once a month with one registration. Offering Sibshops this way can provide a stable group that can form an identity during the months the participants are together. It can be difficult, however, for some participants and families to commit to a series of dates because of conflicts with other activities. More often, Sibshops are offered in a club format with monthly or bimonthly meetings. This format offers families and participants greater flexibility, but participants may vary somewhat from Sibshop to Sibshop. We discuss these and other considerations in Chapter 5.

Registering a Sibshop

To ensure that when parents send their children to a Sibshop, they are sending them to a program that is true to the spirit and goals of the Sibshop model, sibling programs wishing to call themselves "Sibshops" and to use the Sibshop logo must register their program. We describe this straightforward registration process in the Sibshop Standards of Practice (Appendix A).

THE GOALS OF THE SIBSHOP MODEL

 Goal 1: Peer Support in a Recreation Context

Sibshops provide siblings of children with support needs an opportunity to meet other siblings in a relaxed, recreational setting.

The chance to meet other siblings in a casual atmosphere with interactive recreational activities offers several benefits for participants. First, it can help reduce a sibling's sense of isolation. Participants quickly learn that other siblings experience similar joys and challenges. Second, the casual atmosphere and recreational activities promote informal sharing and friendships among participants. Friendships created during Sibshops and continued outside the program offer siblings ongoing sources of validation and support. Third, the recreational aspect of Sibshops makes the events enjoyable to attend. Children who perceive Sibshops as one more thing they have to do because of their sibling may find it hard to be receptive to the information and discussion presented in the workshop. Furthermore, when a workshop does not offer anything that is personally satisfying for a participant, they are unlikely to attend in the future. Recreational activities and the importance of play during Sibshops are discussed further in Chapter 9.

 Goal 2: Healthy Discourse

Sibshops provide siblings with opportunities to discuss common joys and concerns with other siblings of children with support needs.

At Sibshops, participants share stories, experiences, and knowing laughs with peers who truly understand the ups and downs of life with a sibling who has support needs. This opportunity allows participants to learn that they are not alone in their experiences and their often-ambivalent feelings.

 Goal 3: Resilience and Problem Solving

Sibshops provide siblings with an opportunity to learn how others handle situations commonly experienced by siblings of children with support needs.

Siblings of children with health and developmental needs routinely face situations that are not experienced by other children. Defending a sibling from name-calling, responding to questions from friends or strangers, and resenting the time and attention required by the sibling with support needs are only a few of the problems siblings may experience. At Sibshops, participants learn how others handle difficult situations. This experience can offer a sibling a broad array of tried-and-true solutions from which to choose. Activities that promote discussion among sibling participants are presented in Chapter 8.

Goal 4: Knowledge

Sibshops provide siblings with an opportunity to learn more about the implications of their siblings' support needs.

As noted previously, brothers and sisters need information in order to answer their own questions about their siblings' support needs as well as the questions posed by friends, classmates, and strangers. Sibshops offer participants opportunities to learn about the effect that a sibling's illness or disability may have on their life, schooling, and future. We discuss informational Sibshop activities in Chapter 10.

Goal 5: Educating Parents and Providers About Siblings' Concerns

Sibshops provide parents and other professionals with opportunities to learn more about the concerns frequently experienced by siblings of people with support needs.

Because parents and services providers may be unaware of the wide range of sibling concerns, some Sibshop activities attempt to help adults better understand "life as a sib." One activity allows parents and professionals to meet with a panel of young adult and adult siblings to learn about the special joys and challenges of growing up with a sibling with disabilities. Parents learn about what the panelists appreciated in their parents' treatment of the children in their family and also what they wish their parents had done differently. We discuss opportunities for parents and professionals further in Chapter 11.

To advocate effectively for increased services for siblings of people with support needs, it is critical to learn more about issues affecting their lives. The chapters that follow provide an overview of the unique concerns and opportunities experienced by brothers and sisters of people with health and developmental needs.

2

Unique Concerns

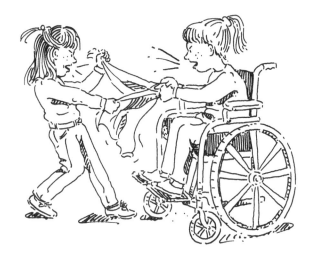

 "We are not heroes any more than we are victims or sufferers. I am just a person, with a brother whose condition makes an added complication in my life. And that, like everything else in life, has both its pluses and minuses." (Pat, in Remsberg, 1989, p. 3)

Is there a relationship more ambivalent than the relationship between siblings? In families with only typically developing siblings, brothers and sisters fight and argue and laugh and hug, often within the same hour. A 5-year-old's name for her 8-year-old brother may be "dummyhead" one minute and "buddy" the next.

 "Having an autistic sibling is basically normal to me. To me, it just feels normal. It's not different to anyone else that I've seen. Once you've been around him for a long time, it's kind of hard to see the difference between having a normal brother and autistic child . . . We make our way in life. It's a pretty simple but good way of life, basically." (Terry, in Gorjy et al., 2017, p. 6)

On the other hand, siblings also experience the traumatic impact that a brother or sister's disability has had on their family.

 "I saw a new psychiatrist a few weeks ago and she asked the standard 'history of abuse, neglect, trauma?' to which I always say, 'no.' After explaining how my family has changed so much in the past few years and how bad things are due to my brother's behaviors, she said, 'You said you've never experienced trauma, but what you're describing with your brother was trauma.' I never realized that, and it was kind of a good feeling to be told that because it felt like a validation of sorts." (D. C., personal communication, 2017)

Siblings, because of their shared experiences, know one another in ways no one else ever will. Being a sibling, someone once told us, is like living in the nude, psychologically. Sisters and brothers know the chinks in each other's armor all too well. Both younger siblings and older siblings alike can be brutal and loving. As another sister told us, "I can always count on my sister to give me an unvarnished view of how I am leading my life. Yet she will be the first to defend me if she feels I am being attacked by someone else."

"There are also other potential outcomes of being a sibling to a brother or sister with disabilities. Some are beneficial, others less so. In many cases, outcomes can be beneficial or challenging at specific times in one's life, or for different siblings." (Hodapp et al., 2017, p. 165)

Given that most brothers and sisters harbor a wide range of feelings toward their siblings, it is not at all unusual to learn that siblings of people with support needs also experience ambivalent feelings about their brothers and sisters (Angell et al., 2012). After all, a relationship in which one sibling has a disability or illness is still a sibling relationship. Adding a support need to the equation appears to enhance the inherent ambivalence for both siblings.

 "Sibling relationships are a crucial axis in the family, a subsystem of their own. Most children demonstrate an impressive capacity for concern about the siblings, although ambivalence intensifies under the stress of illness." (Sourkes, 1995, p. 92)

Although they may be similar, there are important differences when one of the siblings is diagnosed with a health or developmental need. In this chapter, we review the unique concerns that siblings of people with support needs may experience. This overview is based on clinical and research literature and what we have learned working with siblings and parents since 1982. Whenever possible, we let siblings speak for themselves. One unique and paramount concern not covered in this chapter is siblings' lifelong and ever-changing need for information. Chapter 3 includes an extensive discussion of siblings' informational needs. Chapter 4 reviews the equally important but less-reported unique opportunities recounted by siblings of people with support needs.

It is difficult to generalize about siblings who have brothers and sisters with support needs. After all, having a sibling with a disability or illness is only one aspect of their lives. Factors that have nothing to do with disabilities will influence their personalities. And many disability-related variables will make each sibling's experience unique; for example, age, gender, type and severity of the disability, responses of family members, services and supports available, financial resources, and personal and cultural beliefs (Black et al., 2017; Giallo & Gavidia-Payne, 2006; Seltzer et al., 1997; Vermaes et al., 2012; Williams, 1997). Disabilities and illnesses affect people from all walks of life, and siblings will experience these conditions in innumerable ways. If we listen to siblings long enough, however, we hear recurring themes. Here, then, is a discussion of these themes. To be sure, no one sibling will experience all of the concerns discussed in the following sections, but all will share some of them.

OVERIDENTIFICATION

 "Yes, I worry a lot. I worry that my leg will get cut off also. I think about it and then I wake up and I go into the kitchen. All the time I worry about it." (10-year-old brother of a sibling with osteogenic sarcoma, in Sourkes, 1990, p. 6)

- A 4-year-old boy worries that he might catch his sister's cerebral palsy and lose his ability to walk.

- Because her older brother and sister have seizures, a 10-year-old girl wonders when hers will begin.

- Unable to see the blackboard clearly, an 8-year-old boy wonders whether he will lose his vision the way his brother did.

- After doing poorly on a spelling test, a 9-year-old girl thinks that perhaps her brother isn't the only one in the family with a learning disability.

- When her social life is not going the way she would like, a 14-year-old girl is concerned that her twin brother is not the only family member who has autism.

- On the eve of his 16th birthday, a boy worries that he, too, will start showing signs of schizophrenia, just as his sister did soon after her 16th birthday.

Overidentification occurs when a sibling wonders whether they share—or will share—a sibling's problem or fate. Frequently (but not always) irrational, these fears can be very real, especially to young children, who often indulge in "magical thinking" and who have an immature concept of contagion. "Well, we all got strep throat," a sibling may wonder. "Why shouldn't we all catch cancer?" Although younger children are more open about fears of catching a disease or acquiring a disability, Sourkes (1990) doubted that there are many siblings who have not worried about acquiring their sibling's support needs.

Severity appears to influence overidentification. Grossman's 1972 study of college-age siblings of people with disabilities suggested that overidentification is more likely to occur when the disability is mild, and especially if it is "invisible." The logic is apparent: Jennifer's sister has been diagnosed as having epilepsy, an invisible disability. Michelle's sister was diagnosed as having a genetic disorder that causes her to look and act differently from other family members. Because Jennifer's sister is like her in so many ways, Jennifer may be more likely to worry that she, too, has epilepsy.

The risk of overidentification is one of the many reasons that brothers and sisters need accurate information about their siblings' disabilities and illnesses. Children are often excellent observers, but they are not always the best interpreters. Information that may be obvious to adults may not be obvious to children, and lack of information is related to siblings' fear and worry (Deavin et al., 2018). For instance, younger children need to know that they cannot "catch" their sibling's disability. One third of the siblings interviewed by Koocher and O'Malley (1981) said that they worried about getting cancer themselves. Compounding this is the difficulty families often have communicating effectively about a child's disability or illness and the effects it can have on the family (Faux, 1993; Opperman & Alant, 2003; Williams, 1997).

Siblings who are at higher risk for acquiring a disability or illness need to know what their chances are. Usually, their risk is much lower than they might imagine. For instance, siblings who have seen their previously healthy siblings develop serious mental illnesses frequently worry that they also will succumb to the illness, although their chances are only 1 in 10 (compared with 1 in 100 in the general population) and negligible after age 30 (Dickens, 1991). Most siblings appreciate straight talk about their siblings' support needs and, as we will learn later, benefit from parents' and professionals' efforts to provide information proactively.

EMBARRASSMENT

 "My friends and I were watching movies one night and all of a sudden my brother came bolting downstairs with nothing on! I was so embarrassed. My friends are, like, 'Does he do that often?'" (Kathryn C., 14, in Meyer, 2005, p. 86)

 "Embarrassed me? I don't know where to begin. My brother told my friend about a surprise party we were throwing her. He has said VERY inappropriate things to my friends—more times than I can count. He has fully combusted and acted out in front of my friends a million times. He is like a big ball of embarrassment on legs." (Miri L., 16, in Meyer, 2005, p. 86)

A sibling with a disability or illness can be a source of embarrassment for typically developing brothers and sisters. They may get embarrassed by the unwanted attention the child, and consequently the family, receives when the child with support needs has behavior problems:

 "At church, the pastor began to pray. In the middle of the prayer, David started to play his favorite tune—'Happy Birthday'—on the kazoo! (He must have sneaked it in with him!) Everybody laughed! I felt so embarrassed. I was glad when it was time for Sunday school and David went off for a walk with one of his helpers." (Angela, 10, in Burslem, 1991, p. 13)

Differences in appearances can also make siblings feel overly conspicuous:

 "As Red got older, people would stare at him and speak under their breath, as if my brother was some kind of side show. To this day, people still do that." (A. Jones, personal communication, 1991)

In some instances, siblings may be acutely sensitive about the appearance and behavior of their siblings, lest others—peers, especially—conclude that they share their brothers' and sisters' support needs.

 "I was certain that everyone was looking at my brother with his obvious disability and wondering what was wrong with the rest of us." (Marge, in Helsel et al., 1978, p. 110)

In these instances, embarrassment will be more common when the problems are mild or invisible. Visible disabilities, siblings tell us, at least provide an apparent reason for unusual behavior. A brother with a mild learning disability who is given to asking strangers rude questions can be more embarrassing than a sister who uses a wheelchair and makes occasional noises.

 "Even though I am 49 years old, my brother Marty still occasionally embarrasses me. His disability is less obvious than my other two disabled brothers, and I think this has something to do with it. Marty talks very loud, is unkempt, and appears just plain odd to most people. I know I shouldn't feel embarrassed, but I can't seem to help myself." (N. H., personal communication, 2005)

 "My sister can be wildly inappropriate when talking. Everyone laughs it off, but I feel like they're laughing at her and I get annoyed. Or when she has a meltdown and they look at us kind of pitying like or worse when they try to help. Just the thought of it makes me cringe." (S. B., personal communication, 2017)

Siblings may experience embarrassment and unwanted attention when they are asked questions about their brothers' and sisters' support needs. These questions can come from friends, classmates, and even strangers:

 "When I finally found out what happened, it was so hard to talk about it, especially when someone says, 'Hey, what's wrong with your sister? Why is she in a wheelchair?'

People can be such jerks sometimes! They just don't understand!!" (Joanne, 16, in Murray & Jampolsky, 1982, p. 36)

Developing strategies to spare a typically developing child embarrassment first requires analyzing the cause of the embarrassment. Is it something the family can change, such as not using an age-inappropriate bib on a sibling who drools? Is it something like the sibling singing during the church sermon that can be changed with a behavior program? If changeable, then the family can work toward decreasing the sibling's embarrassment and improving the life of the person with support needs at the same time.

It is just as likely, however, that the source of embarrassment is something about which little can be done. In these instances, there are two strategies parents may wish to consider. First, they should remember that most children go through stages when they are easily embarrassed, and these experiences may be unavoidable. Younger adolescents have a particularly strong need to conform. It can make a teenager miserable to be seen with her parents, much less a sister who looks and acts differently.

 "Being in a public place, as a teenager, with my sister who was saying, doing, and/or wearing something inappropriate would have had to have been the worst!" (Seltzer & Krauss, 2002)

During this time of raging conformity, the best strategy may be to give the typically developing child "space"—psychological and otherwise—and model the resilience and sense of humor parents hope their children will someday have. Given permission to walk on the other side of the shopping mall or attend a different church service, most siblings will eventually reintegrate their brother or sister according to their own agendas:

 "As time moved on, I pretended I wasn't embarrassed by Jennifer. But I really was when friends were around. By the time I was 14 or 15, though, I realized my good friends loved her too. I hadn't realized that before. I hadn't given her a chance." (Cassie, 19, in Binkard et al., 1987, p. 16)

 "When I was 10 and 11, I hated going to the mall because she'd scream and try to sit down and just make everyone stare at us. She's completely different now and I hate how I used to be so embarrassed by her doing that. It doesn't even bother me now if she gets a little upset when out shopping. If people are that bored with themselves that they have to stare, let them." (Sarah S., 17, in Meyer, 2005, p. 87)

A second strategy is to acknowledge the embarrassment. Featherstone (1980) wrote that parents can help their children by allowing them some control over situations. One mother told us, "When my son comes up to me and says, 'Mom, I get so embarrassed when she does that!' I tell him, 'Yeah, I really get embarrassed when she does that too!'"

Denying siblings "permission" to be embarrassed by their sibling (as in "He's your brother; you shouldn't be embarrassed by him!") is more likely to evoke feelings of guilt and resentment than to reduce embarrassment. It also will send a message that children cannot bring their concerns to their parents. Acknowledging that a sibling with support needs is sometimes difficult to live with not only reflects reality (after all, what sibling—support needs or not—is always easy to live with?), but it also sends a message that brothers and sisters can feel free to talk about their feelings with their parents. Good communication among siblings and parents is, along with information, the primary means of minimizing siblings' concerns.

"My parents always wanted us to express our feelings. They'd say, 'If you're uncomfortable when Jennifer is around your friends, don't feel guilty. Those feelings are very normal.'" (Andrea, 19, in Binkard et al., 1987, p. 18)

Luckily, for most siblings, embarrassment is transitory. As described in the section on unusual opportunities, most brothers and sisters have a remarkable ability to reframe difficult situations in a more positive light:

 "I'll never forget my brother shouting out in the middle of a crowded movie theater that he had just passed gas. My mom and I both shrunk down in our chairs, embarrassed, but laughing all the way! What else could we have done?!" (Kameron P., personal communication, 2004)

GUILT

 "I often feel trapped by him, as though my life will have to revolve around him. I don't want to be stuck caring for him after my parents are gone, and yet I feel guilty for saying it. I don't like having to take so much care of him, I don't like having to wonder what he would have been otherwise, I don't like that he may keep me from other opportunities. And I don't like that I can't accept it." (Allison S., 17, in Meyer, 2005, p. 99)

Relationships between brothers and sisters and their siblings who have health or developmental needs resemble those of typically developing siblings in most ways. Siblings of individuals with support needs, however, are far more likely to experience guilt than siblings of individuals without support needs (Opperman & Alant, 2003; Shivers, 2019). And guilt, although it represents the darker end of the emotional palette, nevertheless comes in many hues. Brothers and sisters may feel that they caused their siblings' disability, they may experience survivor's guilt, they may feel guilty about their own abilities, or they may harbor less-than-charitable feelings about their siblings.

Feeling Responsible for the Disability or Illness

 "When I was little, I worried that the reason that my sister wasn't learning to talk was because I would often speak for her and tell people what she wanted." (Stephanie G., personal communication, 2004)

Siblings who feel somehow responsible for their brother's or sister's disability or illness may experience irrational, but nonetheless real, guilt. They may feel that they are somehow being punished for something they said, did, or thought near the time of the diagnosis. Koch-Hattem (1986) reported on interviews with 33 siblings of patients with pediatric cancer. Of the 33 siblings, nine reported that when the individual patients were diagnosed, they considered the possibility that the illnesses would not have occurred if they had treated their brothers or sisters differently.

 "I blamed myself [for my sister's illness]. I constantly felt guilty around her. I wanted to punish myself. Somehow, I knew inside it wasn't my fault but I was so hurt, lost, and mixed up that I blamed myself." (Joanne, 16, in Murray & Jampolsky, 1982, p. 37)

One teenage member of a listserv for young siblings wrote that she was responsible for her little brother's autism. When they were younger, she wrote, she had chicken pox. Her brother, then a baby, caught her chicken pox. Shortly after his chicken pox resolved, he began showing behavioral signs later diagnosed as autism. Consequently, she believed (erroneously, of course, as there is no known link between chicken pox and autism) that she caused her brother's autism. The implication of this type of guilt is obvious: Siblings, especially younger siblings, will need to be reassured that the disabilities or illnesses did not result from anything they did.

Survivor's Guilt

Siblings may experience a form of survivor's guilt. A sister's secret prayer might be:

 "Dear God, why did this have to happen to Katie? She's so little and so sweet and now she's in the hospital with all these tubes coming out of her. She has all these seizures and seems in such pain. She doesn't deserve this. Why couldn't it happen to me?"

Three of the siblings interviewed by Koch-Hattem (1986) expressed a desire to trade places with their siblings. One 15-year-old sister of a 9-year-old boy with acute lymphoblastic leukemia said this:

 "Sometimes when I'm in there with him taking shots, I'll just say, 'Why couldn't it be me instead of him?' He's so little and so young that I probably could take shots better than he could." (p. 114)

Siblings may also experience guilt over their abilities or health:

 "Since we were twins, my brother and I were always together. And so from the earliest time I can remember, I had the responsibility of watching after him. A lot of times I felt guilty because I was invited to go to parties, and I went to school. They enrolled him in first grade, but he was only there a very short time. I of course was allowed to go and I felt very guilty about that." (Fish, 1993)

Siblings of people with support needs often learn to value and appreciate their health, independence, family, and other aspects of their lives that their peers may take for granted. Although they appreciate the ability to do things that others—such as their siblings—cannot do and the advantages they have, they sometimes feel guilty for their good fortune.

 "I guess it was in junior high that I started to be aware of some of Tom's disorders and be sad for him. He was falling behind me. When I got to junior high and was having such a good time myself, I realized that the whole experience wasn't going to be the same for Tom as it was for me. I was sad but I didn't know what I could do." (Mark, 24, in Binkard et al., 1987, p. 27)

 "One of the hardest things is leaving for a long period of time. Or going somewhere with my family when I know my sib wouldn't be able to go because of his disability. Whenever I leave, my sib always says, 'Sissy? Sissy?' and it just melts my heart every time." (Cassandra W., 15, in Meyer, 2005, p. 101)

Guilt Over Typical Sibling Conflicts

 "The toughest thing about being a sib is admitting that you don't always like your sib and that sometimes you yell at them and treat them unfairly. It's weird, but you can't fight with them like you could do with a typically developing kid and so you are forced to share your anger with someone else and then you feel like an idiot." (Caitlin M., 14, in Meyer, 2005, p. 141)

Although difficult for parents to watch, teasing, name calling, arguing, and other forms of conflict are common among most brothers and sisters. Even though parents may be appalled at siblings' harshness toward one another, much of this conflict can be a beneficial part of normal social development. Bank and Kahn (1982, p. 199) noted that a "constructive function of sibling aggression is that it forces the participants into a social 'laboratory' where they learn how to manage and resolve conflicts." They further noted the following:

 "The ability to deflect aggression, to use it wisely and at the right moment, to use humor, to surrender without debasing oneself and to defeat someone without humiliating that person are all skills that children and adolescents can eventually use in relationships with peers, spouses, and ultimately with their own children." (p. 199)

Bank and Kahn also reported that children they have interviewed have told them that a moderate amount of aggressive interaction (i.e., not interfered with by parents) is a necessary and positive part of the sibling relationship.

Presumably, lessons learned and relationships built through sibling conflict will also apply to the sibling who has a disability or illness. A brother who has Down syndrome might be better equipped to face life in the community if he has learned to defend himself within the essentially loving confines of a family. A sibling who has shared a rich if sometimes rocky relationship with a sister who has a disability may be more likely to continue that relationship as an adult.

 "It wasn't until I lived with a host family while studying abroad during college that I truly learned that typical siblings really do fight and pick on each other just as much as my sister and I did—that in some ways, my real family was more normal than I thought." (S. G., personal communication, 2004)

Regardless how adaptive or developmentally appropriate it might be, typical sibling conflict is more likely to result in feelings of guilt when one sibling has a health or developmental need. When conflict arises, the message sent to many siblings is, "Leave your sibling alone. You are bigger, you are stronger, and you should know better. It is your job to compromise." Because of their "advantages," brothers and sisters may feel they are not permitted to get angry or tease or argue with their siblings.

 "I remember when I was growing up that my dad told us that individuals with autism didn't lie. If my brother blamed me or one of my other siblings for something, my dad automatically believed him. I resented that he believed anything that came out of my brother's mouth because I knew my brother would say what he needed to say in order to not get in trouble." (F. S., personal communication, 2021)

 "[My sister] would chase me and hit me and bite me all the time. I was not allowed to hit back and she was not ever punished for her aggressive behavior. There were never any words of understanding and support spoken to me in regards to what I was going through with [her] behavior." (K. V., personal communication, 2021)

Although no parent should ever tolerate physical abuse among siblings, brothers and sisters—even those with support needs—should be allowed to work out their conflicts as best they can. Because sibling squabbles can be painful for parents to watch, it is often helpful to remove oneself from the situation. It has been our experience that sibling squabbles resolve in 30 minutes when parents intervene and 30 minutes when they do not. Parents who deny their children the right to have conflicts run the risk that "the children may express their anger in secret and forbidden ways" (Bank & Kahn, 1982, p. 203).

When needed, families learn strategies to help maintain cohesion and reduce stress. This may be even more important in families with a child with a disability such as autism spectrum disorder (ASD) when there may be more serious aggression or violent outbursts (Corsano et al., 2017; Costa & da Silva Pereira, 2019; Mascha & Boucher, 2006; Tsao et al., 2011). A sibling whose brother with autism has challenging behaviors and meltdowns may talk to parents about removing herself and having time and space just for herself (Angell et al., 2012). The family may learn and discuss strategies for redirecting challenging behaviors (Tsao & Odom, 2006).

Guilt Over Caregiving

 "I am Douglas' sibling. I wanted to be a sister and very much wanted a baby brother. But I never planned on being his everything. For years I was just that." (Zatlow, 1992, p. 15)

Some family theorists (Duvall, 1962) have observed that families, like individuals, proceed through a life cycle consisting of overlapping stages. Just as an individual grows, develops, matures, and ages, families also are "born," grow, change, and age. Events such as divorce, desertion, or death will profoundly affect the family life cycle. As noted elsewhere (Meyer, 1986), few changes will have a greater effect on the life cycle than the presence of a child with health or developmental needs.

 "I would give my brother anything. I would love to have him with me, but he needs constant supervision and structure that can be better provided at a residential care setting. I also want to give my children (in the future) all that I have, and if he was with us, I know that would be difficult if not impossible." (Seltzer & Krauss, 2002)

Duvall's (1962) seventh stage, "families as launching centers," begins when a family's first child leaves home and ends when the last child leaves. For a family with a child with support needs, this "launching" stage may take place much earlier (for families who place a child in an institutional setting) or may extend for the life of the child if the child lives with the parents as an adult. Regardless, entering adulthood will be an especially troubling milestone for families of people who have disabilities. For the families Wikler (1981) studied, the 21st birthday for a young adult with a disability was the second most stressful crisis for parents, following the initial diagnosis. The 21st birthday can be a double crisis: Although it normally symbolizes independence, parents may be reminded of their child's many needs before he or she can achieve independence. Furthermore, the 21st birthday will signal a transitional crisis: Schools cease to provide services after this age, and, because they are not federally mandated in the same way as education, adult services are often inadequate and/or difficult for families to navigate.

 "People need to be careful about the responsibilities they place on siblings. I used to feel so guilty because my brother's therapists and some family members would say, 'Carly should be doing (insert difficult task here) with him!' In third grade, my aunt made me put 'spend twenty minutes a day reading to your brother' on my New Year's resolution list. Getting him to sit down for a few minutes was so hard, and I always felt like a failure for never being able to do it and a terrible sister for never wanting to do it. Siblings are charged with so much, and that's not inherently a bad thing. Adults just need to be careful to let sibs pave their own way responsibility-wise whenever possible and develop their own relationships with their sibs. At 18, I am very capable of supporting my brother's needs in a lot of different ways, and I am happy to do so. At age 8, I was not nearly as capable, and it makes me angry to know that I was expected to be, and that so many other siblings are expected to be." (Carly N., personal communication, 2016)

Crises such as these affect other family members as well. Siblings, who would otherwise be planning to "launch" from their families, may feel guilty about moving away from home and leaving their parents to care for their siblings' support needs (Grossman, 1972). One sister commented that going away to college was initially a relief: She did not have to care for her brother who has Down syndrome; she could sleep in. By mid-college, she felt guilty about not helping and felt the need to provide her parents with respite (Nester, 1989, p. 1). Other siblings have expressed similar feelings:

 "I knew I could never move too far away. I always insisted my husband limit his career search to areas within a reasonable driving distance to my Mom's home. Then I would feel guilty that my family limited his career choices." (N. H., personal communication, 2004)

 "It's important for sibs to know that that their families will be okay even if they leave to pursue their own lives. Sibs can feel lots of guilt when their personal desires for school or career or love take them far from home." (A. L., in Meyer et al., 2016)

 "My parents are very proud of me and have never tried to force me to stay near home, but they often tell me how much they wish I was closer to home. It makes me feel like I am directly responsible for hurting them emotionally with my life decisions. Pursuing higher education or living abroad to gain language skills aren't decisions that should create guilt and regret." (A. L., in Meyer et al., 2016)

According to Harland and Cuskelly's (2000) study, siblings who were unable to assume an active role in the lives of their adult siblings with disabilities reported feeling guilty. Even when adult siblings do offer assistance to their siblings, however, conflicting loyalties and needs can produce feelings of guilt:

 "It was grueling; I had no relief, no support, no options. My life was revolving around Kevin and his care. If I wanted to go away for a few days, I couldn't. The guilt was overwhelming. What do you tell your friends? 'No, I can't go out; I have to feed my brother?'" (Pat, in Remsberg, 1989, p. 10)

Torn between loyalty to their sibling and a natural desire for distance and independence, adult siblings frequently experience stress and conflict about caring for their sibling with disabilities. Difficulty finding enough time and managing their brother's or sister's behavior compound this issue (Harland & Cuskelly, 2000). Siblings report that parents' failure to plan often resulted in parents seeking to secure deathbed vows or making assumptions about the caregiving roles their typically developing children would play (Gorelick, 1996, p. 7).

 "I had to go to my parents and make them talk about it. It was always this given that I was going to take the responsibility over, and what ended up happening is that I got really miserable. I love my brother dearly, but I don't want to be a parent. I had to set a very strict boundary: No, he cannot live with me, and I still stand by that. They felt I had really let the family down. They said: 'You're going to let him live on the street!' No, that's not what I'm saying. What I am saying is that we have to look into other options. Living with me is not one of them." (Fish, 1993)

SHAME

Shame, where guilt intersects with embarrassment, is a powerful and painful experience for some siblings. Because of the stigma of a disability or illness, siblings can feel that their family is now "marked" and may wish that their family would just fade into the woodwork (Sourkes, 1980). In addition to feeling embarrassed of their siblings and families for being "different," brothers and sisters may feel guilty for having these feelings about people they also love.

 "Julie went through a long stage of being embarrassed about her sister. This continued into her teenage years. 'There's a constant conflict in you,' she remembers. 'You don't want to say anything because you don't want your parents to feel that you are ashamed.'" (Remsberg, 1989, p. 15)

Shame can have long-lasting consequences. One prominent professional in the field of developmental disabilities told us that much of her success is "shame driven." She grew up with a brother who had Down syndrome, although she did not learn the name of her brother's disability until after his death when they were both in their early teens. Life with a brother who was different was a constant source of embarrassment for her. When her mother would pick her up from school, she would dive into the back seat of the car, afraid that classmates might see her with her brother. After his death, guilty feelings about her embarrassment gave way to shame. Now in counseling, she tells us that her pursuit of academic degrees and work in human services is a means of compensating for her perceived transgressions against her brother. Her shame, she feels, keeps her from enjoying her successes.

Although little has been written about this topic, adult siblings who have shared similar stories seem to share certain characteristics. First, most were born before the 1960s, an era when John F. Kennedy, Hubert Humphrey, and others sought to reduce the stigma of disabilities and illnesses by discussing them publicly. Today, with legislation ensuring access to public education and with increased visibility of people with support needs in popular media, the stigma of having a sibling with health or developmental needs is not what it once was. Siblings report they worry about how their brother or sister will be treated by others, and they expect acceptance and tolerance (Watson et al., 2021).

Second, these individuals came from families where the disability was rarely, if ever, discussed, and the disability was clearly traumatic for the parents.

 "In our family, there exists a way of being, a denial of the truth. There was a strong message that you don't go outside of the family for anything. You stay inside, you keep family secrets, and you don't seek outside help from anyone. I'm the first one in this family to seek therapy and I've had to go through a lot of shame and guilt about doing that." (David, 29, in Leder, 1991, p. 26)

Finally, these instances often occur in families where there are only two children: one who is affected and one who is not. Additional children in the family, as Dyson (1989) and Kazak and Clarke (1986) have found, appear to dilute the consequences of growing up with a sibling who has a disability or an illness. Other siblings can provide a typically developing child other children with whom he or she can identify and a built-in informal means of support.

For the simple reason that they are healthy and their sibling is not, siblings of people with support needs are at risk for a variety of guilty feelings. Although open communication is desirable for any parent–child relationship, it is especially important when that child has a sibling with support needs.

ISOLATION, LONELINESS, AND LOSS

 "It's hard seeing other siblings interact. I watch them talk, exchange advice, confide in each other, and even fight, and I realize: I won't ever have that kind of sibling relationship." (Alethea R., 13, in Meyer, 2005, p. 99)

In *A Difference in the Family,* Helen Featherstone (1980) wrote: "In dealing with the wider world of friends, classmates and teacher, able-bodied children at times feel painfully different" (p. 144). A sibling's disability or illness can cause brothers and sisters to experience various feelings of loss and isolation (Hamama et al., 2000). Some parents may try to protect siblings by not talking about the disability, and this may discourage siblings from asking questions and having information they need (Dixon et al., 2018). Siblings feel isolated when the family is silent about the disability or illness. They may want to talk about their feelings, but they are hesitant and worry they will upset the family. Families nurture positive sibling adaptation when there are opportunities to talk about their questions and feelings (Tsao et al., 2011).

Especially if there are only two children in the family, typically developing siblings may miss having a brother or sister with whom they can seek advice or share their thoughts, hopes, and dreams. They may also long for the rough-but-loving relationship many siblings share:

 "At times, I really missed having a 'normal' sister or brother. Sometimes I wished I had someone to talk to, play with, to tease, argue with, confide in, and have fun with. I could tell my sister and know for sure she wouldn't tell anyone—because she didn't talk! But she never fought with me, never argued. It's not a big thing, but I think I missed out on opportunities to deal with criticism or rejection. I never had anyone yelling at me or telling me I was ugly as most siblings do and therefore didn't really learn how to cope with even the slightest bit of conflict until I entered the workforce after college." (Amy S., personal communication, 2005)

Attention—Isolation From Parents

 "I hate it sometimes, like, I don't like him sometimes because he gets all the attention. I just despise him sometimes because he gets all the attention." (Barr et al., 2008)

When parents are consumed with a child's disability or illness, typically developing siblings can feel neglected and isolated from their parents. These feelings are especially keen during times of stress for the family, such as diagnoses or hospitalizations. Of course, this comes at times when siblings need more, not less, emotional support.

 "When I was 9, my brother had a stroke the same week that my grandpa passed away. It was really scary because my parents had to be out of state with my sib and we were being kind of 'passed around' the family so we would have a place to stay and have someone to talk to." (Cassandra W., 15, in Meyer, 2005, p. 117)

 "Even if you feel bad for your sick brother or sister, you still want your parents too." (12-year-old girl, in Bendor, 1990, p. 24)

"I spent a lot of time with baby-sitters and television, and less with my parents and the relatives who visited only to see Lisa. It seemed as though she were the only one anybody cared about. In this, I was the typical sibling of a victim of childhood cancer." (Ellis, 1992, p. 2)

Cairns et al. (1979), in a study of school-age children with cancer and their healthy siblings, found that siblings showed greater distress than their siblings diagnosed with cancer in the areas of perceived social isolation, perception of their parents as overindulgent and overprotective of the sick child, fear of expressing negative feelings, and (for older-age siblings only) concern with school failure. Siblings of children with cancer have the most difficulty adjusting when their brother or sister has to spend more nights in the hospital, disrupting family life (Sloper & White, 1996). Parents, overwhelmed by a child's many needs, may be too exhausted or simply unable to recognize a sibling's calls for attention (Schorr-Ribera, 1992).

 "Sometimes I feel as though my parents don't care about what I do or don't do. They are so preoccupied with my brother and all his friends that I don't really seem to matter. Almost all my time is spent in my room watching my TV, listening to music, doing homework, or talking on the phone. You would think somebody would notice that I spend all my time in my room, away from everyone else and all the problems that surround their lives." (Alisa A., 18, in Meyer, 2005, p. 119)

Several brothers and sisters of children who have epilepsy reflected on how their sibling's disability caused them to feel ignored by and isolated from their parents:

 "I probably will never forget the loneliness during that period of time. The feeling that I had was that I wasn't worth as much as Jessica. The only way I could get them to pay attention to me was to get mad. That would get their attention. I wouldn't talk to my parents about being lonely because I wasn't sure that they'd understand me—the way I felt. I didn't do my schoolwork. I guess I wanted to see how my parents would react. I wanted to see if they would pay attention or yell at me or ground me or something." (K. Collins, in Collins & Emmerling, 1991)

Other siblings, seeing the pain caused by a sibling's support needs, may elect not to come to their parents with their troubles. Featherstone (1980) wrote,

> These siblings may, then, endure many of [their] feelings alone and without support, even when parents are tactful and eager to help. Conscientious, sensitive parents often have conscientious, sensitive children; seeing how pushed and saddened their parents already are, such children hesitate to burden them further. (p. 61)

Siblings often develop ways to cope with their greater caring roles and their family's increased needs. They may develop what is called "sibling self-sustainability" to avoid conflict and reduce their parents' burden (Bradford, 1997). They may not communicate their own needs for attention or communication in an attempt to avoid increasing their parents' worry (Deavin et al., 2018).

 "When I was growing up, it never crossed my mind to turn to my parents for support. It seemed like they already had too much to deal with, so I didn't want to burden them with my problems as well, since they wouldn't have been easy to fix." (S. G., personal communication, 2005)

One adult sibling we met told us that it took her 5 years to tell her parents that she had been raped. She thought they had "enough to worry about" with her brother, who has autism. Another sister wrote,

"I felt I had to hold my feelings in when I was around my parents. I let my feelings out only when I was with my close friends." (Honey, 16, in Murray & Jampolsky, 1982, p. 54)

When siblings are asked to name the positive experiences that help them, they often say that a close and united family helps, both to meet the needs of their brother or sister and to create a close and sharing family that communicates and works together (Dixon et al., 2018).

 "Small moments of acknowledgment help you not feel invisible and give credence to feelings that you are silently struggling with and may feel guilty or confused about." (K. B., personal communication, 2016)

For many reasons, parents may need to treat their children differently, and more so when there is a child with a disability. However, siblings are less likely to experience their parents' favoritism of the child with a disability when they understand the reasons for this difference (Kowal et al., 2002; McHale et al., 2000). Effective family communication about the child's disability prepares families for times when the child with a disability is facing a health or developmental crisis demanding even more of the parent's time and attention. These are times when families may enlist the support of a favorite relative or adult friend who provides the sibling with time, attention, and an "open ear."

Isolation From Information and "The Process"

 "My parents, my two older sisters, and my grandparents would all leave to go to the hospital while I sat at home with a baby-sitter. All I wanted to know was what was happening and why everybody always left me. No one took the time to explain to me that my sister was basically dying." (Doherty, 1992, p. 4)

Adult brothers and sisters occasionally report growing up in families where they rarely discussed their siblings' disability or illness. They report the irony of this situation: In many ways, they knew their siblings better than anyone, yet they knew little about the illness or disability or its implications.

 "My brother was institutionalized in the 1960s when he was 5 and I was 8. We didn't talk about it much, as our parents followed the prevailing advice to 'place and forget' their son. Visits were entirely forbidden—for my 'protection' apparently. Growing up, I had so many fears, and so many questions. And nobody to talk to. There was a 'correct' silence, enforced, in part, because of my parents' obvious pain about my brother." (M. K. R., personal communication, 2005)

There are several reasons for this situation. Some siblings tell us that their parents wished to protect them from the stress and sadness they experienced and therefore "spared" them information about their siblings' support needs. Some grew up with a sibling whose disability (e.g., epilepsy) or illness (e.g., schizophrenia) was so stigmatizing that their parents sought to keep the problem a family secret. Topics that were taboo outside the home were also frequently taboo inside the home, leaving siblings to feel alone with their questions and concerns.

Other siblings report feeling left in the dark for legal reasons. Foster siblings of children who have complex psychosocial needs have told us of their frustrations: They must live with a foster sibling's often-difficult behavior, yet they are not permitted (interpreted to mean *trusted*) to know details of their foster sibling's background.

Regardless of the reason, when there is insufficient communication about the brother's or sister's problems, a typically developing sibling can experience a unique loneliness. One brother shared what it was like for information about his sister's cancer to be withheld from him. He felt his parents sheltered him, assuring him "not to worry." He now feels that remaining uninvolved and uninformed has a cost:

 "I didn't understand the full extent of my sister's disease—I just thought that the doctors would take care of everything and I didn't think about how tough it was for my sister in other ways." (Peter, in Ellis, 1992, p. 5)

Not understanding the implications of his sister's illness and being reassured that he need not worry caused Peter to feel isolated and confused, especially when his parents left and went to the hospital:

 "I became a latchkey child in a lot of ways—always left by myself—so I feel that essentially I became a peripheral member of my family during that time. I wasn't included at all." (Peter, in Ellis, 1992, p. 5)

Although some parents may accurately estimate their child's need for and understanding of information about a sibling's disability, they may overestimate how well their child understands the implications of the disability (Glasberg, 2000). This underscores the need for ongoing family communication and developmentally appropriate information that matches the sibling's level of understanding. Further discussion on the information needs of siblings can be found in Chapter 3.

Isolation From Peers

 "Until this group, I had never met another sibling [of a person with a disability]. It wasn't until the tender age of 39 that I met another person like myself." (Marilyn, in Fink, 1984, p. 6)

Since the 1980s, we have learned one simple yet far-reaching lesson from the hundreds of parents and siblings we have met, and it is this: Siblings' experiences parallel parents' experiences. Siblings will encounter joys, concerns, and issues regarding the person with support needs that closely correspond to those of their parents. Although siblings often have the longest-lasting relationship in the family, compared to their parents they have far fewer opportunities to gain access to programs, services, and professional support.

Nowhere is this more evident than in the area of peer support. Many parents count on sharing the good times, the not-so-good times, and helpful information with a peer who is also the parent of a child with support needs. Some parents connect with other parents through programs such as Parent-to-Parent, or fathers' programs, or mothers' groups (Meyer et al., 1985). Many parents maintain informal contact with other parents of children who have similar support needs. For most parents, the thought of "going it alone," without the benefit of knowing another parent in a similar situation, is unthinkable. Yet, this happens routinely to siblings. The siblings interviewed by Bendor (1990) made periodic but vain attempts to share feelings of frustration and loneliness with friends. The siblings reported that friends were either uninterested or unable to respond helpfully (p. 25).

"I am part of an online sibling group, so I know lots of sibs from all over the world, but only through the computer. It's nice having people who understand where you're coming from. Most of my friends don't want to hear about it and don't know how to respond when I have concerns or worries about my siblings, health, or home life." (Rebekah C., 17, in Meyer, 2005, p. 91)

Despite the tremendous success of peer-support programs for parents, there remains a dearth of such programs for siblings of children with support needs (Mailick et al., 2009). The need for such opportunities is clear: McKeever's (1983) study of children with cancer revealed that siblings were more in need of support than were other family members. Numerous authors (Cramer et al., 1997; Lobato, 1990; Murphy, 1981; Powell & Gallagher, 1993; Seligman, 1991) have suggested that support groups can provide young siblings with opportunities for "catharsis, support, and insight concerning relationships with family members and others and techniques for managing various situations" (Murphy, 1979, p. 359). Like their parents, brothers and sisters benefit in many ways from support groups in which they can gain information and voice their fears, hopes, and doubts.

"Because I use a sibling listserv, I have met—or rather heard from—tons of siblings from around the world that I would never have otherwise met. It's really great to know that I am not alone." (Laura P., 15, in Meyer, 2005, p. 90)

Groups specifically for siblings demonstrate to them that somebody cares about the issues they face and values the important role they play in the family. Benefits that siblings experience from participating in a support group include increased knowledge about disabilities, a peer network, the opportunity to discuss their experiences and feelings, and decreased loneliness, anxiety, and sadness (D'Arcy et al., 2005; Jones et al., 2019, 2020; Smith & Perry, 2005; Tudor & Lerner, 2015).

"There are millions of children who have disabled siblings like me. It's OK to talk about my brother. I know a lot more about my brother's disability. People want to listen to me and talk to me. It's helped me talk to my family, and think about my family. It's been some special time for me." (Hayden et al., 2019)

As discussed in subsequent chapters, brothers and sisters, although they have unique concerns, do not routinely have negative experiences, as once described in the research literature. Like their parents, the vast majority of siblings of people with support needs do well despite challenges brought about by the siblings' disability or illness (Cuskelly et al., 1998; Dyson, 1996; Eisenberg et al., 1998; Faux, 1993; Ferraioli & Harris, 2009; Hannah & Midlarsky, 1999; Orsmond & Seltzer, 2000). Consequently, programs for brothers and sisters should reflect siblings' and families' strengths while acknowledging their concerns. (To be sure, there will be some family members—parents or siblings—with needs that go beyond what a peer-support group can provide. In Chapter 8, we discuss how to recognize siblings in need of therapeutic programs and where to refer them.)

RESENTMENT

"Someday, if I do marry and have children, I really hope that no one person will have needs that have to be so much more important than everyone else's." (Paul, 21, in Binkard et al., 1987, p. 23)

Sometimes or often in the lives of all siblings, there are things to resent. Resentment, a strong sentiment frequently expressed by brothers and sisters of people with support needs, is unlikely to go unnoticed by parents. A group of parents of children with muscular dystrophy with whom we met said that among the most pressing concerns their typically developing children experienced was resentment. Their observations serve as an overview of the types of resentment mentioned by siblings of children with diverse support needs. The parents volunteered that their children resented the following: the attention the siblings with muscular dystrophy received, the amount of care and time the siblings required, the perceived unequal treatment of children in the family, expectations to do more around the house and help their siblings with toileting and other needs that the siblings cannot do for themselves, and the limitations on their and the families' lifestyle imposed by the disability.

 "Living with my sister [with autism] made my childhood unbearable. Between her physically violent outbursts, to her imposing rules and obsessions, life with her was a constant challenge. As a child (and teenager), I was very resistant to the controls she imposed on the household. I was often filled with resentment toward her, and my parents for trying to appease her demands." (Seltzer & Krauss, 2002)

Siblings also experience resentment when a brother or sister has aggression or severe behavior problems that disrupt the family and home life. When a brother or sister has ASD, it may create more anxiety and daily instability for siblings (Angell et al., 2012; Smith & Elder, 2010; Watson et al., 2021). Siblings may have more difficulty concentrating on school, doing their homework, and dealing with behaviors that disrupt sleep.

 "I'm just too tired to get out of bed because my brother keeps me up nearly every single night, running up and down the stairs and flushing the toilet. Once it was 3 a.m. that I actually got to sleep." (Gettings et al., 2015)

Younger siblings in particular may experience the unequal division of parent time and attention and their increased responsibilities in the family as "not fair." The child with a disability or chronic illness appears to be the favorite, the focus of the family energy. Family relationships and sibling adjustment influence how siblings experience and think about these differences. When siblings understand the reasons for these differences, and when families communicate about sibling needs and responsibilities, siblings are better able to find the meaning for these differences, and they are less likely to experience things as unfair (Gorjy et al., 2017; Kowal et al., 2002; Tsao et al., 2011). Family members help each other create relationships that fit their situations (Stoneman, 2005).

Loss of Parental Attention and Time

 "The toughest thing is always coming second to your sib. Often feelings and wants are put on the back burner so that things work out for your sib." (Amanda M., 19, in Meyer, 2005, p. 142)

One form of resentment occurs when siblings perceive that the child with support needs is receiving more than his or her share of the family's emotional or even financial resources. From the sibling's perspective, the child with support needs becomes the sun in the family's solar system. The siblings of children with cancer interviewed by Koch-Hattem (1986) said that their siblings were receiving more attention, care, and material possessions since having been diagnosed with cancer. Although many were realistic about the need for the changes, all displayed some degree of envy.

"I felt that he was getting all the sympathy and all the attention, and that was all being pinned against me. It's equal now. But, before it felt unfair. To be honest, he kinda needed it though. He needed that extra support that I didn't really need." (Charlie, in Gorjy et al., 2017, p. 5)

When a family has a child with a disability, the sibling may find it more difficult to adjust when the parents are experiencing depression or difficulty balancing the needs of several children in the family. These impacts on siblings increase when the child's disability is more severe—for example, a child with more challenging ASD symptoms and behaviors (Meyer et al., 2011).

Young siblings may lack the cognitive and affective capabilities to appreciate that their parents' behavior is a response to the genuine needs of the child with a disability, rather than a lack of love or appreciation for their typically developing children. Bendor (1990) noted that some children interviewed were frightened by their feelings of anger, and the options available to them for expressing or mastering their negative feelings were limited. Even when they do comprehend their siblings' needs and their parents' stress, however, brothers and sisters may be faced with another dilemma. One sibling to whom Bendor (1990) spoke summed it up this way: "The worst thing about all the anger you feel inside is that there is no one to blame" (p. 24). Without the target that blame provides, siblings may turn inward, feeling guilty about their anger.

Siblings notice, however, when their parents try to be fair in the time and attention they give their children. They value when parents communicate openly and spend time doing things together (Pit-Ten Cate & Loots, 2000). Siblings often express the need for private time with parents, time when they can just enjoy being together.

 "Sometimes, at night time, we go to bed and when my brother is sleeping, I may go downstairs and then my mum and I play a game or watch television together. My brother doesn't know." (Richard, 8, in Moyson & Roeyers, 2012, p. 94)

 "When my brother is away, I have some quiet time with mum and we can play a board game for example. It is nice and quiet when he is not around." (Luijkx et al., 2016)

Unequal Treatment and Excessive Demands

 "I get mad when I get into trouble for things that Vickie gets away with. I try not to get mad because I know that she doesn't know any better about some things, but sometimes I just lose it!" (Michelle O., 17, in Meyer, 2005, p. 109)

Brothers and sisters report resentment when children with disabilities or illness are indulged, overprotected, or permitted to engage in behaviors unacceptable for other family members. Miller's (1974) study revealed that parents were much less tolerant of siblings' negative behaviors toward their siblings with cognitive disabilities than they were of similar sibling behaviors toward other, typically developing siblings.

 "'You should be ashamed of yourself,' her mother told her. 'You should be able to control your temper. She can't help it. You can.'" (Julie, in Remsberg, 1989, p. 15)

Further, Miller found that siblings without disabilities were more likely to be punished if they did not engage in a prescribed activity with a sibling with a disability than if they avoided a similar responsibility for a typically developing sibling. Podeanu-Czehotsky's (1975) study of the families of children with cerebral palsy found that in some families life was normal, whereas in other families, the child with the disability was indulged and became "a tyrant causing hidden or open conflicts among siblings" (p. 309).

"My brother liked to lie on the floor in public places—especially at the mall. As Mom tried to convince Thad to get up, I'd think: 'Why doesn't she just yank him up off the floor so these people will stop staring? I would never be able to get away with this behavior.'" (Kameron P., personal communication, 2004)

Growing up, siblings may find themselves facing a difficult dilemma: They may appreciate that their siblings have bona fide needs, yet, because of their still-egocentric view of the world, they resent them for having these needs. One 16-year-old responded this way when asked what the most difficult aspect of having a sick sibling was: "Having to care so much and being burdened by the responsibility of caring" (Bendor, 1990, p. 28). The girl then described staying home night after night to help her mother when her sick sister had high fevers and was vomiting. She wondered if she was selfish for resenting this role.

When we listen to brothers and sisters at Sibshops or during sibling panels, they sometimes complain that their siblings "get away with murder." Family rules about behavior, chores, bedtime routines, and so forth often do not apply to the child with support needs. Brothers and sisters frequently insist that their sibling could comply with many of the family's rules and requirements "if only my parents would make him [or her] do it."

Siblings' views deserve to be heard, even if, as children, they lack a parent's understanding of the "bigger picture." Their alternative perspective—which almost always focuses on what they believe their sibling can do—can provide parents and service providers with fresh insights regarding a child's actual abilities. "My brother never has to unload the dishwasher because he has Down syndrome," one brother told us. "But he can do it. I know he can, because when my parents aren't home, I make him unload the dishwasher."

Parfit (1975) has recommended that parents avoid overprotecting children with disabilities by discussing with their typically developing children the behaviors that are unavoidable due to the siblings' disabilities and the discipline that can help modify the problem behaviors. Brothers and sisters, then, can advise parents of behaviors for which their siblings should be held responsible: "Children are often more sensible and sensitive about such matters than adults" (Parfit, 1975, p. 20).

Resentment Regarding Failure to Plan for the Future

 "In the planning for my three disabled brothers' future, my mother did not include any of the typical sibs. And the plan she had was outdated and inadequate and forced us into crisis mode when she passed away. This has had a huge impact on our lives and marriages. I was always quite sympathetic about the burden my mom had but this lack of planning made me mad at her at the same time that I was grieving her death." (Nora H., personal communication, 2005)

In the United States, more than 75% of adults with intellectual and developmental disabilities (IDD) live at home with family supporters, more than 25% of whom are age 60 or older (Braddock et al., 2005; Fujiura, 1998). In 2017, 71% of individuals with IDD lived with a family caregiver, and in 2015, more than 871,000 people with IDD lived with caregivers who are 60 years of age or older (Disability Data Digest, 2018). In 2015, only 17% of people with IDD in the United States received long-term supports or services, and only 20% were known to or served by state IDD agencies (Larson et al., 2017). As parents age and pass away, siblings often assume support responsibilities for their brothers and sisters (Burke et al., 2012; Heller & Kramer, 2009).

Sibling research has expanded since the early 2000s, and researchers—many of whom are adult siblings themselves—have turned their attention to the needs of siblings who do or will serve as caregivers for their siblings with support needs. Research suggests that many adult siblings feel emotionally and logistically unprepared to step into the caregiving role (Heller & Kramer, 2009). Siblings have reported the need for disability-related information, support for their caregiving role, and enhanced formal support systems to address their needs (Arnold et al., 2012).

 "I worry a lot about what will happen when my parents die, and somewhat resent that I will be the primary caregiver—which I'm ashamed about." (Seltzer & Krauss, 2002)

In families where there is a child with developmental disabilities, frequently there is an assumption—often unspoken—that brothers and sisters will someday become guardians of their sibling as adults. From parents and siblings that we have met, we know that some siblings are conceived in order to fill a role: someone who will look after the family member with the disability when the parents no longer can.

Not surprisingly, their siblings' future and the role they will play in that future is an especially poignant concern for many adult brothers and sisters. Psychiatrist E. Fuller Torrey (1992), brother to a woman who has schizophrenia, noted: "Demographically, we will outlive our parents; demographically, we will get involved with our siblings."

When parents fail to involve siblings in planning for the future of the person with the disability, resentment is likely to occur. "My parents won't consider letting Bobby try a group home," one sister told us. "That's all well and good now, but what happens when they die? Will he have to come live with me?"

 "My brother lived with my parents until they died. He was about 39 and he was very depressed, not because they died but because he had no life. I am his guardian and I took care of him for a while but came to realize that I could not do a very good job. He needed more stimulation than I could give him. He now lives in a group home with five other people, three guys and two gals. He has gotten so much better since he moved there. But I have to admit that I cried for 6 months trying to figure out what would be best for both of us for the long term. Making the decision was the hardest thing I have ever done. I don't think I will ever get over the anger with my parents for leaving me with the decision." (V. L., personal communication, 2002)

We will never forget the testimony of a young woman who participated in a sibling panel we hosted. This woman, a mother with two young children, clearly loved her parents and her sister, who has cerebral palsy and emotional problems. Her resentment toward her parents, however, was unmistakable. With tears welling in her eyes, she told how her parents, who had grown too frail to take care of her sister's many support needs, "dropped the sister on her doorstep." Her sister's presence and many demands, she said, had been extremely difficult for all members of her young family.

Failure to plan adequately can cause resentment among surviving siblings as well. Adult siblings—generally sisters—have told us how they have somehow inherited all of the responsibilities associated with caring for the sibling who is disabled. "[My siblings] are all patting me on the back, telling me what a good job I'm doing and all that, but they don't help at all" (Fish, 1993).

Even when parents do plan for the future, their expectations can cause guilt and resentment. "My parents never wanted my brother to live outside the family home," one sister told us, "and when we talked about what we would do when they were gone, it was apparent that they wanted Jim to come live with me. I love my brother. I will always be involved with my brother. But I don't want him to live with me." Other adult siblings have told of promises extracted by dying parents that they will take in their sibling with disabilities.

Advanced medical technologies allow people with disabilities to live longer than in previous generations. Social policy and diminishing economic resources dictate that people with disabilities will live closer to their families than in previous generations, when the state assumed an *in loco parentis* role for adults with disabilities. Therefore, it is reasonable to expect that adult siblings of the baby boom and post–baby boom generations will be more involved in the lives of their siblings with disabilities than any previous generation. At the same time, these adult siblings face increasing uncertainty about their own retirement and access to health care. However, siblings continue to be left out of service planning for their brother or sister with a disability, although they want and need more support to be effective advocates (Lee et al., 2020). Unless parents and service providers involve siblings in planning for their children's future, many adults with disabilities will soon have sibling guardians who are both ill-prepared for the job and potentially resentful of the responsibilities placed on them.

 "My mother just passed away after a year-long battle with cancer and my father passed a while ago. I am now my 39-year-old brother's caregiver. He lived at home with her and has never lived on his own. He has no supports in place. I don't even have all of his official diagnosis information. My first questions are related to a trust my parents set up for him. I meet with the lawyer next week. I am doing research to be prepared. I just want to do what is best for him, as well as not get taken advantage of for lack of knowledge." (J. F., personal communication, 2021)

INCREASED RESPONSIBILITIES

 "When my parents went out for the evening, they would hire a babysitter, but babysitters didn't know how to handle a little girl who screamed all night and bit herself and did things like that, so they would get me up to take care of her. So from the time I was 5 years old, I was being responsible and helping and doing things. My two brothers have had a much harder time with it, especially the brother who is less than a year older than my sister. He won't even talk about her, and this has been 30 some years and he will not talk about her." (Fish, 1993)

Early research on siblings of children with developmental disabilities frequently focused on the caregiving demands assumed by siblings—especially sisters. Authors such as Farber (1960) and Fowle (1973) observed that sisters, oldest sisters in particular, were more adversely affected than brothers by the presence of a child with a disability. About caregiving responsibilities, Milton Seligman (1979) wrote,

> The extent to which a sibling may be held responsible for a handicapped brother or sister bears a strong relationship to the perception and feelings children, adolescents, and adults have about their handicapped sibling and their parents. Available research supports the notion that a child's (especially a female child's) excessive responsibility for a handicapped sib is related to the development of anger, resentment and guilt, and quite possibly subsequent psychological disturbance. (p. 530)

Other researchers from this era, including Cleveland and Miller (1977) and Gath (1974), felt that oldest daughters were often pushed into a surrogate parent role for the child with support needs, especially in large and low-income families. This heavy caregiving responsibility, they felt, often isolated them from their age mates. More recent research supports this pattern: Sisters experience greater caregiving responsibilities and a larger role in the caregiving of their adult siblings (Burke et al., 2012; Diener et al., 2015; Hodapp et al., 2010; Krauss et al., 1996).

 "As soon as I could see over the counter in the kitchen, I was making my own school lunch right beside my mother—who was making the exact same lunch for my brother." (Kameron P., personal communication, 2003)

Cleveland and Miller's (1977) research suggested that the oldest female siblings may experience a sibling's disability as a double-edged sword. Their research revealed that, although oldest daughters were often pushed to take on excessive responsibilities, they were also most likely to enter helping professions and to remain involved with the sibling with a disability as an adult. The research also showed that this group was most likely to seek professional help for personal problems.

How much of this older research remains valid? What effect, if any, have programs (e.g., respite care, special sitters, child care for children with disabilities) and movement toward community-based schooling and life had on the caregiving demands placed on brothers and sisters?

In a 1987 study of preschool siblings of children with disabilities conducted by Lobato et al., sisters were found to have the greatest degree of responsibility for child care and household tasks, although the difference was not statistically significant when compared with brothers of children with disabilities and with siblings of typically developing children. The sisters of children with disabilities, however, received significantly fewer privileges and experienced more restrictions on social routines compared with matched controls. Brothers of children with disabilities experienced the opposite—more privileges and fewer restrictions on social activities. According to Lobato and her colleagues, the sex of the typically developing siblings appeared to shape the daily living routines among families with children who have disabilities but not among control families.

Stoneman and colleagues (1991) conducted extensive research on caregiving responsibilities of siblings of children with developmental disabilities. In one study of younger siblings of children with and without disabilities, they found that younger siblings of children with disabilities babysat, monitored, and helped care for their older siblings, whereas the comparison group performed significantly less total child care and never babysat their older siblings.

 "From age 6, I had to help with both my typical and disabled sibs. After coming home from first grade, I fed my baby sister. Starting at age 8, I changed diapers and did laundry. On weekends, I got up early to supervise my three disabled brothers. Starting at age 12, I babysat all seven of my younger siblings by myself." (M. H., personal communication, 2005)

During observational studies conducted by Stoneman et al. (1987, 1988, 1989), children with disabilities (ages 4–8 years) were videotaped with their older siblings (ages 6–12 years). According to the authors, siblings of children with disabilities—especially older sisters—more readily assumed the role of manager or caregiver for their brothers or sisters.

Adult sisters seemed to continue to be more involved in caregiving and planning for their sibling with a disability (Gorelick, 1996). In Orsmond and Seltzer's 2000 survey of adults who had a sibling with cognitive disabilities, sisters reported more involvement with their sibling than brothers. Sisters were more knowledgeable about their sibling's skills and needs, had more discussions with their parents about their sibling, and had more contact with their sibling. These findings—similar to those found by Pruchno et al. (1996)—are echoed in the membership of SibNet, the leading listserv for adult siblings. More than 88% of the almost 6,000 members of SibNet at the time of printing identify as female.

That older sisters assume greater caregiving responsibilities in families where there is a child with a disability is hardly surprising. After all, many oldest daughters find themselves assuming the role of surrogate mother regardless of the presence of a child with a disability in the family. When Stoneman et al. (1988) compared older sisters in families where there is a disability with a comparison group, however, they found that the older sisters of children with disabilities babysat and had more child care responsibilities than any other group of children. Also, the more family responsibilities these sisters assumed, the less they participated in their own activities outside of the homes, and the more conflict was found with the children who had the disability.

 "The toughest thing about being a sib are the sacrifices you have to make. It means being flexible 24/7 and always being aware that there are often changes that need to be made." (Alli J., 15, in Meyer, 2005, p. 141)

In their 1988 study of older siblings, Stoneman et al. found that for brothers and sisters of children with disabilities, an increase in observed sibling conflict and a decrease in positive sibling interaction were associated with child care responsibilities, which was not found with the comparison group. This finding apparently does not apply to other domestic chores. In fact, the authors noted, increased older sibling responsibility for other household chores corresponded to less, rather than more, observed sibling conflict.

As expected, Stoneman and colleagues (1988, 1991) found that responsibilities assumed by the siblings of children with disabilities (e.g., helping with dressing, feeding) tended to be greater when the child with the disability had fewer adaptive skills. Less adaptively competent children, suggested Stoneman and Brody (1993), seemed to place greater demands for caregiving on siblings, regardless of the birth order.

 "The responsibility definitely stinks. I get few privileges for all the work I do for my family and my little brother." (Daniel C., 17, in Meyer, 2005, p. 141)

It would be far too easy and unrealistic to recommend that brothers, and especially sisters, of children with health and developmental needs be spared domestic duties. After all, "support needs" invariably translate into increased caregiving needs and household chores. Besides, the responsible attitudes that many siblings have are in part a result of successfully handling duties performed in service to their siblings and families.

 "As a child, I know I was a very important part of Martha's life. I was the only one she would go potty for. I was the only one who could braid her hair, take her into a store, and stop her tantrums." (Westra, 1992, p. 4)

The research of Stoneman et al. (1988) suggests general guidelines for assigning domestic chores to siblings of children with support needs. The first consideration is the type of chores assigned. Are child care demands causing the conflict described by Stoneman et al. (1988)? If so, parents may wish to consider offering siblings a choice in the household responsibilities they assume. Parents can offer siblings an opportunity to contribute to the family in other ways—shopping, meal preparation, or cleaning.

A second consideration is the number of demands placed on the typically developing child. Parents should be advised to compare their children's level of child care and household duties with those of their peers to determine if their chores are excessive or preventing them from participating in at least some activities outside of the home. Responsibility is good, but so is soccer, being in the school play, or learning to play the saxophone.

A third consideration is who is assuming the caregiving demands. In their research on siblings of adults with cognitive disabilities, Orsmond and Seltzer (2000) found that brothers have the most negative feelings when their sibling with a disability is a sister. The researchers stressed the importance of increasing the involvement and building a strong relationship between these brothers and sisters. It is not surprising that it is sisters who bear the brunt of the caregiving responsibilities (Burke et al., 2012; Diener et al., 2015; Hodapp et al., 2010; Orsmond & Seltzer, 2000). Although this may contribute to sisters often having the closest relationship with their sibling as adults, parents should be encouraged to ensure that the chores and opportunities for interactions are spread equitably among brothers and sisters.

TRAUMA

Increasingly, siblings engaging with our online communities, speaking on panels, and sharing their stories on blogs, podcasts, and social media are talking about trauma—as in, their own. According to the Substance Abuse and Mental Health Services Administration (SAMSHA, 2019), individual trauma results from "an event, series of events, or set of circumstances that is experienced by an individual as physically or emotionally harmful or life threatening and that has lasting adverse effects on the individual's functioning and mental, physical, social, emotional, or spiritual well-being."

Although not every sibling experiences trauma, it is important to consider how having a sibling with a disability may contribute to demographic and other unique environmental stressors for typically developing siblings. It is also extremely important to listen to the sibs we support. Anxiety and depression are common themes among adult siblings who recall childhood trauma. One sister posted this in an online group for adult siblings:

 "Does anyone else struggle with depression and anxiety in their adult life because of this childhood trauma?" (M. R., personal correspondence, 2021)

Her post received 82 affirmative comments (including two perky GIFs exclaiming, "That would be me" and "This girl!") from other sibs who went on to detail their experiences of trauma. Considering some characteristic challenging symptoms of various disabilities, it is not difficult to see how living with a sibling who routinely experiences them could cause physical and/or emotional harm. For example, some behaviors associated with autism, including self-injury (e.g., head banging, skin picking, hair pulling), lack of emotional and social reciprocity, and inflexible adherence to routines or rituals, can be difficult to witness and respond to, to say the least. Growing up watching a sib have unpredictable, dramatic, debilitating seizures can be scary and stressful. Dealing with—or dodging—the aggressive, even violent behavior of a sib who struggles to find less-destructive ways to communicate and interact with the world around them can be harrowing.

 "I'm 24 and have a 15-year-old brother who's autistic. He's very violent and I've spent the majority of my life being scared to live in my own house. As he's gotten older, his episodes have gotten scarier and I do everything I can to avoid him. I've started to resent him and blame him for a lot even though I know it's not his fault. I carry around a lot of guilt and constantly tell myself I need to be a better sister, but can't seem to get myself to spend more time with him. I was recently diagnosed with posttraumatic stress disorder (PTSD)

and it was almost relieving in a way. A lot of my feelings, fears, and avoidance behaviors made sense. I've been told by family and friends my entire life that I need to be nicer, more understanding, spend more time with my brother, etc. No one has ever considered how this has impacted me." (C. K., personal correspondence, 2021)

 "Growing up, [my sister] was an angel about 95% of the time but would have massive episodes of violence and volatility where she would lash out at anyone around (usually our parents, but sometimes me). These were triggered out of nowhere and couldn't be predicted. My parents did absolutely EVERYTHING right to give us both the best child-hood possible, but I couldn't help feeling unsafe in my own home. Since moving out, I've been diagnosed with PTSD and have had a really hard time with it, to the point where I've started to resent my sister, and even my parents for the traumatic childhood." (S. C., personal correspondence, 2020)

 "I was diagnosed with C-PTSD [complex PTSD] when I was about 19. From the violence, but also from the seizures/falls and their triggers and hospital stays. The worst is the seizures. They can be caused by loud sudden noises, so even if I'm not with her, people will do certain movements and I think they're having a seizure. I go into defense mode, ready to catch [my sister] and to defend myself if she gets mad because of the seizure. I also have anxiety and panic disorders, depression, insomnia, and ASD. I am the one she seeks out when she's upset. I believe it's because I see communication where others see violence. So yeah. Lots of baggage here, but I work through it, and cherish the good days when they come." (R. B., personal correspondence, 2020)

 "I can be around my brother but being in the same house overnight brings a lot of trig-gers and I don't sleep. My mom doesn't seem to understand it and whenever I try to ex-plain some of the trauma reactions that I experience due to his behavior, she insinuates that I didn't love him as much." (M. M., personal correspondence, 2022)

Guilt is a common feeling among siblings (see pp. 12–17). For some, acknowledging trauma they have experienced as a result of their brother or sister can cause both guilt and shame. Some siblings have difficulty reconciling their role as the tolerant, patient "good kid" who does not rock the boat with their experiences of, and feelings about, the trauma they have endured.

 "I moved out to go to university and the reality came crashing down because that im-mediate threat was gone. Had years of poor mental health before going to therapy. It was the first time in my life where I was able to talk about the violence I experienced in childhood (which was pretty severe, me being 8 years junior to my brother who is a big, big boy with ASD and intellectual disability). Even then I still didn't accept the fact that what happened to me was traumatic or abusive for months. Because there was nobody to blame and my parents did the best they could. I think in the sibling role we have so much tolerance and sense of duty that when somebody makes you see it in that way, or you start to realize it yourself, it's almost like an attack on your family and identity. But I guess what we did experience was trauma, and we have a right to be safe. That's the hard thing for people to understand and for ourselves to understand without feeling a mountain of guilt." (I. F., personal correspondence, 2020)

 "It breaks my heart to say this out loud. It doesn't sit well that while yes, I adore my sister and will fight to the death for her, she has caused me a great deal of pain and trauma. Does she remember when she choked me? Does she remember when she broke my mom's ribs? Does she remember pulling out my hair? Does she remember when she was only 11, and I was 13, I had her in a full-body restraint at the park? I don't know, and I don't want to ask, but I do want to know if she has any recollection or remorse for the times that she couldn't gain control." (S. A. personal correspondence, 2021)

 "As she grew older [my sister] started showing signs of having a mental illness. She has extreme anger, delusions, hallucinations and other stuff. I was exposed to some difficult situations that I was unable to process. I have been diagnosed with PTSD mostly because of my sister and now struggle with my own mental health challenges. I feel ashamed for struggling with this especially because I am supposed to be the good kid who doesn't have problems." (E. N., personal communication, 2017)

 "It can be really hard for me to reconcile wanting to be an ally for autistic self-advocates and to advocate for siblings like myself. Because I don't want to take away from the work of self-advocates defending their neurodiversity, but also it's not okay to grow up in a house where the kitchen knives had to be locked up (and still are) so my sibling couldn't pull one out of the knife block to threaten us with them. And whether that's because he's autistic, or because of the frustrations of being autistic in a world that's not accommodating of that, or some other reason that's being masked by everyone's seeming insistence that autism is the only diagnosis he needs, I don't know. But there's got to be a way to explain that our experience is not just the frustration of 'my sibling doesn't present as typical' but also the frustration of 'I feel like I'm not allowed to complain about my sibling the way that siblings in most families do' and 'my sibling's behavior is sometimes terrifying and might be classified as abusive if they weren't diagnosed with a disability.'" (E. E., personal correspondence, 2020)

To date, there is very little, if any, research about trauma related to the siblings of people with disabilities. Overall, sibling research from the past few decades indicates that, although most siblings seem to be doing well, experiences are mixed. Many, many more pages could be filled with quotes similar to the ones included here. These are the voices of siblings who have either been diagnosed with some form of PTSD or who struggle with anxiety, depression, and other symptoms consistent with common reactions to trauma. Given their experiences, and the experiences of countless siblings whose voices we have not heard, sibling trauma deserves to be the subject of future research and sibling support efforts. We can begin these efforts in our Sibshops by learning about and applying trauma-informed practices to our work (see p. 2, p. 237, and Appendix F). This is an important step that will support all the young siblings who come through our doors.

PRESSURE TO ACHIEVE

 "Ever since I was a child, I have been put into that role—rescuer, perfect child, the one who would make everything right. And all the time while this craziness was going on in my family, I was trying to maintain my grade point average to go on to college and become a doctor." (David, in Leder, 1991, p. 22)

Over the years, we have had the good fortune to talk to many parents about their children. Some of these parents have told us of a situation they believe to be unusual: One child attends a Special Education program, while another child is enrolled in a program for gifted children. The perceived pressure on siblings of people with support needs to excel in academics, sports, music, or even behavior has long been noticed by clinicians. Earlier writings suggested that parents placed the pressure on their typically developing children, as if to compensate for the "failure" resulting from the other child's disability. Whether consciously or unconsciously, parents can pressure their children to compensate for the limitations of the child with a disability, creating resentment and anxiety for typically developing siblings (Barak-Levy et al., 2010; Murphy, 1979; Schild, 1976).

Grossman (1972) found that this pressure to achieve was especially true when the child with the disability was a son. Older only daughters are particularly prone to dual stresses, suggested Cleveland and Miller (1977). These daughters feel pressured to make up for the parents' unfulfilled hopes for the sibling with the disability; they also experience the increased parent-surrogate responsibilities that are most often delegated to daughters rather than sons.

 "I definitely put pressure on myself to achieve. It's just my brother and me, so I'm the only one who can make good grades, get my driver's license, go to the prom, graduate from high school, college, graduate school, get married, have a career and children—all by myself—of course that's pressure." (K. P., personal communication, 2004)

Although parents may be the source of some of the pressure siblings experience (as one brother told us: "My parents expect me to take up all the slack!"), it may be that siblings place much of the pressure on themselves. Coleman (1990) studied 12- to 14-year-old siblings of children with developmental disabilities and compared them with siblings of children who had (only) physical disabilities and siblings of typically developing children. Specifically, Coleman investigated the siblings' self-concept, their need to compensate for the child's deficit, their actual achievement, and parental demands. Coleman found no significant differences among the groups with regard to the subjects' self-concept. However, there were significant group differences with regard to the need for achievement, with siblings of children with developmental disabilities scoring higher than siblings of children with physical disabilities only or with no disabilities.

For the siblings of children who have developmental disabilities, Coleman (1990) found that as their academic achievement increased, their self-concept decreased somewhat. Coleman speculated that this could be the result of internal conflict and could stem from survivor guilt or setting unattainable achievement goals. No such relationship was found between self-concept and achievement for the other two groups. Finally, Coleman found no significant differences among the three groups regarding siblings' perceptions of parental demands.

 "I put pressure on myself; whether my parents encouraged that stance I don't know." (Cynthia, in Leder, 1991, p. 210)

Suggesting that parents attempt to compensate for the loss associated with having a child who has support needs by placing pressure on their typically developing children may be too simplistic and unidirectional. Siblings may place pressure on themselves for a variety of reasons. This hypothesis would certainly apply to the sister mentioned earlier in this chapter who felt that her success in human services was "shame driven" and who could not enjoy her many accomplishments.

But there can be other reasons as well. The motivation may be attention: As one sister told us, "Growing up I did well in school because that was my way of getting attention from my parents." Another brother said he did well in school to counteract the profound loss that his parents experienced about his sister's disability. Another sister volunteered that success in academics was her way of demonstrating to the world that it was her sister, not she, who had a disability.

 "I never exactly sat down and decided to do this, but I put a lot of pressure on myself to always 'be good' and to excel in school. I think this was, in part, to show the world that I'm different from my sister. It took me a long time to be able to be okay with not being perfect, to allow myself to be human. Trying to keep up the facade of being perfect is an incredibly isolating and tiring experience!" (S. G., personal communication, 2005)

High achievement in academics, sports, or behavior may seem like a dubious "unusual concern." After all, Grossman's (1972) study revealed that not only were there no significant differences between college-age siblings of people with and without cognitive disabilities in academic achievement, overall academic functioning (including social adaptation), intelligence, and anxiety levels, but also that the siblings of people with cognitive disabilities scored higher on measures of overall college functioning.

Indeed, the conscientious attitude some siblings have for their schoolwork would suggest that their need to achieve is, in fact, an "unusual opportunity." And it may well be. Parents and service providers, however, should be alert for siblings whose efforts are compulsive or neurotic (e.g., the sibling who cannot be satisfied with a B+ average), or for siblings who are unhappy despite many successes.

Those who wish to support siblings who may be putting undue pressure on themselves to be "perfect" should also consider the healing power of validation from parents, professionals, and peers. As with many sibling concerns, the self-imposed pressure to achieve may be alleviated for sibs by the simple recognition that they are seen, heard, and not alone.

 "Growing up, I was always told I was the lucky one, and that I should be thankful I am not disabled. There are many negative feelings associated with being the sibling of a person with developmental delays. Growing up, those feelings were viewed as very negative, or labeled as being selfish. As the sibling, I felt I always had to be the strong one, the perfect one, I was the lucky one. I fear failure, and feel that I am a burden at times. After connecting with more siblings with similar situations, I have been able to express my feelings of resentment in a safe place, with people who understood. This made it much easier to process those feelings, and know that it is totally okay to feel how I am feeling. Connecting with other siblings has helped tremendously. Connecting with others of similar backgrounds has created a safe place for me to talk about my feelings, and know I am not alone. When parents or professionals have asked me how I am doing, that made me feel very supported. Just the acknowledgment that being a sibling of a person with developmental delays is hard has helped me feel heard. When others ask about me, and my experience, that truly helps." (Chelsea A., personal communication, 2021)

3

Information Needs of Siblings

 The hardest thing is the uncertainty—not knowing what's coming next—and the feeling of vulnerability if something does happen and that you're open to being really hurt. Also, not knowing if my little brother will wake up in the morning, or when a kiss I give him will be the last. (Rebekah C., 17, in Meyer, 2005)

Throughout their lives, brothers and sisters will have a need for information about their siblings' condition. Their needs will closely parallel the informational needs of their parents, and yet parents have distinct advantages. As adults, parents' understanding of the world and the way it works is more mature and benefits from a lifetime of experiences. Also, parents have far greater access to information—written and otherwise—about their child's condition and its implications than their children do.

 "It's kind of frustrating not always knowing what they are saying about him. I am a member of the family, too, and I deserve to know what's going on with him just as much as they do. I mean: What if they aren't always there to take care of him? How am I supposed to be able to take care of him if I really don't know anything about him or the problems he has had in the past? Or what meds he is allergic to? That kind of stuff. I need to know, too, and I don't think that they realize that." (Alisa A., 18, in Meyer, 2005)

Siblings of children with disabilities have a compelling need for information about the condition of their brother or sister with a disability and its implications. They need information for reassurance, to answer their own questions and questions posed by others, and to plan for their future. Unless their sibling has a terminal condition, the need will be lifelong and the topics ever-changing. Throughout their lives, the types of information siblings need—as well as how it is optimally presented—will vary according to the siblings' age.

INFORMATION NEEDS ACCORDING TO AGE

Preschool-age brothers and sisters will have a need for information about their siblings' support needs—and so will siblings who are senior citizens. What they will want and need to know will evolve throughout their lives and their family's life span.

Preschoolers

Debra Lobato (1990) has written that children's understanding of their siblings' support needs "will represent a unique blend of what they have been told, overheard, observed, and conjured up on their very own" (p. 21). When siblings lack adequate, age-appropriate information, and a mature understanding of the world, misunderstandings will be neither unusual nor surprising.

 "I remember walking into my sister's room one morning [and] seeing large clumps of blond hair on her pillow. 'Mommy, why is Lisa's hair falling out?' I asked. 'She's sick,' was the only reply possible from my mother; she had no time for lengthy explanations for a 3-year-old. So, I was left to solve the mystery by myself." (Ellis, 1992, p. 1)

Typically, young children interpret their world in terms of their own immediate observations. Because they have a limited range of experiences from which to draw, they frequently engage in magical thinking.

 "'My kitty is sick!' said a 6-year-old girl who came to me, crying. Her cat had been coughing up hairballs, and this little girl was afraid that it caught cancer from her brother, who had been throwing up from his chemotherapy treatments. She looked at me, sighed deeply, and said, 'This chemo has been hard on all of us.'" (Schorr-Ribera, 1992, p. 2)

To prevent such misconceptions, preschoolers need to know that they cannot catch their siblings' disability and that they did not cause the condition. These concepts—although obvious to adults—may not be clear to a young child who has caught her sister's cold and has a preschooler's sense of causality. If she can catch her sister's strep throat, she may reason, it is possible she may also catch her spina bifida.

Children ages 2–6 are concrete thinkers. Explanations of disabilities or illnesses to children at this age should be as clear as possible. Debra Lobato (1990) noted that children as young as 3 years can recognize some of their brothers' and sisters' problems, especially when they have had contact with other children and their siblings are older.

 "John plays cars with me and he loves to break dance. Sometimes he pulls off a shoe and I have to put it back on, but he is just slower than us, that is all." (4-year-old brother, in Fink, 1984, p. 6)

Lobato counsels that 3 years is not too early to share comments about a child's disability or illness. One means of explaining a disability is to describe it in terms of differences in behavior or routine. Thus, a 4-year-old who accompanies his 2-year-old sister to an early intervention program may understand his sister's disability this way: "Down syndrome means that you have to go to school to learn how to talk." To another preschooler, cerebral palsy might mean "you have a hard time walking, and a lady comes to your house to help you learn how to eat." Although clearly incomplete, these definitions can be the foundation for more involved explanations at later ages.

School-Age Children

During their grade-school years, typically developing siblings need information to answer their own questions about the disability or illness as well as questions posed by classmates, friends, or even strangers. Older children may harbor private theories to explain their siblings' problems—even when accurate information has been provided. Sourkes (1990) recounted the observation of a 10-year-old boy whose teenage sister had a leg amputated due to osteogenic sarcoma:

 "My sister hurt her leg on the chain of her bike. She didn't even notice it until I pointed it out to her. I don't ride my bike anymore. I'm afraid to. One night I went out and I broke the chain on my bike so that I couldn't ride it. I told my mother that the bike broke by itself, but I really broke the chain." (p. 3)

Other siblings may hold beliefs about the cause of the condition that place the blame on the child with support needs. "She probably got it because she never drank water or something," said one 13-year-old sister of a 7-year-old patient with Wilms tumor. Blaming the patient "may be a reflection of the sibling's own anger, a part of the belief system of the sibling or family, or a projection of guilt onto the patient" (Koch-Hattem, 1986, p. 113).

 "My sister's diagnosis is very strongly connected in my mind to nail polish. She was getting into that kind of stuff and I wasn't and so I thought it was kind of gross. I thought she got a rash because of the nail polish, which then caused the cancer." (Naomi, 22, in Sourkes, 1990, p. 12)

 "I always knew that Nick had spastic quadriplegia. But it took years for me to know what that meant." (Barbara, personal communication, 2005)

School-age children may have more specific questions than preschoolers may. They may ask, "Why does she have to go to the hospital?" "Why can some people with cerebral palsy walk and some can't?" "What does amniocentesis mean?" "What's physical therapy? Does it hurt?" "Why is Stephanie getting so fat?" "What does cognitive disability mean?" Yet, obtaining this information can be a problem for siblings of this age.

Teenagers

Even teenagers may have misconceptions about their siblings' problems. Some may assign a psychological or metaphysical reason for the diagnosis. One teen commented:

 "Well, I think maybe it was God's way of telling our family to pull together. There had been a lot of arguing and a lot of dissension in my family and maybe this was his [sic] way to bring us together." (Sourkes, 1990, p. 4)

Like preschoolers and grade-school children, teenagers often have specific questions about the support needs of their brothers or sisters.

 "Why was his hair falling out? Why was he going to the hospital all the time? Why was he getting bone marrows all the time? It never occurred to me that he might die. What was happening? I didn't get to go to the hospital to see him. What was leukemia? Why was he getting so many presents?" (Chet, 14, in Murray & Jampolsky, 1982, p. 35)

 "Jake has had three seizures today. I have reached my breaking point. My mom has cried ALL day and Jake is so confused and keeps asking why this is happening to him. I just feel so bad for my sib tonight." (S. M. personal communication, 2012)

AVOIDING MISCONCEPTIONS ABOUT THE CONDITION

 "My mother didn't tell me what was going on because she wanted to protect my feelings. I was so angry because Jeana and I were so close. I was so terribly afraid. I didn't know what was happening; I was afraid of the unknown. If you know what the problem is, you can face up to it and work it out; but if you don't understand, you can't handle it." (Joanne, 16, in Murray & Jampolsky, 1982, p. 36)

How a family handles the dissemination of information about the disability or illness will greatly influence a typically developing sibling's adjustment to the condition. Some parents, seeking to protect their children from the sadness they are experiencing, choose to tell their children as little as possible (Canary, 2008; Kao et al., 2012). Siblings tell us that they think parents should avoid this strategy. When left in the dark about what is happening to a brother or sister, siblings may make up their own stories that will be worse than the truth. They may even blame themselves for their siblings' conditions. Obtaining information, then, can be reassuring, even comforting, for a sibling. They tell us that they still worry, but their concerns will be easier to manage because they are based on facts rather than fantasies.

 "My advice is that doctors and parents ought to give information to the brothers and sisters straight! Sometimes, instead of telling them the truth, parents and doctors tell siblings a lot of baloney. It is easier to handle when at least you have all the facts." (Maria, 15, in Murray & Jampolsky, 1982, p. 43)

Or, as Callahan (1990) noted, "Information, even concerning a painful subject, is preferable to ignorance distorted by imagination" (p. 157). Traditional sources of information available to parents usually are not available to siblings. With rare exceptions such as the resources provided on the Sibling Support Project website (www.siblingsupport.org), most books, websites, and materials about disabilities and illnesses have been created for adults, although more resources address the information needs of young siblings.

 "After he got diagnosed, it got a lot easier. I knew what to expect and ways to deal with him. We've read a lot of books which have been a big help on that subject, like on that particular autism. They've been like a big help and it makes you realize how they're feeling rather than like how you deal with someone else without autism. There's a big difference." (Jackson, p. 6, in Gorjy et al., 2017)

Siblings are also frequently excluded from another traditional source of information: the teachers, physicians, therapists, nurses, and other providers serving children with health and developmental needs. Brothers and sisters seldom accompany their parents to clinic visits or individualized family service plan (IFSP), individualized education program (IEP), or transition planning meetings, and if they do, providers are unlikely to seek their opinions, thoughts, and questions. Left out of the loop or relegated to waiting rooms, siblings report feeling ignored or isolated.

 "I went with Lisa and my mother several times a week to the hospital where Lisa would get finger pokes and sometimes bone marrows (which I thought of as 'bone arrows' because the procedure entailed being punctured in the back by a large needle). She lost all her hair. Sometimes she threw up and sometimes she stayed overnight at the hospital. I remember not understanding at all what was happening to my sister, and not receiving any explanations." (Ellis, 1992, pp. 1–2)

"Once when I was little, Monica had a seizure in the middle of the night. My parents had to rush her to the hospital because she was not breathing and left me at home with a babysitter. My mother and sister stayed in the hospital for a week while I sat at home wondering what had happened. My parents had not informed me so I was not sure what was going on." (Martha P., age 13, in Meyer, 2005)

 "My sister came here for therapy. She got to go on these scooters, but I had to sit in the waiting room with my mom the whole time. Why isn't there something for brothers and sisters to play with while they're there? When you are a kid, you don't understand. All your parents are telling you is that she is special and has to go to these special programs. Well, I wanted to be special too!" (Fish, 1993)

 "My parents sometimes include me in conversations, but most of the time I have to listen in on discussions with doctors or discussions between my parents. For example, I had to find out about one of Sarah's surgeries from when the doctor called to remind my parents of the surgery and I answered the phone. I do wish that my parents would include me more because I'm going to find out what's going on eventually." (Stephie N., age 15, in Meyer, 2005)

 "I've been talking to my mom a bit, about how I feel left out. She says that [my brother] has been left out and excluded all these years. But she doesn't understand the hardships of being a sibling." (M. B., personal correspondence, 2012)

The isolation, loneliness, and loss some siblings experience will be complicated by a lack of information about their siblings' support needs (Seligman, 1983). In some families, siblings receive a clear (if unspoken) signal that the family doesn't discuss the condition, leaving siblings to feel alone with their concerns and questions. A sibling wrote about growing up in an extended family in Hawaii:

 "Joyce was born soon after me. Joyce, Sharon, and I sunbathed together and explored the property between the houses, with cousin Miles as our fearless leader. Then Joyce got very sick and didn't 'grow up' like the rest of us. . . . Joyce was no longer at home. We would ask, 'Where is Joyce' 'How is she?' 'What's Joyce doing?' Simple questions from children. We received no answers, except, 'Don't ask those questions anymore.' 'Never ask Aunty Florence about Joyce.' How were we to know any better? Our friend, our neighbor, our cousin, was no longer in the front house. We were only 8 and 10 at the time." (A. T., personal communication, 1992)

Even when parents are happy to answer questions, some siblings will keep their questions and concerns to themselves. These brothers and sisters are reluctant to ask questions, having witnessed their parents' sadness caused by the disability or illness. "Why would I ask my parents about something which makes them cry?" one sister told us. When parents are so busy with caring for the child with a disability, siblings feel reluctant to talk to parents about their concerns and questions (Gorgy et al., 2017).

 "Mum notices her hit me at the time but we don't talk about it. Mum is too busy to talk; I ask her and she says, 'I'm busy.'" (Gettings et al., 2015)

 "I'd like to be told what's going on and have explanations. I get told stuff but not explanations." (Gettings et al., 2015)

Some parents are unaware that their children harbor questions they feel will cause discomfort for either the child with a disability or the parents. Often, parents are willing to answer any question their child asks, but when the child does not ask the questions, parents may assume that the child has no interest in the topic. Siblings tell us that parents must be proactive in offering information:

 "I would like people to understand that children need information [and] have feelings and fears. I would like to let people know that they need to be open with their children, all their children, that just because the sisters and brothers don't ask, it doesn't mean that they don't want to know." (Pat, in Remsberg, 1989, p. 4)

PROVIDING BROTHERS AND SISTERS NEEDED INFORMATION

What, then, are the best ways to provide a sibling with information? Siblings, young and not so young, recommend a variety of approaches. Few, however, are as important as the family's attitude toward the topic.

Keep the Sibling's Disabilities an Open Topic

 "Parents have to sit down and talk to the brothers and sisters about [the disability]. Kids don't automatically understand it by themselves. Maybe the other kids need some help, too, understanding that it won't go away, that it will be there and is a fact of life. I love my brother, but I'd like to understand more..." (Beth, 16, in Binkard et al., 1987, p. 5)

Although Beth encourages parents to "sit down and talk" to their typically developing children, many siblings report that this is an uncomfortable situation for all parties and have likened it to being told about the birds and the bees. A far better way, they tell us, is to keep the topic of the support needs open and to offer information frequently, preferably in small doses. If siblings observe their parents openly discussing the disability or illness, they will learn to do so as well.

Answer Siblings' Questions About the Condition

If parents answer children's questions about siblings' support needs in a forthright manner, and if they make their children feel glad that they asked, their children will not only gain an understanding of their siblings' support needs but will also become confident enough to approach their parents whenever they have questions. Of course, not all siblings will ask questions. Parents need to adopt some strategies that can help all siblings—school-age and older—acquire the needed information.

Provide Siblings With Written Materials

 "My lack of information about my brother's disability led me to read everything and anything about cerebral palsy, including the novel *Karen* [Killilea, 1952] and textbooks on cerebral palsy and speech. When I was in college studying to become a speech-language pathologist, I laughed when I learned I was going to read the revised versions of the two textbooks I had read as a sixth grader." (B., personal communication, 2005)

Another way to help siblings learn more about their brothers' and sisters' support needs is to utilize print and web-based materials on the disability or illness. The Sibling Support Project website (www.siblingsupport.org) provides lists of books—both fiction and nonfiction—that can help young readers learn more about various disabilities. In addition, parents, family members, and service providers can contact agencies or associations representing the child's disability or illness and request information prepared for young readers. If the agency does not have such materials or web content, parents should challenge them to create these materials or provide links to them.

Include Siblings in Visits With Service Providers

 "Let him be as involved in the medical side as he wishes to be. Ask him if he would like to visit his brother or sister in the hospital. Let him ask questions and discuss treatments with you and the medical staff." (Schorr-Ribera, 1992, p. 1)

There has been a growing recognition that a child's disability or illness will affect more family members than the child and their parent(s). The professional literature today more often refers to the family unit, whereas in the past, the focus was primarily on the mother, or the parents, and the child with the disability or illness. Research on families tells us that siblings' attitudes toward their brother or sister with a disability, as well as siblings' adjustment, mood, and self-esteem, are strongly influenced by family cohesion and family supports (Williams et al., 2002). However, even when an agency claims to offer family-centered service, siblings are rarely invited to clinic visits or involved in the IEP, IFSP, or transition planning process. Service providers who fail to address siblings' concerns squander valuable opportunities and resources.

Inviting—but not requiring—siblings to attend meetings with service providers can benefit all parties. When included, siblings can obtain helpful, reassuring information about a sibling's condition (e.g., behavior, schooling, future planning) (Lee et al., 2020). Brothers and sisters can contribute to the team by providing information and a unique, informed perspective. Their views on issues such as barriers to inclusion with same-age neighborhood peers, or a sibling's ability to share household responsibilities are likely to be insightful—if frequently unsentimental. Siblings often have a good sense of the strengths and abilities of their brothers and sisters despite their disabilities and can make valuable contributions to a strengths-based approach to support, goal setting, and overall wellness. Parents gain a fresh perspective on the siblings' concerns, which can result in improved communication about the child's disability.

 "I wish the doctor had told me his hair would fall out. It surprised me when I saw him bald. It would scare me when he was throwing up because I thought he was dying. Later on, I found out that his baldness and his throwing up were side effects of medicine. My advice to others is to try and get as much information as you can. I was one of the last ones in my neighborhood to find out he had cancer." (Kurt, 13, in Murray & Jampolsky, 1982, pp. 38–39)

Furthermore, when invited to meet with service providers, siblings are brought into the loop. This sends a message to family members and service providers alike that siblings are valued members of the child's team. Including brothers and sisters acknowledges the important roles they currently assume in their siblings' lives and, for many, roles they will have as adults.

Finally, information can promote understanding. Iles (1979) found that when healthy siblings had sufficient knowledge of their siblings' illness and treatment, they had increased empathy for their parents and greater compassion for their ill brothers and sisters. To be sure, it will not always be appropriate to invite a brother or sister to a meeting: A sibling may be too young, or a meeting may be about delicate issues best discussed first with parents. Whenever possible, however, parents and professionals should invite the child's siblings. At the very least, this will prevent siblings from experiencing the emotional exclusion of sitting alone in a waiting room.

Determine the Sibling's Knowledge of the Condition

Although these strategies—keeping the topic open, answering siblings' questions, providing written materials, and inviting siblings to meetings—will go a long way toward meeting siblings' informational needs, the only way to be certain siblings understand the disability or illness will be to have them explain it to someone else. One time-tested strategy is for parents to check in with their typically developing children approximately once per year during the school years.

To do this as unobtrusively as possible, parents should choose a time when they are alone with their children, perhaps on the way to soccer practice or play rehearsal. As the child with support needs naturally enters the topic of conversation, parents pose a hypothetical situation to the typically developing sibling: "If someone asked you, 'What's the matter with David?' what would you say?" Asking the question like this will provide the parent with a fairly accurate window on the child's understanding of their sibling's disability. Because the question, as asked, is typical of questions asked of most siblings at one time or another, siblings are likely to be interested in discussing what a satisfactory response might be. Parents then listen carefully to their child's response. If the child seems to have a good grasp for their age, parents should compliment the child for their knowledge and consider adding a few facts to the knowledge base. If the answer needs some adjustments, this will be an ideal chance to improve the child's understanding of the sibling's condition. If the typically developing child does not have a satisfactory answer, parents can provide some elementary information. Even a "canned" response will help the child respond when asked this question.

WHEN SIBLINGS THINK ABOUT THE FUTURE

 "I am terrified to have a child with a disability such as my brother's. I don't think I could handle it. Genetics counseling before planning pregnancy is definitely a necessity." (Seltzer & Krauss, 2002)

 "We all have to worry. Who else is going to be there? I will have to worry and it will be my responsibility; I think about it all the time. I think about the person I am going to marry. When I meet someone, they are not going to just marry me, but they are going to have to love my brother and know he is going to be around all my life." (Fish, 1993)

One very difficult topic for siblings to discuss with their parents is their concern about the future. A typically developing child may wonder, "Will my own children have disabilities?" and "What responsibility will I have to my sibling when my parents die?"

Childbearing Concerns

Siblings' concerns about their childbearing potential may be rooted in their often unexpressed but real fears about the hereditary nature of the disability (Parfit, 1975). Often, these fears are unfounded, but siblings need information and reassurance to that effect. In the event that the condition does have a hereditary basis, older siblings, prior to their childbearing years, need an opportunity to learn about genetic implications of the disability (Ferraioli & Harris, 2009; Murphy, 1979).

 "I really don't know what we'd have done if the tests had shown I could pass on osteogenesis imperfecta. I've always loved kids and assumed I'd have some someday. I hadn't really thought about what my mother's and sister's osteogenesis imperfecta could mean for myself. But my husband did bring it up when we were engaged and thought it was something to explore. Luckily, we found out there was no way I could pass it on." (Rachel, 21, in Binkard et al., 1987, p. 20)

Concerns About Future Responsibilities

 "The future is so unpredictable. Most likely, my parents will care for Nathaniel and Sophia as long as they are capable. I'll probably go off to college, start a career and a family, and visit whenever it's possible. When my parents can't care for them anymore, I'll probably help choose a place for them to live because I don't think I'd be able to provide the care they need as much as I would like to. It's painful to think about, but I will still make them a priority in my life." (Althea R., 13, in Meyer, 2005)

 "I have a lot of fear inside for Allen. I think I have a good future ahead—I work very hard in school and do well—but what will happen to him? I'm sure he'll stay at home with my mom and dad a lot longer than I will, but will he ever be able to get married and have kids?" (Beth, 16, in Binkard et al., 1987, p. 7)

 "Sometimes it is scary, because if someone would try to kidnap him, he wouldn't know what to do. He is not going to be able to scream and shout like me or somebody else would. It's kind of scary. Same with swimming. I get nervous if he is swimming by himself, like if me and my friends aren't out there or something. Like I do have occasional bad dreams about him drowning or dying because I cannot help him." (Breanna, age 11, Angell et al., 2012, p. 6)

It is not unusual for school-age children to express a desire to care for their sibling when they become adults. They may reveal this sentiment in statements such as, "When we all grow up, I want Alicia to come live with me." And siblings with a close relationship are likely to be more involved in future caregiving (Burke et al., 2012). Like other children when they reach their teens, however, it is also common for them to dream of a life beyond their immediate family. Unlike other teens, siblings of people with disabilities or illnesses may feel that their future options are limited by their siblings' many needs. They may feel that whom they marry and where they may move will be restricted because of their sibling with support needs.

 "I asked my mom. 'I don't really want to do this all my life when I'm older; when I'm married, have kids.' And she said, 'That's why we try to help and all that good stuff. And just, you're supposed to have your life and he's supposed to have his. We're not saying blow him off, but keep in touch, have help, be there once a week.' 'Yeah, okay.'" (Mitch, age 10, Angell et al., 2012, p. 6)

 "My sister and I have this picture of the future, this plan. We are going to buy a house together. Neither of us will get married. When we get jobs, one of us will work days, the other will work nights. That way we can take care of our brother around the clock." (17-year-old sister, at a sibling panel)

Siblings' concerns about their future options are compounded when they are unaware of their parents' plans for their siblings' adult years. Siblings are often not involved in future planning for their brothers and sisters (Heller & Arnold, 2010; Lee et al., 2020). Fish and Fitzgerald's (1980) work with adolescent siblings revealed that 9 of 10 siblings lacked an understanding and awareness of future plans for their brothers or sisters. Siblings have concerns about their own future as well as their brother or sister's future care (Corsano et al., 2017; Eisenberg et al., 1998; Harland & Cuskelly, 2000; Pavlopoulou & Dimitriou, 2020).

 "Even though my mother asked my husband and me to care for my brothers, I was not allowed any input into the planning. She even wanted us to move into her home and take over her business so my brothers wouldn't have to move. As it turns out, her financial planning was not done correctly. This almost forced us to assume caregiving as soon as she died. The only other alternative was emergency placement, which we feared would not give my brothers good care or would place them far from family." (Margaret, personal communication, 2005)

Many siblings tell us that their family does not discuss the future. Parents, perhaps unaware of their children's concerns, or reluctant to confront their own mortality, often fail to make adequate plans for the child's future. They may not share whatever plans they have made with their typically developing children. Many brothers and sisters assume that they will someday shoulder many more responsibilities than their parents actually intend.

 "I've been thinking very, very hard recently about the care my brother will be under when my parents pass. Although this event will take place most likely in 30–40 years from now, this is the #1 worry that haunts my conscious and unconscious thoughts. My parents say that I have no obligatory responsibility to take care of him, and that they will figure it out. But I can't help but feel like a terrible sister, family member, and person when it comes to not offering to care for him. I love him and I want him to be happy. Most of all I never want him to be alone—I never want him to have to face life alone. I'm crying as I write this because it puts such a hole in my heart. But I don't want him to depend on me. I don't want my life to stop to care for him, I want to move on, I want to have a go at life with fair opportunity. I'm so confused and hurt by these decisions I need to make, and I don't know how to handle this." (C. D., personal correspondence, 2016)

Many families do plan for the future, involving siblings in this process. In these families, there is a spoken and accepted agreement about the responsibilities that siblings will one day assume. Unfortunately, in other families, there is an unspoken assumption that brothers and sisters will take over the roles previously assumed by the child's parents.

 "I don't know the options. I would watch him, but I can't do it alone. I would need help." (Seltzer & Krauss, 2002)

Older adult siblings who care for their brothers and sisters with disabilities have an additional concern: What will become of our siblings if we die before they do?

 "I worry that at my age, I'm not going to be here forever and who is going to take care of her when I'm gone. I can see if she were worked with a bit more, she could go into a smaller group home or semi-independent living. I hate the thought of her living with 23 other adults on a third-floor dorm for the rest of her life." (Fish, 1993)

Unless parents make specific arrangements, responsibility for care of the family member with support needs may ultimately rest with the typically developing siblings. When this happens, siblings can become resentful and may not take adequate measures to meet their sibling's ongoing needs.

 "It is like no one else wants to do it. I'm just thrown into the role which, you know, I don't actually like a lot. I have three brothers and three sisters. They could help out a little, but they don't, actually." (Fish, 1993)

McCullough (1981), in a study of 23 middle-to-upper-class families of children with developmental disabilities, learned that 60% of the parents said they had not made plans for someone to care for the child with support needs if they could not. Sixty percent of the siblings from these families, however, assumed that their parents had made plans. Similarly, 68% of the parents had not made financial arrangements for the child's future, and an equal percentage of siblings had assumed that their parents had made those plans. The picture that emerges from McCullough's study and other more recent research (Burke et al., 2018) is one of parents who have not prepared for their children's future and, if they have made plans, have not shared this information with their typically developing children. Barriers include limited services, financial barriers, and the emotional nature of planning for the future. Various authors (Burke et al., 2018; Murphy, 1979; Parfit, 1975; Powell & Gallagher, 1993) have strongly urged parents to "openly and firmly" face the question of the future, perhaps with the assistance of a specialist, before the need is at hand.

 "I worry about my brother many times during the day, and I confess that in the darkness of night I pray that I may outlive him so I can advocate for him during his lifetime. No matter how good a facility or staff may be, I contend that nothing can take the place of the love and caring of family members." (Liska, 1996, p. 10)

When they interviewed young adult siblings who had a brother or sister with a disability, Harland and Cuskelly (2000) found that the siblings had many concerns about the future. They realized that their parents could not indefinitely care for their brother or sister, and they felt unprepared to take over. Yet, the siblings expected to help manage the finances and advocate for the welfare of their brother or sister. Siblings reported that their biggest contribution would be the emotional support they provided to their brother or sister. Several studies confirm that siblings continue to provide emotional support to their adult brother or sister with a disability (Harland & Cuskelly, 2000; Krauss et al., 1996; Seltzer et al., 1991). Because they can envision a life beyond their parents, teenagers and young adults will require additional information about their siblings' future and what role they will play in that future. If parents have not made plans, it is critical that they begin to and that they encourage the siblings to be a part of the planning. During their teen years, siblings must be able to discuss their perception of their future roles with their parents.

 "I just keep thinking that even if I do move away, if I go away to school or if I have a job away, I am going to have to come back to Columbus. Gilbert is only comfortable in certain surroundings. If you take him away from those surroundings, he won't function. So this is going to be my home someday."

Interviewer: "Do you think about this a lot? How much?"

"Well—now planning my major—very much. There are only so many jobs in Columbus." (Fish, 1993)

When parents plan for their family's future—by writing wills that address the family members' future needs, naming a guardian, setting up trusts—they can reassure their children. They can allay worries by telling them at an early age, for example, "If you want Alicia to live with you when you grow up, that's fine, but if you don't, that's okay, too, because Mommy and I are planning for when Alicia grows up."

In other words, brothers and sisters need to know that when they are adults, there will be a continuum of ways for them to remain lovingly involved with a sibling with support needs. Parents need to be reassured that many, if not most, siblings will choose to remain actively involved in the lives of their brothers and sisters with support needs, especially if they are given choices and a voice throughout the process of providing and planning support.

 "I will be there whenever I can. I don't want him to forget me at all or think I don't love him." (Kathryn C., 14, in Meyer, 2005)

INFORMATION AT SIBSHOPS

 "I know I'm not exactly alone and there are other people that have the same difficulties as me."

"I've made new friends like me."

"It has helped me knowing there are other people like me."

"It's a chance to talk about problems freely." (Gettings et al., 2015)

Siblings' ongoing need for information creates the rationale for the fourth Sibshops goal (see Chapter 1): to provide siblings with opportunities to learn more about the implications of the support needs of their brothers and sisters.

Ultimately, attempts to provide siblings with information at Sibshops are limited: Many Sibshops serve siblings of children with various disabilities or illnesses, precluding an in-depth look at any single condition. Although this type of information is usually best provided by parents and primary service providers, Sibshops can provide participants with overviews of services, therapies, and conditions (as further discussed in Chapter 10). Sibshops can also be a safe place to seek information.

 "I never really understood what my sister's sickness was. My mom and dad didn't ever talk to me about it but I knew something was real unhappy. [At the group] I got to ask things I never asked before." (Forrest, 10, in Murray & Jampolsky, 1982, p. 16)

Each sibling experiences a personal mix of challenges, needs, and opportunities, and support groups and programs like Sibshops extend a range of benefits (Tudor & Lerner, 2015).

 "I don't have to keep things to myself. That it is not my brother's fault; he is how he is. I have learnt that I can share things." (Hayden et al., 2019)

ADULT SIBLINGS

 "Mike has only one sibling, a brother Chris. Chris, who has Down syndrome, lives at home with his mom in another state. Mom is in her late seventies; Dad died last year. Mike and his parents have never really discussed what will become of Chris after his parents are no longer around to care for him. Mike figures that because Chris has Down syndrome, his parents always assumed they would outlive Chris. Mike, who has a young family, worries deeply about Chris's future. Should he bring Chris to live with his family or in his community? What would be the impact on his own family? What services are available for a person with a disability, especially one who is new to the state?" (Meyer & Erickson, 1993, p. 1)

Of all the age groups, adult siblings frequently have the most compelling need for information. Many will find themselves increasingly responsible for meeting the ongoing needs of their siblings. Consequently, adult siblings express a desire to learn more about services for their brothers and sisters (Eisenberg et al., 1998; Harland & Cuskelly, 2000). They say that they need this information to help their siblings make informed choices and to plan for a future that considers the needs of all family members. Few programs exist specifically for adults whose siblings have support needs, but each program attempts to address the participants' need for information. According to organizers of one such program in

New Jersey, many members are "apprehensive about what will happen when their parents die" (Meyer & Erickson, 1992, p. 3) and wish to learn about options available for their siblings. One Seattle-area program for adult brothers and sisters surveyed 60 adult siblings to determine their informational needs. They identified the following topics, which are listed in decreasing order of interest:

- Recreation and leisure opportunities

- Community living and residential options

- Sexuality, socialization, and friendship

- Family communications

- Employment and day-program options

- Eligibility for services

- Legal issues

- Advocacy

- Respite care options (Meyer & Erickson, 1992)

The New York City–based disability organization AHRC NYC (https://www.ahrcnyc.org/) periodically hosts meetings for local adult siblings on specific topics, including family teamwork and future planning, guardianship, the caregiver experience, entitlements and benefits, and family and professional partnerships. Despite their need for information, and although similar organizations are increasingly aware that siblings often step into caregiving roles, few agencies serving adults with disabilities reach out to adult siblings. Some agencies find it difficult to attract parents of adults with disabilities to meetings, workshops, and other events. Parents may be aging, have difficulty attending meetings in person or navigating technology for online meetings, or feel they have already attended enough meetings to last several lifetimes. Agencies should instead market their informational efforts to siblings—the family members who will have increasing involvement and responsibility in the life of the person with the disability.

The good news is that a growing number of disability organizations, health care providers, and social services providers recognize the importance of building relationships, and sharing information, with siblings. We are increasingly encouraged by the inquiries we receive from agencies, health care practices, and trade organizations that want to learn more about how to effectively connect and cultivate relationships with siblings of all ages. Professionals from a variety of health care and social services backgrounds who seek training on the Sibshop model represent an expanding population of providers who acknowledge the value of communicating with and supporting siblings of all ages. Participants in a Sibshop Facilitator Training shared the following feedback after completing the workshop:

 "How can we say we offer family-centered services when there aren't specific services or opportunities for the siblings? I will be an advocate in the organization to ensure we are truly family centered."

 "I'm excited to bring this certification back to [our organization] to create space for siblings. This training has invigorated me as a sib and social worker to be mindful of ways we can engage sibs in all aspects of our work."

"While I work primarily to serve and support adolescents in my work, I am often also supporting parents. This training has encouraged and equipped me to better address the needs of siblings as well."

 "I now have a deeper understanding of the struggles and triumphs of siblings. I will continue to advocate for both the child with support needs and their siblings, as well as connect with other allies and providers to better support the families I serve."

 "[I will] try to incorporate them more in the educational components of our structure so that they get the information they need to feel less stressed and more prepared for their potential future responsibilities."

 "I previously never considered the siblings of children with disabilities but now it is something I am very aware of as a necessary piece of my future work as a speech-language pathologist."

 "I'm a pediatrician, so I would like to advocate the importance to support siblings of children with disabilities."

 "I learned so much about including siblings. I can go back and work with our different departments to give time to address the sibling on their own and answer their questions. Also to educate our staff on praising siblings as individuals, rather than for how good they are with their sib. There are so many opportunities we can take to be more inclusive of sibs daily, and I plan on bringing that to all [our organization's departments] EI [early intervention], OT [occupational therapy], PT [physical therapy], speech, family support, and respite!!"

 "We meet with parents and the youth with the disability on an annual basis. During these meetings we talk about plans for the future (including employment, living arrangements, etc.). Parents will be encouraged to have siblings attend these meetings and include siblings in discussions at home regarding the youth's future (what will happen when parents are no longer living)."

 "We tend to place so much focus on the person with the disability. We provide regular support to parents, professionals, and extended family members, but not specific to the siblings. We will make changes to include siblings and train more people to do this important work."

4

Unique Opportunities

 "My overriding impression of siblings is of amazing resilience. They go through the experience with the same intensity as the patient and the parents, but often on the sidelines. They come out whole, with a maturity, with a different view of things." (Sourkes, 1990, p. 11)

When asked to reflect on how their children's needs have changed their lives, most parents will acknowledge that, in addition to the many challenges, there have also been unique, significant, and often unexpected rewards. These parents have told us that, as a result of having a child with disability, they have met the person who is now their best friend or spouse, helped create services for people with disabilities, edited a newsletter, written a book chapter, testified at a state legislative hearing, or embarked on a new career. Having a child with support needs was, perhaps ironically, an opportunity for meaningful connection and personal growth.

Previous research about siblings of people with disabilities, and the families in which they grow up, focused almost exclusively on their concerns, taking a pathogenic, glass-half-empty perspective. The child with the disability was seen as a burden to the family, and the family itself was assumed to be dysfunctional, experiencing chronic sorrow and pervasive guilt. Positive traits, such as optimism and resilience, were frequently interpreted as signs of denial, not as signs of strength. Families, of course, knew better.

 "We are a very close family, and are all heavily involved with Special Olympics, which is a direct impact from my brother. Having him in my life reminds me not to take my health, sanity, or freedom for granted." (Seltzer & Krauss, 2002)

Parents, especially the growing number of parents who work in social services, medicine, education, and academia, were the ones to begin challenging this paradigm (see Gerdel, 1986). On a daily basis in their homes, they witnessed dynamics that apparently had eluded many researchers. They knew that their families and the vast majority of the families of children with support needs they knew were—all things considered—doing quite well.

 "If Tracie wasn't autistic I wouldn't know anything about autism. I wouldn't know as much as I do now. And it's like a life skill, knowing about autism." (Joseph, in Gorjy et al., 2017, p. 4)

More recent research suggests that sibling experiences are not, in fact, all bad. Sibling studies paint a more positive, balanced, and complex picture of the lives of brothers and sisters. In 2017, researchers from Vanderbilt University reviewed decades of sibling studies to determine outcomes in four key areas of siblings' lives: problems–advantages and life successes, life choices, adult sibling relationships, and caregiving and anticipated caregiving. In summarizing their findings, they describe sibling experiences as being mixed:

> There are also other potential outcomes of being a sibling to a brother or sister with disabilities. Some are beneficial, others less so. In many cases, outcomes can be beneficial or challenging at specific times in one's life, or for different siblings. (Hodapp et al., 2017)

More recent research also describes the close relationships that develop between siblings and the child with support needs, as well as the self-reliance, tolerance, sensitivity, and prosocial behaviors siblings develop (Marquis et al., 2019; Orm et al., 2021; Williams et al., 2010). These are aspects of family relationships overlooked in the early literature. Today, research more often considers broader social influences on family adjustment and the severity of disabilities. A life-span perspective supports the idea that there are both positive and negative effects of living in a family when a child has a disability (Marquis et al., 2019). Rather than painting family experiences with a broad negative brush, research helps uncover the finer influences on families, such as the negative effects a sibling may experience when the child with a disability has higher levels of behavior problems (Hastings, 2007; Neece et al., 2010). Research on moderators of sibling relationships also reveals findings such as the greater compassion, social maturity, and empathy siblings develop that lead them to be more civic minded in adulthood and to be more likely to enter human service careers (Martins, 2007; Salena et al., 2018).

 "My experience with my sister has been one of the most important in my life. It has definitely shaped my life and channeled my interests in ways I would not have otherwise pursued." (Itzkowitz, 1990, p. 4)

Beginning in the 1980s, researchers and parents such as Ann and Rud Turnbull and their many colleagues began to seek a fresh, balanced view of families of people who have disabilities and health impairments. They sought a view that acknowledges the challenges faced by these families but one that also appreciates families' many strengths. This view, described as a salutogenic perspective (Antonovsky, 1993; Deavin et al., 2018; Ylven et al., 2006), has been proposed as an alternative to the pathogenic view of families that has dominated the research and clinical literature.

> The salutogenic perspective calls for theorists, researchers, families and service providers to identify factors that contribute to families' successful functioning. This perspective assumes that families inevitably will be faced with stressors but have the potential for active adjustment. Accordingly, the role of service providers is to enhance family strengths rather than to focus solely on deficits. For families, the salutogenic perspective implies discovering and learning how best to use one's resources to meet the challenges of life. (Turnbull & Turnbull, 1993, p. 11)

Like their parents, siblings are not the at-risk population described in the early clinical and research literature. Empirical investigations and clinical observations are beginning to substantiate what most family members have believed all along: siblings of people with disabilities display many strengths and report many opportunities. Research evidence has increasingly shown that siblings are less negatively affected in families with a child with a disability than previously reported, and there is support for the psychological strengths that siblings develop (Drotar & Crawford, 1985; Hastings & Petalas, 2014).

What follows are some of the unique opportunities reported by siblings. Because viewing families from a salutogenic perspective is a more recent research paradigm, this section is briefer than the previous section, and we will rely more on siblings speaking for themselves. We look forward to more research on siblings that proceeds from a salutogenic perspective. In order to help those families who are truly burdened by the challenges imposed by an individual's disability or illness, it is critical that we understand how so many families adapt and, in fact, thrive. We must learn what strategies, philosophies, and resources have sustained these families during difficult times. Appreciating the family members' many strengths and opportunities for growth should not be viewed as interpreting their lives from an idealistic perspective. Many of the insights and opportunities, although invaluable, are hard earned.

MATURITY

 "Because I had a lot of responsibility as a child, I have become a responsible, loyal, even-tempered adult. However, I also worry a lot!" (Seltzer & Krauss, 2002)

Simeonsson and McHale (1981) noted that siblings of children with support needs are often well-adjusted and characterized by greater maturity and responsibility than their typical age peers.

 "When my sister got sick, I kind of became a big brother. I was younger, but I felt like I had to take some initiative and take care of her myself." (Chad, 16, in Sourkes, 1990, p. 13)

There are several ways in which siblings' experiences can shape their frequently observed maturity.

Their Experiences Are Different From Those of Their Peers

 "When I was in high school, I remember thinking that I was far more mature than the people around me but also less mature at the same time. I was very responsible and thought that my peers focused on such petty and insignificant things. But I also had never dated and didn't know how to fit in. I felt like such an odd mix of old and young." (Stephanie, personal communication, 2005)

Because of the impact of their siblings' needs, some siblings may feel that their peers' current concerns appear trivial by comparison.

 "I guess I've always felt I've been 10 years older than my peers when it comes to responsibilities." (Seltzer & Krauss, 2002)

 "I have a different outlook on life than many other people my age. I understand that you can't take anything for granted. And you have to be able to look at the positives.... With Jennifer, there are negatives, but there's so much more that is good." (Andrea, 19, in Binkard et al., 1987, p. 19)

"I think after something large like this happens in your family, you feel a lot more mature. When I went back to school after the summer, it seemed like everybody else was so immature. How could they be moaning because they lost a girlfriend or something like that? I felt I had real adult problems now." (Chad, 16, in Sourkes, 1990, p. 15)

A Loss of Innocence

Like Chad, a sibling's maturity may also be coupled with a loss of innocence. This loss is frequently mentioned by parents who have a child with a serious illness, such as cancer, or who has experienced a traumatic injury. For these siblings, maturity will be hard won: They learn early that life can be unfair, things might not get better in the long run, bad things do not always happen to other people, and they, like their brothers and sisters, are not indestructible.

 "I have a greater sense of compassion and sensitivity toward people who are different from the norm, but I am acutely aware of ignorance and prejudice through inflictions on my family. I may have acquired maturity at an early age, but in the process lost a degree of my innocence and childhood." (Cobb, 1991, p. 3)

Increased Responsibilities

 "I definitely felt I had more responsibilities compared to friends. I grew up faster because of it." (Seltzer & Krauss, 2002)

A child's support needs are usually synonymous with increased caregiving demands, and, as we saw earlier, siblings—especially sisters—are frequently expected to assume an active role in that care. Successfully handling the tasks assigned them can increase siblings' sense of maturity and pride.

 "I learned to be responsible, and I know what it's like to have people rely on you." (Seltzer & Krauss, 2002)

 "One day, a girl comes up to me and says, 'Why are you so mature?' and 'Isn't it hard to be mature?' I just said, 'I don't know, not really.' I feel like we have to be more independent, which makes us more mature." (L. E., personal communication, 2014)

Gaining Perspective

 "I've become a lot more mature and see things a whole new way." (J. L., personal communication, 2021)

Siblings of people with support needs inevitably gain a unique perspective into the human condition. This expanded understanding frequently adds to their mature view of the world.

 "Deaf-blindness causes you to look at yourself. You see how much he has affected your life; being around you all the time and helping you grow up. By dealing with his deaf-blindness, it causes you to become more mature. It causes you to deal with life in an 'adult' manner. You also find out just how much you love your brother and how much a part of life he is." (Harkleroad, 1992, p. 5)

"I can't really separate what's just me and what's been a part of my experience as a sib. I am mature for my age and have learned a lot about the world. I like to think that knowing Caroline has made me less of an oblivious teenager." (Caitlin M., 14, in Meyer, 2005, p. 50)

As Dudish (1991) noted, siblings of children with a disability or illness have multi-dimensional lives. They see that life has many, varied facets. From and with their families they learn determination, patience, and other qualities that can help them grow into mature, sensitive adults.

 "He has helped me appreciate the freedom I have—whenever I do something or go somewhere new and exciting. I get sad knowing he'll never be able to do such things, but at the same time, I am reminded to appreciate it doubly for both of us." (Seltzer & Krauss, 2002)

Although maturity is certainly an attribute desired by parents (and many siblings we have met have been delightfully mature for their years), we realize that maturity is an attribute on a continuum: early maturity can also be a source of concern. On occasion, we have met young siblings—usually sisters—who have little in common with their same-age peers and seem to act as very young adults instead. Most of these siblings are involved in many aspects of their siblings' lives, especially their care. A reasonable amount of responsibility, it seems, can help develop a sibling's sense of maturity; however, excessive demands can cost a sibling their childhood (Angell et al., 2012; Hoskinson, 2011). These children (and their parents) will need to be encouraged to attend to equally important aspects of their development that have little to do with the sibling who has the support needs.

 "There have been times when I have had to tell my parents, 'I am not the parent, you are!' Because when I was ten years old, I was probably giving them advice on how to help her out and how to raise her." (Fish, 1993)

 "For as long as I can remember, people have always told me that I 'seem so mature for my age.' I took pride in that when I was younger. I wanted to be more mature. But as I get older, this isn't such a compliment anymore. Some days I don't want to be 'more mature' than usual." (K., personal communication, 2005)

SELF-CONCEPT AND SOCIAL COMPETENCE

 "Growing up, I enjoyed linking my identity to my brother. I always asked my parents to bring him to school assemblies, after-school activities, birthday parties, etc. I liked the praise, support, and attention that I got from teachers and friends after they met him. And, of course, my parents were usually beaming with pride at my request. To this day, my self-concept is largely intertwined with his presence in my life." (K., personal communication, 2005)

For many, being the sibling of a person with a disability shapes the way they identify, perceive, and view themselves, as well as their capacity to build successful relationships with others. For example, siblings may identify as a "brother," a "sister," a "kind, compassionate person," a "good friend," or a "hard worker." Their ideas about who they are and what they are about often impact the social connections they make.

Self-Concept

Children's self-concept describes their sense of competence, both cognitive and physical, and their social acceptance by family and peers. Researchers have studied many influences on children's self-concept, including their gender and age. Self-concept is often studied by having children complete self-report measures, rating how they feel about their math and problem-solving skills, their appearance, or their physical ability. It includes how children feel about themselves in different areas of their lives—in their family, their school lives, and their expanding social networks.

Growing up with a child with a disability or chronic illness in the family can influence how siblings think about themselves. Existing studies on the self-concept of siblings of children with support needs are inconclusive; however, most studies suggest that siblings' self-concepts compare favorably with those of their peers in the community. For instance, Harvey and Greenway (1984) found that brothers and sisters of children with physical disabilities had lower self-concepts than did controls. Coleman (1990), however, found no significant differences in the self-concept of siblings of children with physical disabilities when compared with siblings of children with cognitive disabilities and siblings of children with no disabilities.

Kazak and Clarke (1986) compared 8- and 9-year-old siblings of children with spina bifida with a control group. Subjects completed the Piers Harris Self-Concept Scale (Piers, 1984), which measures their self-concept as well as their perspectives on their own happiness, popularity, level of anxiety, physical appearance, school performance, and behavioral functioning. The authors' results indicated that there were no differences in self-concept between the two groups.

Coleman's (1990) finding that siblings of children with cognitive disabilities were not significantly different from a control group concurs with studies by Dyson (1996), who found that siblings of children with disabilities displayed the same levels of self-concept, behavior problems, and social competence as matched siblings of children with typical development. Other studies (Dyson & Fewell, 1989; Hannah & Midlarsky, 1999; Lobato et al., 1987) also have reported that siblings of children with disabilities do not display lower self-concepts.

Studies of the self-concepts of siblings of children with chronic illnesses are similarly inconclusive. Spinetta (1981) found that 4- to 6-year-old siblings of children with cancer had lower self-concepts than did the patients. Tritt and Esses (1988) found that preteen siblings of children seen at three specialty clinics (diabetes, juvenile rheumatoid arthritis, and gastrointestinal) had significantly more behavior problems than did controls; however, their levels of self-concept did not differ.

 "Having an autistic sibling is basically normal to me. To me, it just feels normal. It's not different to anyone else that I've seen. Once you've been around him for a long time, it's kind of hard to see the difference between having a normal brother and autistic child. . . . We make our way in life. It's a pretty simple but good way of life, basically." (Terry, in Gorjy et al., 2017, p. 6)

Social Competence

In virtually all studies of the subject, siblings' social competence compares favorably with peers who do not have siblings with a disability or illness. One study (Abramovitch et al., 1987) revealed that both younger and older siblings of children with Down syndrome were significantly more prosocial than children in the normative sample. Ferrari (1984) compared siblings of boys who had diabetes or pervasive disabilities or were healthy. Comparing the three groups, Ferrari found no overall group differences in self-concept or teachers' ratings of self-esteem. He found that the siblings of children with diabetes were reported by teachers as displaying the most prosocial behaviors toward other children in the school, and the siblings of children with pervasive disabilities were given the highest ratings of social competence. He concluded that his study fails to support the view that siblings of children with a health impairment or disability are uniformly at greater risk of psychosocial impairment than siblings of children who are healthy.

 "If Pete wasn't so unique, I probably wouldn't have a brother I could talk to. My brother, I can tell secrets to and he can just be a very cool role model. It is amazing what he does." (Ruby, 14, in Angell et al., 2012, p. 5)

Gruszka (1988) as reported in Lobato (1990) compared 45 siblings (ages 3–17) of children with cognitive disabilities with a control group of equal size. Mothers of these children were asked to rate the children's behavior problems and social competence, and the children completed a standard assessment of their own self-concepts. Gruszka found that the two groups did not differ in their mothers' ratings of their social competence, or in the number and type of behavior problems. The children held similar positive views of their cognitive and physical abilities and their relationships with their mothers and peers. The author concluded that the way they thought about themselves, and the way they thought that others felt about them, was not influenced by the presence of their sibling.

 "Once, I was away during one week on a school camp and my mother sent me a letter, saying that my brother was well-behaved. I remember I felt happy and proud!" (David, 12, in Moyson & Roeyers, 2012)

Dyson (1989) also found that children with siblings who had disabilities were better behaved and less aggressive and hyperactive and tended to have fewer acting-out behaviors than did controls. In a later study, Dyson (1996) reported the positive self-concept of siblings with a brother or sister who had a learning disability. In a study that compared equal numbers of siblings of children with either autism, cognitive disabilities, or no disabilities, McHale et al. (1986) found that, as a group, siblings of children with autism or cognitive disabilities were significantly less hostile, less embarrassed, more accepting, and more supportive than siblings of children with no disabilities. The authors did note, however, that there was a much wider variation in the attitudes of the siblings of the children with disabilities than in the control group—that is, some attitudes were extremely positive and others much more negative.

 "I have learned to be less self-conscious and less concerned with what others think about me. It made me defend the disabled more than I probably would have otherwise. It made me feel better about myself and any problems I might have." (Seltzer & Krauss, 2002)

INSIGHT

 "Sometimes, I want to be just like him, because I want to know what he wants, how he feels, what he thinks. So I will be more considerate with him." (Nell, 9, in Moyson & Roeyers, 2012)

Perhaps the greatest of opportunities experienced by any family member of a person with a disability or illness is the insight one gathers on the human condition. Brothers and sisters frequently mention how their siblings have influenced their perceptions and philosophies, giving them reason to reflect on aspects of life that their peers may take for granted. For instance, young siblings frequently discuss the meaning of friendship during a Sibshop. A friend, they often say, is not someone who makes fun of a person with support needs. Brothers and sisters, first as grade schoolers, then as teenagers, and later as adults, may use the treatment of a sibling with support needs as a "litmus test" when screening potential friends, dates, or even spouses.

 "When my husband asked me to marry him 6 years ago, I answered with an excited 'yes,' and then stepped back and said I wanted him to really think it over because I was a package deal. My sister will always be a priority to me. If he marries me, he must understand that at some point if my parents are gone that my sister will need our support and I will be there no matter what. That is the thing: I think you learn early on to spot out quality people. Somehow, and without many words, my sister taught me what was important in relationships and life. She taught me to accept people for who they are, to accept and appreciate myself, how to be quiet and enjoy someone's company, to slow down and to look at what's around you. She did all this without trying." (Summers, 2004)

 "I tend to pick friends who are likely to get along with Nathaniel and Sophia because it's easier that way. And besides, my take on it is that if they're not going to try to get along with Nathaniel and Sophia, they're really not my friends." (Alethea, 13, in Meyer, 2005, p. 58)

 "When I was in my early 20s, I met a girl and fell in love. After a few months I brought her home to meet my family. When my mother went to the kitchen to prepare dinner, I asked the girl, 'Would you like to see Oliver?' for I had told her about my brother. 'No,' she answered. Soon after, I met Roe, a lovely girl. She asked me the names of my brothers and sisters. She loved children. I thought she was wonderful. I brought her home after a few months to meet my family. Soon it was time for me to feed Oliver. I remember sheepishly asking Roe if she'd like to see him. 'Sure,' she said. Today Roe and I have three children." (de Vinck, 2002, p. 33)

Appreciating the distinction between mere ignorance and actual rudeness at a young age, many brothers and sisters can be philosophical (and sometimes forgiving) even of those who do not appreciate their siblings' qualities.

 "When I started a new school, I showed him to my new friends. It was a bit uncomfortable because they didn't know how to respond. I do get it. He's really disabled; you can see it in his face. And perhaps it would scare me too if I were one of them." (Luijkx et al., 2016)

 "The people who know him don't tease him. The kids who are my age and my sister's age are more curious than wanting to ridicule." (Bill, 16, in Binkard et al., 1987, p. 8)

"There are a lot of people who don't understand. The people who are just being 'ignorant' I usually don't waste my time with. But people who try to understand, I usually explain the situation. Then they get the full picture and see that he is a person, just slower than others. This taught me to respect people, because I can understand how it feels not to be wanted, held, and cared for." (A. Jones, personal communication, 1991)

Many siblings, realizing how their families differ from others in the community, often express appreciation for things that may go unnoticed or unappreciated by their peers, and the desire that others be accepting and tolerant (Deavin et al., 2018; Malcolm et al., 2014).

 "Among people we know, we were unique in having an autistic sibling. We're proud of him, proud of my mother for all her support of him, proud that he's part of a close-knit family." (Seltzer & Krauss, 2002)

Appreciation for Their Siblings' Abilities

 "Peter was the golden thread that held our family together." (Peter's sister speaking at a sibling panel)

Perhaps because they perceive that there is a societal emphasis on their siblings' disabilities, brothers and sisters frequently describe their siblings in terms of their strengths, not their deficiencies (Mascha & Boucher, 2006; Petalas et al., 2009, 2012).

 "The label *autism* does not cover the breadth of my brother's personality. It does not explain why he prefers contemporary jazz to other types of music, why he will spontaneously initiate verbal games with my fiancé, or why he chooses to bond with certain peers over others. If the word *autism* were the sum total of my brother's personality, would he have learned to be affectionate and communicative?" (Shanley, 1991, p. 2)

 "I'd like people to know that although my brother may express his skills differently, he is very talented. And although he may not be able to carry on a philosophical conversation, he ain't stupid." (Carly, 17, in Meyer, 2005, p. 41)

 "Sometimes nothing makes Ray happy and it is frustrating. Then there are days when he is so happy. He can be listening to music or, you think, to your conversations. You really marvel at how your brother copes with deaf-blindness. You appreciate the fact that he 'loves' to work as often as he can. (How many people feel this way?) These are some of the things that make me feel he is a very special person." (Harkleroad, 1992, p. 5)

 "My brother loves to draw. I think he's an awesome artist, although he does not think so." (Cabot, 10, in Angell et al., 2018, p. 6)

 "My brother attends a day program and one of the things that they have taught him to do is to weave. I did not know that they had an Instagram where they sell his work. They are truly art. Proud of him." (L. M., personal communication, 2020)

"Even now, 5 years after his death, Oliver remains the weakest, most helpless human being I ever met, and yet he was one of the most powerful human beings I ever met. He could do absolutely nothing except breathe, sleep, eat, and yet he was responsible for action, love, courage, insight." (de Vinck, 1985, p. 28)

Siblings and family members often come to appreciate the skills and abilities of a brother or sister with a disability who has access to strength-based programs, and when siblings come to share common interests (Diener et al., 2015). For example, siblings of children with ASD enrolled in a technology education program discovered new ways to interact with each other, as well as a new appreciation for a brother or sister's talents:

 "I think [his projects] were pretty cool, because I don't know how to do any of that stuff and he does. And he's good with games and stuff." (Caroline, 14, in Diener et al., 2015)

 "Kevin possesses virtues that I lack. He is not judgmental and he is quick to forgive. He does not expect too much out of people or bear grudges Although I am the 'oldest' in my family, it is his example I follow. He has the virtue of simplicity. It's too bad that simple is often considered a synonym for stupid. They are worlds apart." (Cobb, 1991, p. 3)

Many say that life with a sibling who has support needs has profoundly influenced their values. These brothers and sisters claim that their siblings have taught them at an early age that there are human qualities to appreciate in a person besides intelligence, popularity, and good looks. Their siblings have taught them about compassion, humor, loyalty, and unconditional love.

 "She taught me how to love without reservation, without expectation of returned love. She taught me that everyone has strengths and weaknesses. Martha is no exception. She taught me that human value is not measured with I.Q. tests." (Westra, 1992, p. 4)

 "Here's what I have learned as a sib: The odds may be against you, but if you strive for success, it will come to you. I have watched Stephen beat the odds many times, and I remember that when the odds are against me." (Kevin, 14, in Meyer, 2005, p. 133)

Appreciation for Family

 "I don't have my own children yet, but when I do, I will aspire to be at least half the parent that my mother and father were to my brother and me. My brother is living at home once again after being in a group home for 7 years. My parents' love, support, and dedication to him is unwavering and continues to amaze me. They absolutely personify the definition of 'good parents.'" (K., personal communication, 2005)

The involvement of family members in learning and living together often leads to strong sibling relationships.

 "Because he had his sister, I think, as such a close friend, and they are very close. She's sorta like the cavalry on the hill I say. She comes and rescues him a lot and will explain things and he relies on her heavily." (The mother of a son with a speech impairment, in Barr et al., 2008)

Adaptation to the support needs of a sibling with chronic health needs or a disability is a process, and family roles and activities change and evolve (Glasberg, 2000; Williams, 1997). Adaptation includes learning effective ways for family members to communicate and to problem solve, and these create resilience and sibling adjustment (Giallo & Gavidia-Payne, 2006). Families learn together how they can work and enjoy time together in ways that everyone can participate.

 "We have a special bike for the wheelchair, you can put the wheelchair behind the bike and so she can come along when we are cycling." (Luijkx et al., 2016)

Because they and their families experience challenges unlike those faced by others in the community, siblings often express gratitude for their parents' efforts during difficult times.

 "My parents treated us equally—but to be equal, Jennifer had to have more direct attention from our parents. We never felt shut out because of her needs though. Our whole family always got attention." (Cassie, 18, in Binkard et al., 1987, p. 17)

 "My parents went out of their way to give me significant attention. I understood that sometimes my mom needed to take care of my sister's problems. My parents would take turns taking me out to eat or to the park. I would get time alone with them away from my sister. I also went to Sibshops." (Ty, 17, in Meyer, 2005, p. 56)

 "People tend to think in simplistic terms, not in reality. My mother, for example, is not a saint. In some ways she has still not come to terms with my sister's disability. Yet I see her as a tower of strength. I don't know if I would have that much strength." (Julie, in Remsberg, 1989, p. 3)

Appreciation for Health and Capabilities

 "I have a greater appreciation for my opportunities and capabilities. Yet, I am painfully aware of what I, and others as fortunate, waste. My 'special' brother has taught me through his life that my dreams are only as inaccessible as I let them remain." (Cobb, 1991, p. 3)

Many children grow up feeling indestructible. Brothers and sisters who have witnessed their sibling's struggle to learn or simply stay alive are often less likely to take the blessings of good health and abilities for granted.

 "Most of my friends have lived very sheltered lives—and I admit I have as well. But because they have never suffered a loss, they don't appreciate the little things." (Catherine, 13, in Meyer, 2005, p. 48)

 "Jennifer wasn't going to have all the positive things the rest of us would. I was never jealous. I couldn't be. I have so much, can do so many things, and have all the friends that I do." (Cassie, 18, in Binkard et al., 1987, p. 17)

 "Living with Melissa's handicaps makes me so much more cognizant of my own blessings. She provides a constant reminder of what life could have been like for me if I had been my parents' oldest daughter. This encourages me to take advantage of my mental capacities and to take care of my healthy body." (Watson, 1991, p. 108)

TOLERANCE

 "Lucy is constantly teaching me stuff. She has taught me to be more patient in accepting people where they are and not putting my expectations on them." (Skrtic et al., 1983, p. 18)

The college-age siblings that Grossman (1972) studied reported that the benefits of growing up with a sibling who has a disability include greater tolerance, understanding of people, compassion, and a dedication to altruistic goals. Parents, as well as brothers and sisters themselves, have reported that siblings of people with support needs are more tolerant and accepting of differences than their peers are. The siblings of children with chronic illnesses that Tritt and Esses (1988) studied remarked that they had developed more patience, understanding, sensitivity, and awareness about how to deal with someone who is sick.

 "In spite of his I.Q., Kevin has taught me many valuable lessons. Growing up with a handicapped brother has fostered perseverance and patience. I am accepting of not only the shortcomings of others, but those in myself as well." (Cobb, 1991, p. 3)

They are more tolerant, siblings frequently note, because life with their brothers and sisters has made them keenly aware of the consequences of prejudice. Intolerant of intolerance, brothers and sisters bristle when others make assumptions about their siblings based on their physical appearances.

 "Sometimes kids at school look at Elizabeth and say, 'Is that your sister?' 'Who is she?' They think because she looks different that she's different inside. But she's just like us inside. And she doesn't want to be stared at and laughed at or ignored." ("Jennifer," 1990, p. 2)

PRIDE

Due to their tendency to focus on their siblings' abilities, brothers and sisters frequently testify to the adaptations their siblings have made to their disabilities or illnesses:

 "When my brother had his leg amputated, I wondered if he would ever be able to skateboard or ride a bike again. Then the first day out of the hospital he rode a skateboard. Now he can ride a bike, a horse, and do anything. My brother Tony's ability to deal with the problem helped me to have the strength to deal with it too." (Eric, 16, in Murray & Jampolsky, 1982, p. 41)

 "What makes me proud of my brother? He has dreams and goes after them. Some people sit around just thinking about what they want to do with their life, and Alex makes an effort to make his dreams become reality. Alex is also an incredible bowler, and a great friend." (Stephanie, 16, in Meyer, 2005, p. 53)

 "Jennifer has probably achieved more than I have. She's been through so much. She couldn't even talk when she started school; now she can, and she can understand others. She's really fulfilling her potential. I'm not sure the rest of us are." (Cassie, 18, in Binkard et al., 1987, p. 17)

 "Chelsea graduated from cardiac rehab today!! What a rollercoaster the last 8 months has been. So proud of her (and myself) for getting here. I cried when we got in the car, not sure why exactly, but it felt cathartic." (N. L., personal communication, 2021)

"I have an older sister (by 19 months) who has autism. Even though she struggles sometimes, I am very proud of her and her accomplishments." (P., personal communication, 2021)

In SibTeen, an online group created and moderated by the Sibling Support Project, a member posted this:

 "Let's start a proud moment thread! I'll start. My sister (15 with Down syndrome) has been working with an OT and has finally learned to tie her shoelaces and do her hair in a ponytail all by herself." (F. G., 2019, post from personal Facebook group)

Replies to this post included the following:

- That's great! My sister (16 with cerebral palsy) has recovered dramatically from a major hip operation.

- I'm super proud of my brother for having his bar mitzvah.

- My sister (17 with cerebral palsy) is learning how to feed herself, and it's been really exciting seeing her progress.

- My brother (13 with Down syndrome) just rode a bike around our block!

VOCATIONAL OPPORTUNITIES

 "As I plan for my future, I realize how much of my life, of what makes me unique, is the result of having Alison as my sister. My desire to become a doctor, my ability to work well with children, all can be attributed to Ali's presence." (Rinehart, 1992, p. 10)

Siblings, as well as Gorelick (1996), have noticed that brothers and sisters of people with support needs frequently gravitate toward the helping professions. Among siblings of people with disabilities, Cleveland and Miller (1977) found oldest daughters most likely to enter helping professions. Grossman's (1972) study of college-age siblings revealed that young adults who grew up with a brother or sister who had a disability were more certain of their own future and about personal and vocational goals than comparable young adults without a similar experience.

 "My brother [with autism] has such a different perspective on life, and he makes life much more interesting. It gave me more of a focus for helping people in my career." (Seltzer & Krauss, 2002)

In a 1993 study, Konstam et al. did not find differences in the career choices of siblings with and without brothers or sisters with a disability. The authors speculated that economic and social changes since the earlier studies may influence siblings' career choices. When siblings do enter professions in social services, education, or health care, their motivations are varied. One brother of a person with mental illness noted: 'It can be therapeutic to help others if you cannot help your family member' (Dickens, 1991). Another acknowledged that 'Part of the reason I've chosen law as my career is to enable myself to deal with some of the problems that Tom will always face' (Mark, 24, in Binkard et al., 1987, p. 28).

 "I have found my upbringing to have been very positive, in spite of the emotional hardship that [my sister's] cystic fibrosis placed on the family. At the age of 9 I perceived myself as being a vitally important participating member of the family. My parents encouraged me to assist in the care of my newborn sister, and I learned to crush pills and mix them in applesauce, do postural drainage, and clean and fill the mist tent. Through this experience, self-esteem was enhanced, responsibility was learned, and maturity was developed. Although I occasionally feel that I grew up too fast, for the most part the experience gave me a personal insight and compassion that I carry with me in my practice as a pediatric specialist." (Thibodeau, 1988, p. 22)

Many siblings have told us that having a brother or sister with support needs has made them feel comfortable with disabilities and appreciate the diversity of the human condition. As a result of their many years of informal education on disabilities, chronic health impairments, or mental illness, these siblings feel that they have much to share. Like the growing number of parents of children with support needs who are assuming leadership roles in education and health care, the siblings who seek careers in these fields bring a welcome reality check to their professions.

 "I am very open to 'different' people or situations. I have patience with young children or disabled people, and I always choose to work with the 'black sheep' of the group." (Seltzer & Krauss, 2002)

ADVOCACY

 "We have not fought this hard for Douglas to be thwarted by a termination of programs. Personally, I have not given so much of myself and my life to Doug only to see his existence end in despair. . . . My brother WILL have an option." (Zatlow, 1981, p. 2)

Many siblings are natural-born advocates. Their efforts to advocate for and with others often extend beyond their own brothers and sisters, and manifest through both formal and informal roles. Some siblings assume formal advocacy roles as professionals in disability and other social services organizations, championing, creating, and executing services and supports for people with various needs and their families. Siblings' life experience of living 24 hours a day/7 days a week with someone who has support needs often makes them adept, passionate, and uniquely qualified to serve in these roles (Orm et al., 2021).

 "I tell them that my brother has Down syndrome, which affects him physically and mentally. Sometimes they ask questions and I am always pleased to answer. Questions only mean that they are interested and want to learn more. I take it as a positive sign." (Lindsay, 17, in Meyer, 2005, p. 60)

Equally important are the many ways that siblings advocate informally, every day, on playgrounds and sidewalks; in school cafeterias, coffee shops, and workplaces; and elsewhere throughout their communities, to stand with those they feel are being treated unjustly. Through small acts, such as sitting with the ostracized new kid at lunch or explaining to a colleague who dropped the "r-word" in a meeting how hurtful it can be, siblings can and do make a big impact in demonstrating and promoting what they believe to be just.

 "Melissa also gives me a sense of responsibility to inform others about the realities of Down syndrome. Although speaking in front of a class usually makes me literally stop breathing and grow dizzy, I have faced large groups without fear, arguing the right to life of babies with Down syndrome." (Watson, 1991, p. 108)

"If I see someone with a disability walking down the street, I don't think *AHHHH!* or *eww*, I think that person is out, taking care of herself, being independent. I feel proud of them, even if I don't know them because I understand, a little, some of the things they have to overcome." (Erin, 14, in Meyer, 2005, p. 48)

Because of the value they place on their siblings' abilities and contributions, and perhaps because they will likely assume increasingly active roles in the lives of their siblings, brothers and sisters often become ardent advocates for people with support needs (Hall & Rossetti, 2017; Kramer et al., 2013).

 "Today, not because of guilt, but because I genuinely want to, I am helping my mom monitor and coordinate Kim's programs. I think that things go better for people like Kim when service providers know there is a family member on the scene and paying attention." (Marsha, 28, in Binkard et al., 1987, p. 31)

Programs serving siblings can provide participants with information and pre-advocacy skills. Sibshop discussion activities and informational activities acquaint participants with the services, therapies, career, and residential opportunities available for adults with disabilities. This information provides a foundation that siblings can draw on in future advocacy activities.

LOYALTY

 "I don't have my own family yet, but when I do, they will know that there is no question as to where my brother will be when my parents are no longer able to care for him. He will absolutely be close to me, wherever I am—this is not negotiable." (K., personal communication, 2005)

Like most siblings, brothers and sisters of children with support needs frequently fight and argue within the family. Outside of the family, however, siblings of children with developmental disabilities or chronic health impairments may feel required to defend their brothers and sisters from cruel comments and stares. This loyalty can cause problems for some siblings.

 "Now that she is older, people treat her just fine. When we were younger, a few kids teased her and called her a retard. Once I got kicked out of Boy Scouts because this punk kid called her a retard. I punched him in the face. No one calls my sister a retard. They know I will kick their ass." (Ty, 17, in Meyer, 2005, p. 93)

 "I'm used to being kind to my brother and sister, so I'm kind to everybody else. But, if someone starts a fight, I will fight. I won't put up with anyone teasing Wade or Jolene." (Morrow, 1992, p. 4)

 "When my brother turned 4 or 5 years of age, I was a very defensive person. I felt people were treating my brother differently. I used to get into fights with other kids." (A. Jones, personal communication, 1991)

 "She caused problems for me at school too. I'd get into fights because of her, so I held her responsible for most of my problems." (Marsha, 28, in Binkard et al., 1987, p. 29)

Yet, for many other siblings, these incidents can be a reason to reexamine the relationship they have with their brothers and sisters and to reflect on the meaning of friendship and society's tolerance of differences.

 "I decided that I had to stop being worried about how friends might react. There were two boys whom I'd met at school and thought were my friends. The first time they met Jennifer, though, they laughed. I told them to leave our house." (Cassie, 18, in Binkard et al., 1987, p. 16)

 "My sisters and I can turn into three really big monsters in public if someone makes fun of her when we're around. But we don't want pity for her. She deserves respect as a person." (Andrea, 19, in Binkard et al., 1987, p. 19)

 "Disabilities make life rich and experiences different; they're not all bad. It's the reactions to them that cause problems." (Rebekah, 17, in Meyer, 2005, p. 125)

CONCLUSION

 "We all love my brother very much. My siblings and I have and continue to support my brother to the best of our abilities. He unites us." (Seltzer & Krauss, 2002)

As the brothers and sisters quoted in this chapter make clear, many siblings of people with support needs experience unique opportunities throughout their lives. We can better appreciate siblings' many strengths and coping strategies if we complement their testimony with research that proceeds from a salutogenic viewpoint. As McConachie (1982) noted,

> Most [scales] do not evaluate positive traits. When the researcher has given parents greater freedom to comment, they tend to demonstrate their strength, resilience, and sense of humor in coping with their own reaction . . . and also with the reactions of their family and neighbors. (p. 161)

In addition to research that respects the complexity of their experiences, siblings deserve more immediate considerations. These considerations should begin when siblings are young and be offered proactively throughout their lives. Parents and providers should become familiar with the wide range of issues siblings may experience growing up. All of those who work with people who have disabilities should understand the important role that siblings play and create policies that include brothers and sisters who wish to be involved in the lives of their siblings with support needs. Programs should be widely available for brothers and sisters who wish to meet and talk with their peers. When siblings receive these considerations, it is possible to minimize the "unique concerns" they experience and maximize their "unique opportunities."

5

Getting Started

In this chapter, we discuss the component activities required to create a Sibshop. If the information that follows appears daunting, please remember that any activity—even something as mundane as cleaning a refrigerator or washing a car—can seem surprisingly complex when broken down into component tasks. Use this chapter as a blueprint for planning your Sibshop.

COSPONSORS

As mentioned in Chapter 1, we strongly encourage cosponsorship of Sibshops and feel that the benefits of cosponsoring Sibshops are many.

The first benefit is that you can serve more siblings. Frequently, individual agencies will not have a sufficient number of siblings in the identified age range to create a viable Sibshop. Working with other agencies helps ensure that all potentially interested families in your community will learn about a Sibshop and, as a result, you will be able to register more siblings.

An enthusiastic response and a healthy enrollment help create a vibrant program. Second, as discussed later in this chapter, cosponsorship allows agencies with limited resources to share costs and pool resources.

Third, Sibshops offer an extraordinary opportunity for collaboration among diverse agencies. Agencies that have worked together to cosponsor Sibshops include autism societies, chapters of The Arc and United Cerebral Palsy, children's hospitals, developmental disabilities councils, early intervention programs, Parent to Parent (P2P) programs, parks and recreation programs, Ronald McDonald Houses, school districts, schools for the Deaf, and University Centers for Excellence in Developmental Disabilities (UCEDDs).

We have also witnessed examples of agencies with previously competitive and even acrimonious relationships working together to cosponsor Sibshops. Sometimes, community businesses that donate to a local Sibshop are cosponsors. We know of one Sibshop that is cosponsored by a community hospital, three early intervention programs, a P2P program, and a local grocery store! A "village" approach often works well.

Of course, any agency or organization serving families of children with support needs can sponsor a Sibshop provided it can offer financial support, properly staff the program, and attract a sufficient number of participants. Single-agency sponsorship may be most appropriate if the Sibshop is to be a component of a larger event, such as a statewide conference for families of children with support needs, or if it is for a specific disability, such as for children with hearing impairments, sponsored by a state school for the Deaf.

Educate Community Partners About Sibshops

Agency staff may want to learn more about the need for Sibshops before they attend a planning meeting. With your invitation to cosponsor a Sibshop, send them information, such as A Brief Description of the Sibshop Model (Appendix B) and What Siblings Would Like Parents and Service Providers to Know (Appendix C)—both are also available at no cost at www.siblingsupport.org—and follow up with a phone call to answer any other questions they might have.

Ensure Family Participation in Planning for Sibshops

In many communities, Sibshops are spearheaded by what Florene Poyadue, a founder of California's Parents Helping Parents program, calls "monomaniacs with a mission": people who have a vision of what ought to be. Often, these visionaries are parents. If the representative body of your cosponsoring agencies does not include a parent or sibling of a person with support needs, please do invite a family member to be a part of your planning committee. You will be "selling" your Sibshop to parents. Consequently, it helps to involve them from the start.

Invite Community Partners to a Planning Meeting

Once you identify your cosponsoring agencies, each agency should appoint a representative to be a part of the Sibshop planning committee. Ideally, the agencies will send representatives who work closely with family members of people with support needs or are family members themselves. We recommend that all members of the planning committee read this chapter and the Sibshop Standards of Practice (Appendix A) prior to meeting. The committee may find the Sibshop Planning Form (see Figure 5.1) a helpful tool as you plan your community's Sibshop.

As your committee begins planning, keep in mind that each interagency Sibshop collaboration will be unique; the arrangements will reflect the resources each partner has to offer. Arrangements might be "potluck" style, depending on available resources. For instance, Agency A, although committed to the program, has no funds to support the program. It does, however, have an excellent facility or online meeting platform that the Sibshop can use. It agrees to handle the registration. Agency B has a similar lack of funds but is sufficiently committed to the program and will offer the services of its family specialist, who will take "comp time" for time spent on Sibshops. Agency C has neither staff nor space to support the program, but it does have $1,500 in a gift fund to help defray costs, and so on.

PARTICIPANTS

Once you settle the question of sponsorship, it will be easier to make decisions about service populations. You and the planning committee will need to identify the siblings you wish to reach with your Sibshop.

Sibshop Planning Form

Use this form as you plan for a Sibshop in your community, and update it as needed. With your planning committee, discuss the following questions to determine audience, resources, and responsibilities.

1. The sponsoring agencies and planning committee:

   What agencies will cosponsor the Sibshop?

   _____

   _____

   Who are the identified representatives from these agencies on the planning committee?

   _____

   _____

   Which members of the planning committee are also parents or siblings of people with support needs?

   _____

   _____

2. Identifying the siblings you wish to serve. Please define your population with regard to:

   The support needs of the siblings of the children you wish to serve

   _____

   _____

   The ages of the children who will attend your Sibshop _____

   The geographic area you wish to serve _____

   The maximum number of children you wish to serve _____

   Will enrollment be limited to families served by the cosponsoring agencies, or extended to the general community?

   _____

   _____

   _____

Figure 5.1. Sibshop Planning Form.

(continued)

3. Identifying resources. Please discuss what financial or other resources may be available to support your Sibshop for the following areas:

Potential costs _____

_____

Sibshop facilitators _____

_____

Materials and food _____

_____

Facility/Online meeting platform _____

Other (postage, stationery, printing, photocopying, processing registrations, etc.)_____

_____

Potential sources of income:

Registration fees _____

Grants, donations, and other sources of income _____

_____

4. Identifying Sibshop facilitators

What is your desired facilitator-to-participant ratio? _____

Who will be your Sibshop facilitators? _____

5. Where will your Sibshop be held? _____

6. When and how frequently will your Sibshop meet? _____

7. Who will publicize the program and recruit participants? _____

8. Who will register participants and manage the Sibshop budget? _____

_____

What Are the Support Needs of Siblings of Children Your Sibshop Will Serve?

Will this Sibshop be for siblings of children who have a specific disability (e.g., Down syndrome) or illness (e.g., cancer)? Or will it be for siblings of children with various developmental disabilities, chronic health impairments, or perhaps mental health concerns? We have also seen Sibshops for children whose siblings are involved in the foster care or juvenile justice systems. Focusing on a specific disability or illness can offer participants a wonderful opportunity to learn more about their siblings' condition. Unless you can ensure sufficient numbers of participants (at least six), however, we recommend offering the Sibshop to siblings of children who have various developmental disabilities or chronic illnesses. Although there will be some differences in their experiences, there will be many more similarities. Besides, differences will afford participants not only a richer understanding of the diversity embodied in the term support needs, but also insight into their own families. For participants who may lose a sibling to disability or illness, we encourage you to keep your doors open and invite them to decide, when they are ready, whether they wish to continue with Sibshops.

What Are the Ages of the Children Who Will Attend Your Sibshop?

Avoid the temptation to offer a Sibshop for children of all ages. Sibshops hosted for children ages 4 through 16 will confuse the 4-year-olds and bore the 16-year-olds, and the confusion and boredom can adversely affect the experience of the Sibshop for the children who fall in between. Although Sibshops can be adapted for younger and older children, they were designed with children ages 8–13 in mind. Restricting the age range ensures that the siblings share the common interests and levels of emotional maturity that make Sibshops successful.

By 8 years of age, most brothers and sisters know a little about their siblings' disability and can talk about their life, their feelings, and other people. Children younger than 8 may not even be aware that their sibling has support needs, and younger children often have a difficult time grasping the topics discussed by the older children. The typical 3- to 4-hour in-person Sibshop, or 90-minute online Sibshop, will be too long for children younger than 8. It is far easier to expand the target range of 8 through 13 to include older siblings. Many programs have successfully incorporated teen siblings as "junior facilitators." In a leadership position, teen volunteers can help with recreational activities and model the behaviors you will want from your young Sibshoppers. Further, they will benefit from support activities, and they may even fulfill service hours needed to graduate from high school. It is a win-win-win relationship!

If the committee determines that they want a program for siblings other than the target range of 8–13 years, there are alternatives. One option is to hold two Sibshops, one for younger siblings (i.e., 6–9 years) and another for older siblings (i.e., 10–13 years). Or sponsor a Sibshop specifically for younger children (i.e., 4–8 years) or for teenagers. Chapters 7–10 include activities that will be helpful with younger children and teens. Sibshops for younger children will need to be shorter in duration than typical Sibshops.

How Many Children Do You Wish to Serve?

Sibshops should be large enough to offer participants a vital, exciting program yet be small enough to ensure that everyone gets to participate in the discussion activities. Ideally, there will be enough children in the group for a participant to find another child—a future friend, perhaps—close in age to connect with outside of the Sibshop. Between 12 and 20 kids seems to be a good number for many Sibshop facilitators.

With a recommended ratio of one facilitator per five or six participants (and ideally more with younger children), the number of facilitators you have—as well as the space available in your facility or online meeting account—will influence how many siblings you can serve.

Open or Closed Enrollment?

You will need to consider whether you will have a closed enrollment (more like a class) or an open enrollment (more like a club) for your Sibshop. Each has advantages and disadvantages.

A Sibshop with a closed enrollment might meet once per week for 6 weeks. The advantage of a closed enrollment is that the "cast of characters" remains constant and a group identity can be nurtured. The disadvantage of a closed enrollment is that families and kids have very busy schedules. Consequently, if they can attend only four of the six meetings, they may not sign up at all. Another potential downside of closed enrollment is that families who learn about your Sibshop mid-session will need to wait until you offer a new session.

A Sibshop with an open enrollment might meet once per month throughout the school year. The advantage of open enrollment is that if a Sibshop participant cannot attend a meeting in November due to a conflict with his soccer schedule, they can rejoin the group at the December meeting. Furthermore, families who hear about the program mid-year will learn that it is not too late to enroll their children. The disadvantage of open enrollment is that the participants will change slightly from Sibshop to Sibshop. Usually, however, there are enough familiar faces to make a Sibshopper feel at home after having missed a session, and veteran members enjoy welcoming new sibs to the group. See Appendix D for an example of how one Sibshop successfully uses an open enrollment format.

What Geographic Area Do You Wish to Serve?

Will your Sibshop be for kids from all over the county, or just from a specific town, city, or school district? This question will have a greater impact on Sibshops that meet in person than those that meet online. Online Sibshops began in 2020, when the coronavirus pandemic prevented people from meeting in person. Since then, many Sibshops have continued to offer online Sibshops, sometimes in a hybrid model that includes less-frequent in-person meetings, because of the convenience they offer. Online Sibshops eliminate the need to commute as well as geographic barriers, and they reach more potential participants. This decision may affect, among other things, how you publicize your program and when you host the program.

Will Sibshop Enrollment Be Limited to Siblings
From Families Served by the Cosponsoring Agencies?

Will your Sibshop be available for all appropriate brothers and sisters in your community, regardless of where their sibling receives services? Is this Sibshop just for the cosponsoring agencies' families? Will they get priority? Although there are no right or wrong answers to these questions, we encourage you to decide ahead of time and consider supporting as many siblings as possible in your community.

FINANCIAL ISSUES

Most communities, organizations, and agencies have limited funds for family support programs, regardless of how valuable they may be. This is true for traditional family programs (i.e., programs for parents), and even more so for less-traditional programs such as Sibshops. Consequently, most programs for brothers and sisters have budgets and funding bases that are both creative and individualistic.

Sibshops rarely happen because there are readily available funds. Sibshops exist because individuals and agencies share a belief that siblings deserve peer support and education opportunities despite a lack of designated funds. This enthusiasm encourages agencies to seek innovative approaches to fundraising: Where there is a will, there is a way. Although a robust Sibshop budget may be elusive, many local programs arrive at similar low-cost strategies for success.

Agencies' abilities to share costs and pool resources will greatly affect a Sibshop budget. Some programs relying on volunteers and donated food and materials have achieved a zero-based budget. Others pass on all costs to participants. Most fall somewhere in between. A discussion of costs associated with hosting Sibshops follows.

Costs

According to a survey in 2022, most facilitators lead Sibshops as part of their job or they are hired to conduct the programs, often with the help of adult or teen sibling volunteers. Much rarer are Sibshops run by volunteers alone. Volunteers can be a wonderful asset to a Sibshop. Because they donate their time, however, volunteers may be less reliable than paid staff. Hiring staff to conduct the Sibshop can help ensure reliability and accountability, assuming that funds and/or comp time are available. Some programs have volunteers who receive a small stipend. Designating someone who is already on staff to conduct a sibling program is perhaps the best option. This eliminates the need to identify new funds, and the staff member who will coordinate Sibshops can take comp time for their involvement in a Sibshop. Many agencies profess—and truly wish to fulfill—a commitment to serving people with support needs and their families, when, in practice, they may only be serving the client with support needs and their parents, neglecting the sibling. By committing staff to facilitate sibling programs, agencies acknowledge siblings' critical role in the family and move closer to achieving their goal to provide comprehensive, even cutting-edge, family support.

Materials, Food, and Facility

The Sibshop model was created with the goal of incorporating activities that require minimal materials. There are two reasons for this: to reduce costs and to streamline planning. Sibshops often are conducted by facilitators who do not work at the facility where the Sibshop is being held. Consequently, facilitators will need to bring their own materials or, at the very least, seek permission to use the facility's materials.

Food—even if it is just a snack—is an essential part of Sibshops. Local pizzerias, sandwich shops, and other community businesses are often happy to donate food to your Sibshop once they understand why and how you are supporting young siblings who participate. When facilitators' time and the facility are donated, Sibshop registration fees can cover or supplement materials and food.

Frequently, one of the cosponsoring agencies will contribute the use of a facility or online meeting platform. Later in this chapter, we discuss preferred locations for Sibshops.

Miscellaneous Costs

Postage, stationery, printing, photocopying, and processing registrations are miscellaneous costs that vary greatly from program to program. Generally, one agency assumes responsibility for all of these costs.

Income

Although some agencies offer Sibshops free of charge, it is reasonable to ask parents to pay a fee for their children to attend. Most Sibshops cost far less than childcare for the same amount of time, and these fees can help offset costs associated with running a Sibshop. Perhaps most important, fees help ensure that parents follow through and bring their children to the Sibshop that they have paid for and that facilitators have worked so hard to make rewarding.

Make a significant effort to ensure that Sibshops are accessible to families who cannot afford the set fee. On the registration forms of many Sibshops is a statement similar to the following: "A limited number of Sibshop scholarships are available on a first-come, first-served basis. Check here if you would like your child considered for a Sibshop scholarship." (See Appendix D.) On the same form, other families who have greater means can be offered the opportunity to contribute to the Sibshops scholarship fund.

Other local Sibshops have successfully applied for grants from community mental health boards, Developmental Disability Councils, local businesses, fraternal and community-based organizations, local private benefactors, and city block grant programs.

Sibshop Budgets

There is no typical Sibshop budget. Tables 5.1–5.3 outline sample budgets for three different Sibshops and provide some ideas on expenses you may incur. For the purposes of comparison, each sample Sibshop uses four facilitators and offers a 4-hour meeting once a month for 5 months. The first two Sibshops serve 20 children; the third serves 10.

FACILITATORS

We believe that Sibshops are best facilitated by at least two people. Ideally, one facilitator will be an adult sibling of a person who has a support need similar to the siblings of the participants. The involvement of an adult sibling can keep the program "honest," credible, and focused on issues important to the participants. On occasion—and as appropriate—adult sibling facilitators can share the experiences and insights that they had growing up. For young Sibshoppers, having a facilitator who has successfully adapted to life with a sibling who has support needs can be tremendously reassuring.

The other member of the team will be a service provider (e.g., a social worker, special education teacher, professor, psychologist, child life specialist, nurse) who will be aware of issues, resources, services, and the support needs represented in the Sibshop. This person, frequently employed by one of the cosponsoring agencies, can also serve as the liaison between the facilitators and the planning committee.

Parents, of course, can be excellent facilitators, but ideally, they would not facilitate Sibshops that their own children attend. Parents are often the driving force for creating community-based Sibshops: They appreciate the value of peer support and witness on a daily basis the concerns experienced by siblings. Even if they are not facilitators, parents can make many behind-the-scenes contributions to ensure a successful Sibshop.

Based on years of conducting programs for siblings, we believe that Sibshop facilitators should share some varied core skills. Both facilitators, for instance, should be

Table 5.1. Budget for Sibshop A

Facilitator 1	Services donated by Agency 1 (employee)
Facilitator 2	Adult sib "paid volunteer" services donated by Agency 1 ($300: $15/hour × 4 hours per session × 5 sessions)
Facilitator 3	Volunteer, works for Agency 2
Facilitator 4	Services donated by Agency 3 (employee)
Food	$500 ($5 × 20 participants × 5 meetings)
Materials	$400 ($4 × 20 participants × 5 meetings)
Facility	Donated by Agency 3
Other (e.g., mailing, printing)	Donated by Agency 1
TOTAL	$1,200
INCOME	$900 registration ($5 per session × 18 paying participants × 5 sessions. Two scholarship participants.)

Sibshop A is in person for 20 participants. For online Sibshops, "facility" is replaced by "online meeting platform," and food/recipes and materials might be secured by families or delivered by staff to participants' homes before the event.

Table 5.2. Budget for Sibshop B

Facilitator 1	Community volunteer
Facilitator 2	Community volunteer
Facilitator 3	Services donated by Agency 1 ($300: $60 per session × 5 sessions)
Facilitator 4	Services donated by Agency 1 ($300: $60 per session × 5 sessions)
Food	Donated by local grocery stores and individuals ($500: $5 × 20 participants × 5 meetings)
Materials	Donated by Agency 1 ($400)
Facility	Donated by Agency 2
Other (e.g., registration, mailing, printing)	Donated by Agencies 1–4
TOTAL	$0
INCOME	N/A (no registration fee)

Sibshop B is in person for 20 participants.

Table 5.3. Budget for Sibshop C

Facilitator 1	$125 ($25 per session × 5 sessions)
Facilitator 2	$125 ($25 per session × 5 sessions)
Facilitator 3	$125 ($25 per session × 5 sessions)
Facilitator 4	Volunteer, works for Agency 2
Food	$200 ($4 × 10 participants × 5 sessions)
Materials	Donated by Agency 1
Facility	Donated by Agency 2
Other (e.g., registration, mailing, stationery, printing)	Donated by Agency 1
TOTAL	$575
INCOME	$600 ($15 × 8 paying participants × 5 sessions; two additional participants received scholarships)

Sibshop C is in person for 10 participants.

as comfortable leading discussions as they are organizing a game of Ultimate Nerf or a cooking project for 14 children. We strongly recommend that Sibshop facilitators:

1. Have a working knowledge of the unique concerns and opportunities experienced by siblings of children with support needs. At the very least, future Sibshop facilitators should read Chapters 2–4 of this book, which were written in order to fill in this background for facilitators. Facilitators and the planning committee, however, should not stop there. The sibling panel and the books, videos, social media groups, and newsletters discussed in Chapter 11 are excellent ways to learn more about sibling issues.

2. Attend a Sibshop training offered by the Sibling Support Project. At least one member of your Sibshop team will need to complete the Sibling Support Project's Sibshop Facilitator Certification Training, per the Sibshops Standards of Practice (Appendix A). These trainings, offered in person and online, offer facilitators in-depth information about siblings' lifelong issues and the implications these issues will have for facilitators, parents, and service providers. Equally important, they provide participants with detailed information on the Sibshop model and an opportunity to experience a demonstration Sibshop. These trainings are the best way to learn what Sibshops are all about. Completing a certification training on the Sibshop model is required to use the Sibshop name and logo (see Appendix A).

3. Have personal or professional experience with people who have support needs and their families. They should also possess knowledge of the support needs represented at the Sibshop. Therefore, a special education teacher, despite their experience with children with developmental disabilities, may not be the best candidate to run a Sibshop for siblings of children who have cancer. A colleague knowledgeable about the impact of childhood cancer on families (e.g., a child life specialist, clinical nurse specialist, pediatric social worker) should be there to provide assistance.

4. Be familiar with active listening principles. These skills will be valuable throughout the Sibshop, especially during discussion activities. If there is a P2P program in your community, you are encouraged to attend the workshops offered by the program to train "helping parents." Active listening is a key skill taught at these training sessions, and these same principles can be used with Sibshop participants. (Of course, P2P trainings are also a great way to learn about the impact a child's disability has on families and to get the word out about your Sibshop to a key audience.) If P2P trainings are unavailable, consider reading Adele Faber and Elaine Mazlish's (2012a) excellent book *How to Talk So Kids Will Listen and Listen So Kids Will Talk*.

5. Have experience leading groups, preferably groups of children.

6. Convey a sense of joy, wonder, and play. Having fun is an important component of a successful Sibshop. Even though Sibshops are about learning, they are not school. Even though we talk about our feelings, Sibshops are not therapy. All potential facilitators should truly enjoy the company of children. Anyone who has ever taught in a classroom, run a kids' rec program, or served as a camp counselor knows that kids can intuitively assess within seconds—with startling accuracy—their adult leaders' comfort, enthusiasm, and commitment. A self-deprecating sense of humor helps too!

7. Be available to meet at the times and dates identified by the planning committee.

8. Connect with other Sibshop facilitators. Sharing activities, challenges, questions, and successes with other Sibshop facilitators—some who have offered Sibshops for many years—can be tremendously helpful. We believe so strongly in the power of connecting to the Sibshops community that we require at least one facilitator from your Sibshop team to join our online Sibshop Facilitator Forum. See Appendix A or www.siblingsupport.org for details on how to join.

9. Be somewhat physically fit. Sibshops are lively, exciting events, with many high-energy activities. Even online Sibshops require a healthy dose of movement! Facilitators will be expected to model and participate in these activities.

10. Appreciate that Sibshop participants, not the facilitators, are the experts on living with a sibling with support needs. One of the rewards of facilitating the program is what we can learn from the kids we serve.

LOCATION

An ideal facility will be centrally located and kid friendly. It will have a gym or a large, open multipurpose room for games; a quiet meeting place for discussions; and a working kitchen that accommodates all participants. Ironically, although public schools may seem the best choice (as they certainly meet the qualifications mentioned previously), they can also be the most difficult to access. Although some districts will donate the use of a school, others will charge fees to cover general rent or to pay for a custodian. In some instances, stringent contracts with food-service unions will prevent use of a school kitchen without paying an employee overtime. In this case, you should inquire whether the district has a living-skills classroom with a kitchen. It may be easier and less expensive to meet in a church or temple hall, a community center, a library, an early intervention program site, and so forth. If you are meeting online, consider secure technology platforms available to host organizations, and provide parents with guidelines on setting up a private space in their home where siblings can participate via computer, tablet, or smartphone without distractions or interruptions (see Appendix B).

TIMES AND DATES

We encourage you to survey the families you wish to support through Sibshops to identify days and times that work for the majority. Although many in-person Sibshops are held on Saturdays from 10:00 a.m. until 2:00 p.m., this time may not be ideal for all families. Many programs have found that this time slot is simply the "least worst time" for most families, participants, facilitators, and agencies. Smaller communities often have greater flexibility in meeting times than larger communities. If all the participants attend the same school district, Sibshops can be held on teacher in-service days. Sibshops are sometimes held on Friday evenings in communities where Friday afternoon traffic is not a nightmare, or on Sundays if Friday nights and Saturdays are not an option for religious reasons. Online Sibshops, which are shorter in duration (typically 60–90 minutes) and eliminate commuting time, may be easier to schedule after school or on weekday evenings. How often your Sibshops meet will be determined by the needs and resources in your community. The following section offers guidelines for different meeting frequencies.

Annually

Some Sibshops meet only once a year. Examples of this are a 6-hour Sibshop that is part of a national conference for families who have children with a specific disability or illness, or a 4-hour Sibshop that is a part of a statewide conference for families who have children with various disabilities. Another example is the Sibshop that is a component of a camp for children or families of children who have disabilities or illnesses.

Every 6 Months or Quarterly

In rural communities, where long-distance travel would prohibit meeting in person more frequently, some Sibshops are offered once every 3–6 months. Sometimes, a simultaneous program is offered to parents. Some Sibshops offer a hybrid of in-person meetings every 3–6 months with online meetings in between.

Monthly or Every Other Month

Many Sibshops find that meeting every month, or every other month, is manageable for facilitators while providing consistency for participants and enough time between events that siblings look forward to attending. Sibshops using an open enrollment format typically meet monthly on a reliable schedule that is easy for parents to follow. Often, these Sibshops meet during school months only. One community does it this way: The September, November, January, March, and May Sibshops are for 6- to 9-year-old siblings; the October, December, February, April, and June Sibshops are for siblings ages 10–13. Other communities meet once a month and split the day into two Sibshops by age group; for example, the first Saturday of every month, 9:00 a.m.–12:00 p.m. for 6- to 9-year-olds and 1:00–4:00 p.m. for 10- to 13-year-olds. Sibshops with sufficient staff may also offer one Sibshop, 10:00 a.m.–2:00 p.m., and split the large group by age (6- to 9-year-olds and 10- to 13-year-olds) for some activities and then bring together the entire group for lunch, snacks, and recreational activities.

Weekly

Some Sibshops, especially those held for a limited time (e.g., 4–6 weeks) with a closed enrollment, are held weekly. Usually, these are much shorter in duration (1–1.5 hours) and are often held after school.

Other Meeting Options

Of course, there are many variations on the theme. As noted previously, some Sibshops are held on teacher in-service days, and still others are held during the summer, perhaps every day for 3 days or even for an entire week.

Finally, when deciding how often to meet, remember this rule: It is better to meet less frequently and have Sibshops that are well-planned, exciting, and meaningful events than to meet often and have programs that become routine and stale.

PROMOTING YOUR SIBSHOP VERSUS RECRUITING PARTICIPANTS

There is a big difference between promoting your Sibshop throughout your community and recruiting siblings to attend it, and you will need to do both to build a successful program. Promoting your Sibshop and informing parents, siblings, local government agencies, community organizations, and the public of your services for brothers and sisters is an important and ongoing effort! Find various ways to promote your Sibshop: on your website, in flyers, in email blasts, in social media campaigns, and through the Sibling Support Project's online directory (see the Sibshops Standards of Practice, Appendix A). It is important to repeat messaging about your Sibshop multiple times. Tammy Besser, a longtime Sibshop Facilitator in Chicago, has found that it can take six or seven rounds of messaging before it "clicks" and parents are truly aware of your program. If you offer your sibling program in a series (e.g., one meeting a week for 6 weeks), expect to publicize your program multiple times prior to each series before registration closes. If your program is ongoing (e.g., monthly meetings with open enrollment), plan on publicizing the entire program once per year and sending rounds of reminders before each meeting. If you hold the program infrequently or as a one-time event, plan on promoting consistently prior to each event.

Successfully recruiting children to attend your Sibshop is a more targeted effort. Invitations by phone calls, personalized emails, texts, and direct messages to specific families that you or your colleagues directly support are the most effective ways to invite siblings to participate. Parents are more likely to accept a personalized invitation from a trusted professional or friend who can speak to the benefits that Sibshops can provide to their children. Inviting parents to attend a 60-minute information session about Sibshops prior to your first meeting is a great way to engage parents, explain what your program is about and how it can benefit young siblings, and recruit participants. See Chapter 6 for a further discussion of awareness activities, sample awareness materials, and timelines.

REGISTRATION AND BUDGET MANAGEMENT

A detailed registration form and process can help you plan for your Sibshop, collect the participant information that will help you effectively support them (see example in Appendix D), collect fees, and store contact information for communication with families. Registration can be conducted online and/or on paper, depending on available resources, and is usually handled by the agency that manages the Sibshop budget or donates the facility where the Sibshop will be held.

CONCLUSION

Once you have answered the questions outlined on the Sibshop Planning Form (Figure 5.1) discussed in this chapter, you should have a clear idea of the following:

- Who your cosponsors are
- Who will be served by your Sibshop
- What your financial and other resources are
- Who will facilitate your Sibshop
- Where your Sibshop will be held
- How frequently it will meet
- Who will promote the program
- How you will recruit participants
- Who will register participants

If you can answer all or most of these questions, congratulate yourself and your planning committee. If you can't, hang in there! There is a good chance that no one in your community has ever tried to organize anything like a Sibshop before. As pioneers and history makers, you and your colleagues will need to be creative, resourceful, and occasionally monomaniacal. If you get stuck, seek the counsel of other Sibshops in your state and the Sibling Support Project. When you resolve the logistics, the fun begins. In the next chapter, we provide detailed information on planning your first Sibshop.

6

Putting It All Together

PENCILS AND SCISSORS
STRING
CRAYONS
BALLOONS
BANDANAS
ROLL OF PAPER
PLASTIC EGGS
HUMAN BINGO
FELT PENS
TAPE
DONUTS

As we noted previously, Sibshops are logistically no more difficult to organize than other groups for kids (e.g., Camp Fire, Cub Scouts, Brownies). They may, in fact, be easier! In this chapter, we guide you as you plan your first Sibshop. We provide you with a timetable for promoting your program and with sample awareness materials. Furthermore, we give you and your colleagues tested and detailed Sibshop schedules that can help you plan your very first meeting, in person or online. At the end of this chapter, we suggest ways to evaluate the satisfaction of parents and participants with your program. In providing the information in this chapter, we are assuming the following:

1. You and your planning committee have read Chapter 5.

2. You have identified and met with representatives from cosponsoring agencies and family member representatives.

3. You have defined the population of children you wish to serve.

4. You have identified the necessary financial resources.

5. You have identified and secured a site for your Sibshop.

6. You have identified facilitators for your Sibshop who meet the qualifications discussed in Chapter 5.

7. You have read and agreed to the Sibshop Standards of Practice (see Appendix A).

8. Dates for your Sibshop have been set.

PROMOTION AND RECRUITMENT ACTIVITIES

How to recruit children to attend Sibshops remains one of the most common questions from newly certified facilitators. Promotion activities—web pages, flyers, emails, social media blasts, and notes sent home to families—are good ways to get the word out about your Sibshop. However, as discussed in Chapter 5, they are not enough. Especially in your Sibshop's early years, you will need to personally invite parents to bring their children to your Sibshop. You will also want to encourage your colleagues to do the same. After you have developed effective word of mouth strategies through parents and service providers, these personal invitations may become less necessary.

Timeline

Once you have identified resources, dates, facility or online meeting platforms, and facilitators, you will want to develop a timeline for promotion and recruitment activities. We suggest the following:

8 weeks before—Create a flyer and seek opportunities to speak to groups of parents, special education parent–teacher associations, and service providers about your new Sibshop. Send out the first social media blast. Invite parents and providers to a Sibshops information session, either in person or online.

6 weeks before—Send flyers and letters to agencies via email and "snail mail." Send a second social media blast.

5 weeks before—Send flyers, letters, and emails to parents of children served by cosponsoring agencies. Invite parents to a Sibshops information session, either in person or online.

4 weeks before—Send press releases to local media. Send out a third social media blast.

2–6 weeks before—Send links to online registration forms, or paper forms, to parents who have requested registration materials. Make phone calls and send personalized emails to colleagues who work with families, and to parents of siblings. Continue weekly social media blasts until registration closes.

This chapter contains sample awareness materials you may use to promote your upcoming Sibshops. You should, of course, adapt these in any way you see fit.

Expanding Awareness of Sibshops

An effective way to create general awareness of your Sibshop program is to present information at local programs for parents of children with support needs and colleagues interested in the well-being of those children and their families. You may wish to request a chance to speak at staff meetings and parent support groups sponsored by your organization or by local chapters of The Arc, early intervention centers, schools, hospitals, disability-specific groups and providers, or P2P programs. This does not need to be a lengthy presentation. Remembering the dictum to "be brief, be bright, and be gone," you can plug your program in 15 minutes or less. You may use the Brief Description of the Sibshop Model (see Appendix B) and What Siblings Would Like Parents and Service Providers to Know (see Appendix C) as a basis for your talk and as a handout, and you may show short videos about Sibshops that can be found at www.siblingsupport.org or elsewhere online.

Promoting Your Sibshop

Letters, emails, flyers, social media blasts, and press releases are effective methods of getting the word out about your Sibshop. Because parents may not know what you will offer their typically developing children, be sure to emphasize Sibshops' wellness approach and the fun and camaraderie experienced by participants.

A Sample Press Release

Sibshops and the young participants who attend them have been featured in many local newspapers and on their websites, podcasts, blogs, and social media. Besides calling

---

Subject Line: New Program Dedicated to Life's Longest-Lasting Relationship
Date: 10/31/2023 FOR IMMEDIATE RELEASE
Contact: Sarah Marshall, Sibshop director, DayStar Developmental Center, 555-368-4911; www.daystar.org/sibshops

Sibshops
A Program Just for Sibs of Kids with Support Needs

Brothers and sisters will have the longest-lasting relationship with a sibling who has a disability—*one that can easily exceed 65 years.* During their lives, they will experience most of the unique concerns and joys their parents do. However, few siblings of kids with special needs ever have a chance to talk about their issues with others who "get it"—until now.

Siblings of kids with support needs from Brighton County now have a program that is just for them called Sibshops. At Sibshops, they'll have a chance to meet other kids whose brothers and sisters have support needs and talk about the good and not-so-good parts of having a sibling with a disability. Most important, they will have fun!

Sibshops are an exciting new support, information, and recreation opportunity for siblings ages 8–13. Brighton County's Sibshops are cosponsored by Children's Hospital, the DayStar Early Developmental Center, and The Arc of Brighton County. Sibshops will be held at Olympic View Elementary School, 504 NE 95th in Lake Stevens. For more information and to register, call Sarah Marshall at the DayStar Developmental Center at 555-368-4911 or visit www.daystar.org/sibshops.

The first meeting will be held on Saturday, February 22, from 10 a.m. to 2 p.m. Additional meeting dates are March 21, April 25, May 16, and June 13 [year].

In addition to receiving peer support, Sibshop participants will play lively "new games," learn about their siblings' disabilities and the services they receive, participate in cooking and craft activities, and make new friends. Sibshops are spirited celebrations of the many contributions made by brothers and sisters.

Many siblings have feelings that can be difficult to express, even to a friend: sadness that a sister struggles to learn things that others take for granted, anger when a brother's behavior prevents the family from doing things other families do, the special pride when a sibling with a disability learns a basic but important life skill after months or years of practice. At Sibshops, they will share these feelings with others who truly understand.

Figure 6.1. Sample press release.

attention to an especially deserving community, the media can be a great way to get the word out about your Sibshop. You can let local news organizations (including newspapers, podcasts, and radio and television stations) know about your Sibshop by calling their "news tips hotlines" or submitting an online form through their "Contact Us" webpages. Drafting a press release can help you gather the important information about your Sibshop in a format that is easy to share. Media relations professionals we have consulted suggest sending out press releases no later than 3 weeks prior to the event or registration deadline for maximum impact (a sample press release is shown in Figure 6.1).

If your agency does not already have a list of contacts and addresses for local media, consider asking well-connected colleagues or parents in the community for their lists.

A Sample Flyer

All registered Sibshops (i.e., those that have read and agreed to uphold the Sibshop Standards of Practice [Appendix A] and joined the online Directory of registered Sibshops at www.siblingsupport.org) may use the Sibshop name and logo in their promotional materials. Included in this chapter is a blank flyer with empty boxes that you may use to publicize your program (see Figure 6.2). The box on the left may be filled in with information about the sponsoring agencies, and the box on the right may be filled with contact phone numbers, websites, and emails, as shown in Figure 6.3. This flyer can then be used in several ways. It can be copied onto the back of the letter you send to parents, included with your press release, or saved as an image to post on social media. If dates are not included, it can even be distributed to agencies for children with support needs and their families to post indefinitely.

Sibshops: A program just for brothers and sisters of kids with support needs!

Sibshops are a celebration of the many contributions made by brothers and sisters.

Here's what kids say about Sibshops:

"At **Sibshops** you get to meet other brothers and sisters of kids with support needs."

"**Sibshops** have outrageous games!"

"At **Sibshops** you can talk about the good and not-so-good parts of having a brother or sister who has support needs."

"**Sibshops** are a place to learn about cool things."

"**Sibshops** have great cooking activities!"

"**Sibshops** have some of the greatest kids in the world!"

"**Sibshops** are fun!"

Sibshops are for kids who have a brother or sister with special health or developmental needs. **Join us!**

Figure 6.2.   Blank Sibshop flyer.

Sibshops: A program just for brothers and sisters of kids with support needs!

Sibshops are a celebration of the many contributions made by brothers and sisters.

Sibshops are cosponsored by: Children's Hospital and Medical Center, The Arc of King County, and Seattle Public Schools.

Here's what kids say about Sibshops:

"At **Sibshops** you get to meet other brothers and sisters of kids with support needs."

"**Sibshops** have outrageous games!"

"At **Sibshops** you can talk about the good and not-so-good parts of having a brother or sister who has support needs."

"**Sibshops** are a place to learn about cool things."

"**Sibshops** have great cooking activities!"

"**Sibshops** have some of the greatest kids in the world!"

"**Sibshops** are fun!"

Sibshops are for kids who have a brother or sister with special health or developmental needs. **Join us!**

For information and registration call 368-4911.

Figure 6.3. Filled-in Sibshop flyer.

Dear Parents,

It gives us great pleasure to announce Sibshops, an exciting program just for brothers and sisters of kids with support needs. At a Sibshop, brothers and sisters will:

- Meet other brothers and sisters of children with support needs

- Have fun

- Talk with others who "get it" about the good (and sometimes not so good!) parts of having a sib with support needs

- Learn more about disabilities and the services that people with disabilities receive

- Have some more fun!

Who are Sibshops for? Sibshops are for 8- to 13-year-old brothers and sisters of children who have support needs.

Who sponsors Sibshops? Sibshops are a collaborative effort of Children's Hospital, the DayStar Early Developmental Center, and The Arc of Brighton County.

Who runs Sibshops? Our Sibshops are run by a team of people who have a professional and, in some cases, a personal understanding of the impact a child's support needs can have on brothers and sisters. Equally important, they all have great kid skills! We also have junior facilitators who are sibs in their late teens.

When and where are Sibshops held? Sibshops will be held from 10 a.m. to 2 p.m. on the following dates: February 22, March 21, April 25, May 16, and June 13. Sibshops will be held at Olympic View Elementary School, 504 NE 95th in Lake Stevens.

What is the cost of a Sibshop? Each Sibshop is $15, which includes lunch. A limited number of scholarships are available.

Sounds great! How do I register? For more information and to register, call Sarah Marshall at the DayStar Early Developmental Center at (206) 555-0100 or visit www.daystar.org/sibshops. But hurry—space is limited!

Figure 6.4. Sample letter to parents.

A Sample Letter to Parents

The letter you send to parents provides them with details pertaining to the "who, what, when, where, and how much" of the program (see Figure 6.4). It also reassures parents about the program in which they will be enrolling their children. The letter to parents, like the flyer, should present the program as a positive, fun experience for a deserving population. Common ways to disseminate these letters are to ask agencies to email them to the families they serve, or to send them home with children who attend special education programs.

Other ways of distributing the letter include obtaining mailing lists of families from P2P programs, The Arc, and other parent-driven organizations, or requesting that these organizations include a copy of this letter in their routine mailings to families.

A Sample Email Message to Agencies Announcing Upcoming Sibling Workshops

The letter in Figure 6.5 may be sent to other agencies serving people with support needs. It asks agencies to post a flyer and offers further information on your program. An alternative to sending this letter is to send agencies a press release and a flyer.

PLANNING FOR YOUR VERY FIRST SIBSHOP

Whether you are planning to host your first Sibshop in person or online, the following information is designed to assist the planning committee and facilitators in planning

---

Dear Colleague,

We are pleased to announce that Children's Hospital, the DayStar Early Developmental Center, and The Arc of Brighton County are cosponsoring Sibshops for 8- to 13-year-old siblings of kids with support needs. Please share this email with parents and others who may be interested!

Our Sibshops are lively, action-packed, 3-hour workshops that celebrate the many contributions made by brothers and sisters of kids with support needs. Sibshops acknowledge that being the sibling of a person with support needs is for some a good thing, for others a not-so-good thing, and for many, somewhere in between. They reflect a belief that brothers and sisters have much to offer one another—if they are given a chance. The Sibshop model mixes information and discussion activities with new games (designed to be unique, offbeat, and appealing to a wide ability range) and special guests.

We are attaching a flyer on the Seattle-area Sibshops and ask that you post it where parents and other interested professionals might see it. A letter to parents describing the program is also attached. Please feel free to photocopy it and distribute it to families.

For more information and registration materials, visit www.daystar.org/sibshops or write to me at smarshall@daystar.org

Sincerely,
Sarah Marshall

DayStar Developmental Center
555–368–4911

P.S. We'd welcome an opportunity to share information about Sibshops at your next staff or parent support meeting!

Figure 6.5. Sample letter to agencies.

a Sibshop for 8- to 13-year-old siblings of children with health or developmental needs. The annotated schedule for each format describes, in detail, Sibshop discussion, recreation, and food activities as well as component tasks and materials that need to be purchased or gathered. We are confident that after you have conducted a Sibshop using this schedule, you will have no problem planning subsequent Sibshops with these activities and/or activities of your own. At the end of this chapter, we discuss a planning sheet that will simplify planning for future Sibshops.

The schedule shown in Table 6.1 is intended to make your first Sibshop as smooth and successful as possible. Set a time to meet with the other co-facilitators to work through the packet and assign responsibilities as needed. It is critical that you and your co-facilitators read carefully the Annotated Sibshop Schedule for an in-person or online Sibshop. You and your team, of course, can feel free to substitute other activities of your choice.

Table 6.1. A Sibshop schedule

Time	Activity	Materials needed
9:15	Setup	☐ Signs
		☐ Tape
		☐ Coffee, anyone?
10:00	Trickle-In Activity:	☐ Sibshop Registration Form
	For parents: Enrollment	☐ Face Tags sheet
		☐ Pencils
	For sibs: Face Tags	☐ Sticky-back name tags
		☐ Felt-tip pens
		☐ Scissors
		☐ Music and speaker
10:20	Introductory Activity:	☐ Strengths & Weaknesses sheet
	Strengths & Weaknesses	☐ Pencils
10:45	Knots	
10:50	Lap Game	
11:00	Last Kid Standing	☐ Clothespins
11:10	Group Juggling	☐ Beanbags, stuffed animals, rolled-up socks, or—during warm weather—water balloons!
11:30	Triangle Tag	☐ Wristbands or bandanas
11:40	Sightless Sculpture	☐ Bandanas
		☐ Rectangular table
11:50	Lunch prep	
12:00	Lunch	
12:20	Lunch cleanup	
12:30	Dear Aunt Blabby	☐ Letters in envelopes
12:55	Pushpin Soccer	☐ Large balloons
		☐ Large, clean garbage bags
		☐ 2 pushpins
		☐ 2 large rectangular tables
1:15	Scrabble Scramble	☐ 62 sheets of 8 × 11 paper
		☐ 2 large felt-tip pens (different colors)
		☐ 2 rectangular tables
1:30	Sound-Off	☐ Sound-Off sheet
		☐ Pencils
1:55	Closure	☐ Day's schedule to take home
2:05	Debriefing and planning for next Sibshop	☐ Activity Planning Form

AN ANNOTATED SCHEDULE FOR AN IN-PERSON SIBSHOP

This section describes in detail what will happen during the first Sibshop. You will need to photocopy some materials, gather other materials, and decide who will present activities.

Times on the Schedule

We list approximate times on the Sibshop schedule and this annotated schedule assuming that your Sibshop will run from 10:00 a.m. until 2:00 p.m. You may not have time for all activities, or you may try a different game suggested by a sibling or a cofacilitator.

PLEASE NOTE: This schedule does not include a guest speaker or other learning activity. During the first Sibshop, participants usually spend extra time getting to know one another. If you are hosting your Sibshop at a conference for a specific population (e.g., siblings of children with spina bifida), you may wish to amend the schedule to make room for an informational activity or guest speaker (e.g., Ask Dr. Bob!). All facilitators will need a copy of the complete schedule for Sibshop day. For each schedule item we describe below, we call out a question. These are decisions you need to make about facilitators' roles for each activity.

ANNOTATED SAMPLE SIBSHOP SCHEDULE

Who will photocopy the schedule?

9:15 a.m. Setup

It is a good idea for all facilitators to arrive 45–60 minutes before kids are scheduled to arrive. This provides time for staff to ensure that the building and rooms are as you wish (i.e., open and clean), arrange furniture, post directional signs (e.g., "Welcome to SIBSHOPS! Use front door"), ensure that you have all your materials and that they are set up, and confer briefly before the festivities begin.

Materials: Signs, paper, tape, coffee

Who will gather materials?

10:00 a.m. Trickle-In Activity: Face Tags (p. 108) and Registration

Invariably, some participants arrive early, some arrive late, and a few might even arrive on time. It is always helpful to have a few activities available while kids are trickling in. Besides keeping participants busy, trickle-in activities go a long way toward making kids feel welcome and at ease. Examples include group juggling, a pickup basketball game, a craft project, or helping the facilitators set up the food activity for the day. As mentioned in Chapter 7, Introductory and Trickle-In activities, a great way to add excitement and instant atmosphere is to stream world-beat music. Because this is the first meeting, facilitators will be asking participants and their parents for information during the trickle-in time. If the participants' parents have not completed and returned registration forms online (see example in Appendix D) or any photo consent forms or waivers, they will be asked to do so when they drop off their children. At least one facilitator should be available at every Sibshop to welcome kids and parents and to help participants with name tags. For the first Sibshop, however, all volunteers will welcome families and help participants create their Face Tags. Of course, each facilitator will make a Face Tag too!

Materials: Sibshop registration forms, Face Tags sheets, pencils, sticky-back name tags, felt-tip pens, scissors, music and speaker

Who will gather materials?

10:20 a.m. Introductory Activity: Strengths & Weaknesses

For our first Sibshop, we will get to know one another using a simple activity called Strengths & Weaknesses (see p. 114, p. 147). In addition to introductions, this activity gives participants permission—from the start—to say flattering and, should they wish, not-so-flattering things about their siblings with support needs.

Materials: Photocopies of Strengths & Weaknesses for each participant and facilitator, pencils

Who will make photocopies and gather materials?

Who will present Strengths & Weaknesses?

10:45 a.m. Knots

The entire group ties itself into one big knot. Can it be untied? You'll find out! (see p. 115).

Materials: None

Who will present Knots?

10:50 a.m. The Lap Game (see p. 173)

This game doesn't require anyone to run laps, nor does it hail from Lapland in Finland. This lap refers to (as the dictionary defines it) "the front region or area of a seated person extending from the lower trunk to the knees." In short, participants and facilitators will attempt to sit on one another's lap—all at the same time. Can it be done?

Materials: None

Who will present the Lap Game?

11:00 a.m. Last Kid Standing (see p. 174)

Favorite Sibshop activities require few materials, are easy to "pitch," and feature a healthy dose of barely contained chaos. Last Kid Standing meets these requirements handily! In this game, each participant is given a clothespin. With the help of friends, clothespins are pinned to the back of each player's shirt. To play, all players simultaneously attempt to remove the clothespins from other players' backs—while not allowing other players to remove their own. Once a player's clothespin has been taken, the player moves to the side. Continue until you have only one player left.

Materials: One clothespin per participant

Who will present Last Kid Standing?

11:10 a.m. Group Juggling (see p. 110)

Although it can be difficult to juggle three balls by oneself, it's easier with a little help from your friends. Or is it? In a circle, we pass a ball and establish a pattern. Once established, we add another ball. And then another. Then, we'll try it a different way entirely.

Materials: Three beanbags for each group of five to six

Who will gather materials?

Who will present Group Juggling?

11:30 a.m. Triangle Tag (see pp. 186–187)

A geometrical twist on Tag. Three players hold hands to make a triangle. One wears a wristband or a bandana around the wrist to identify her as the "target." A fourth player attempts to tag the target while the triangle moves around to protect the target.

Materials: One wristband or bandana for each group of four

Who will gather materials?

Who will present Triangle Tag?

11:40 a.m. Sightless Sculpture (see p. 182)

Can a person who is blind be an artist? Sure, she can—she can even be a sculptor! This activity requires three participants: one who will be a model, one who will be a blob of clay, and one who will be a blindfolded sculptor. This can be done in groups of three. It is even better when groups of three sculpt in front of the rest of the Sibshop.

Materials: Bandanas or blindfolds, rectangular table

Who will gather materials?

Who will present Sightless Sculpture?

11:50 a.m. Lunch: Super Nachos

If you plan on making lunch instead of bringing in pizzas or putting together a few subs, we suggest Super Nachos for the first lunch. Most kids love nachos, and compared with other cooking activities, they require little in the way of equipment and preparation. After you use the kitchen and get to know its strengths and shortcomings, you can attempt something more adventurous. Although nachos are easy to make, they can be difficult to prepare if you forget an important ingredient or piece of equipment. You will need the following:

Food

- Tortilla chips
- Yellow cheese (in blocks, so kids can grate)
- Mild salsa
- Black olives (optional)
- Sour cream (optional)
- Tomatoes (optional)
- Green pepper (optional)
- Mild onion (optional)
- Refried beans (optional)
- Juice, cider, or other beverage
- Fruit or dessert (optional)

Equipment

- Working oven
- Hot pads
- Metal spatula
- Bowls for salsa, grated cheese, olives, and so forth
- Cheese graters
- Can opener
- Cutting boards
- Kid-friendly knives
- Cookie sheets
- Pan for heating refried beans (or a microwave and a suitable bowl)
- Cups
- Paper or other plates
- Napkins
- Cleaning equipment and soap

Who will shop?

Who will visit the kitchen to determine equipment needs?

Who will gather the remaining equipment?

12:30 p.m. Discussion Activity: Dear Aunt Blabby (see pp. 138–139)

A visit with Dear Aunt Blabby puts the participants in a rarely recognized role: as experts on what it is like to live with a brother or sister who has support needs. Write out five to seven letters from Appendix E and place them in individual envelopes addressed to Dear Aunt Blabby.

Materials: "Dear Aunt Blabby" letters in envelopes

Who will copy the letters and place them in envelopes?

Who will present Dear Aunt Blabby?

12:55 p.m. Pushpin Soccer (see pp. 177–178)

Soccer with a point and a caution: This game requires two players to use pushpins! Teams swat balloons toward the "popper" in their goal, who pops the balloon to score a point. For safety's sake, poppers cannot reach outside of the goal box and other players cannot reach inside. If the thought of participants plus pushpins is more than you can bear, or if you have noise-sensitive Sibshoppers, substitute an equally lively activity such as Blob Tag (p. 164), Islands (p. 172), or something outrageous, like The Dangling Donut Eating Contest (p. 165).

Materials: Two large balloons per participant, two pushpins, four or more large garbage bags (to store balloons after they are blown up), two large rectangular tables (to serve as goals). When shopping, aim for balloons at least 8 inches when inflated; in this game, bigger is better. Dollar stores can be a good resource for balloons.

Who will gather materials?

Who will lead Pushpin Soccer?

1:15 p.m. Scrabble Scramble (see pp. 180–181)

A fast-paced variation of the world's most popular crossword game. Watch out, though: Adults are likely to be every bit as competitive playing as the kids!

Materials: 62 sheets of 8.5″ × 11″ paper, two large felt-tip pens (different colors), two rectangular tables

Who will lead Scrabble Scramble?

1:30 p.m. Discussion Activity: Sound-Off (see pp. 135–137)

Sound-Off provides participants with an open-ended structure to hypothetically tell a friend, teacher, parent, or the whole world whatever they wish about being the sibling of a person with support needs. Responses generally cover a wide range of experiences.

Materials: Sound-Off sheet, pencils

Who will photocopy the Sound-Off sheet?

Who will lead Sound-Off?

1:55 p.m. Closure

Closure is a good time to check in with participants. You may wish to ask, "If your friends ask you what you did today, what would you tell them?" (Inevitable answers: "We played games!" "We ate nachos!" Continue to rephrase the question; eventually they will mention that they had a chance to talk about their siblings.) An alternative question might be, "You know, there are probably some brothers and sisters who knew about the Sibshop but weren't sure whether they wanted to attend. What would you say to them to encourage them to come to the next Sibshop?"

Finally, closure is a good time to ask participants to suggest food activities, recreational events, or guest speakers. Accommodating the group's wish to, say, make pizza or play Freeze Tag at the next Sibshop can encourage continued participation. At the very end, you may wish to have a group cheer. If this is to be your only meeting, it is also a great time to take a group picture or to hand out the official Sibshop certificate (see Figure 6.6). Group pictures are a wonderful way of extending the Sibshop experience. We know participants who were involved in Sibshops 10 years ago who still have their Sibshop group picture and can still identify many of the kids in the group. If you are holding a series of meetings, plan on taking a group picture during your next-to-last meeting. At your last meeting, hand out copies of the picture, along with participants' names, addresses, phone numbers, and email addresses (be sure to get parents' permission to share this information in advance).

Who will lead Closure?

Figure 6.6. Sibshop certificate.

2:05 p.m. Debriefing and Planning for Subsequent Sibshops

This is an opportunity to discuss what went on while it is still fresh in your mind. Even though you will have had a long day, consider spending a few minutes planning for the next Sibshop. A few minutes spent at this time may mean that the group will not need to meet again before the next Sibshop. The Activity Planning Form can help you plan your next Sibshop.

THE ACTIVITY PLANNING FORM

The Sibshop Activity Planning Form (see Figure 6.7) can greatly simplify the process of coming up with the next meeting's agenda, for both in-person and online Sibshops. For each activity, the form asks you to estimate time and identify a leader, materials needed, and which materials may need to be purchased. Here is how it is done:

1. Flipping through Chapter 8, identify the peer support and discussion activity you want to try at your next Sibshop. For a 4-hour Sibshop, three will be plenty; two may be enough.

2. Decide on information activities or a guest speaker, either one proposed in Chapter 10 or as identified by the facilitators. Of all activities, planning this one should get top priority; potential guest speakers need as much lead time as possible. You may wish to identify a backup speaker or activity. Also, the times that a guest speaker is available may influence the rest of your schedule.

3. Select an introductory activity (see Chapter 7).

4. Select a food activity from Chapter 9 or, better yet, create one of your own. Think through the ingredients, materials, and equipment you will need.

5. Select three or four high-energy activities and two or three quieter recreational activities from Chapter 9.

6. If you are having special events or other activities, include the estimated time, activity leader, and materials needed on the Activity Planning Form.

7. Using the completed form, begin to build a schedule around timed activities such as introductory activities, lunch, and perhaps your guest speaker. It is often best to hold the discussion activities after lunch, when full tummies predispose participants toward quiet conversation and contemplation. Follow up the high-energy activities with a more restrained activity.

Materials: Activity Planning Form

Who will photocopy the Activity Planning Form?

Who will develop the schedule for the next Sibshop (based on activities suggested on the Activity Planning Form)?

Sibshop Activity Planning Form

Planning for a Sibshop need not be difficult or time-consuming. Use the following form to record the activities you select for your next Sibshop. After deciding upon your core (discussion and information) activities, decide upon complementary recreational activities. Once completed, use this information to build a schedule.

Date: _____

Discussion/Peer Support Activity: _____
Estimated time to complete activity: _____
Activity leader: _____
Materials needed: _____
Shopping list: _____

Information Activity/Guest Speaker: _____
Estimated time to complete activity: _____
Activity leader: _____
Materials needed: _____
Shopping list: _____

Introductory/Warm-Up Activity: _____
Estimated time to complete activity: _____
Activity leader: _____
Materials needed: _____
Shopping list: _____

Food Activity: _____
Estimated time to complete activity: _____
Activity leader: _____
Materials needed: _____
Shopping list: _____

High-Energy Recreation Activity #1: _____
Estimated time to complete activity: _____
Activity leader: _____
Materials needed: _____
Shopping list: _____

High-Energy Recreation Activity #2: _____
Estimated time to complete activity: _____
Activity leader: _____
Materials needed: _____
Shopping list: _____

Figure 6.7. Sibshop Activity Planning Form.

(continued)

High-Energy Recreation Activity #3: _____

Estimated time to complete activity: _____

Activity leader: _____

Materials needed: _____

Shopping list: _____

Quieter Recreational Activity #1: _____

Estimated time to complete activity: _____

Activity leader: _____

Materials needed: _____

Shopping list: _____

Quieter Recreational Activity #2: _____

Estimated time to complete activity: _____

Activity leader: _____

Materials needed: _____

Shopping list: _____

Special Event: _____

Estimated time to complete activity: _____

Activity leader: _____

Materials needed: _____

Shopping list: _____

Other #1: _____

Estimated time to complete activity: _____

Activity leader: _____

Materials needed: _____

Shopping list: _____

Other #2: _____

Estimated time to complete activity: _____

Activity leader: _____

Materials needed: _____

Shopping list: _____

NOTES: _____

_____

_____

_____

_____

CONSIDERATIONS FOR PLANNING ONLINE SIBSHOPS

While many considerations for planning an online Sibshop are the same as a traditional Sibshop, there are a few unique factors to think about as you plan:

1. **Technology platform.** There are several online meeting platforms to choose from. Some are free, others require a paid subscription, and some offer both free (basic) versions as well as paid subscription services with more features. You will want to follow your organization's guidelines regarding teleintervention confidentiality, and make sure that you obtain written permission from parents for their children to participate. Some online meeting platforms offer HIPAA-compliant contracted services.

2. **Audience.** Online Sibshops remove geographic barriers, and families who live too far to drive to a local Sibshop may have greater access to an online meeting. For this reason, consider expanding your reach to all families within your organization's service region, and possibly beyond, especially if you are one of only a few Sibshops in your state. Cosponsoring with another agency in your state can expand your resources and the number of sibs you support.

3. **Participant ages.** Sibshops are sib-only spaces, and participants must be old enough, or technologically savvy enough, to participate independently. Children younger than 7 may require an adult's support throughout an online Sibshop, which will change the group dynamic. If you consider including children who are younger than 8, consult with parents to make sure that their children are able to participate independently.

4. **Duration.** While in-person Sibshops usually range in duration from 2 to 4 hours, your online sessions will be shorter. Best practices suggest offering an online session that is 60–90 minutes in duration, depending on how many children participate.

5. **Number of participants.** For an in-person Sibshop, we like anywhere from 12 to 20 participants. This size ensures greater likelihood that kids meet at least one other person who laughs at the same jokes and shares the same feelings about pepperoni pizza. This size is manageable enough to get through a good number of activities, including meaningful discussions. For an online Sibshop, we recommend aiming for 8–12 kids, unless you have enough facilitators to use breakout rooms for smaller groups to do discussion activities. Aiming to register 15 participants will likely result in a manageable number of attendees, considering the typical attrition rate.

6. **Equity and accessibility.** Although online Sibshops remove geographic barriers for some families, they create technological challenges for others. Consider the resources of your organization and/or local community to explore opportunities to help families access technology if necessary.

COMMUNICATING WITH FAMILIES BEFORE ONLINE SIBSHOPS

After families have registered their children for your online Sibshop, you will need to send them information about the event, including date, time, and online meeting link. It is also helpful to send parents a schedule of activities that they can share with siblings (and use as a springboard for discussion after the Sibshop; "Feelings-on-a-Screen? What was that activity about?"), and tips to prepare for the Sibshop. Often sent via email, this "welcome" message is also a great way to gently remind parents that, while we like and appreciate them, this Sibshop is one party to which they are not invited. Suggested language for a pre-online Sibshop welcome email can be found in Figure 6.8.

Dear Parents,

Welcome to Sibshops! We are excited that your child will be joining us for an online Sibshop on:

[DATE, YEAR]

[TIME]

Sibshops are fun events just for brothers and sisters of kids with developmental, health, and/or mental health concerns. They are special times for siblings only to shine.

Here is what you can do to support your child's participation in our online Sibshop:

1. Ensure that your child has a quiet, private space to set up a computer or tablet to participate in the online Sibshop. The child will need enough room to stand and stretch. We ask that you please respect the privacy of the group by keeping all other family members, including parents and siblings with support needs, away during the Sibshop. Having even one parent or family member present (even if you are off camera), can disrupt the balance of the group.

2. Read the attached activity schedule, which includes the materials you will need to gather for the Sibshop. You will also find information about [INSERT YOUR ORGANIZATION'S NAME], and contact information for our Sibshop, should you have any questions prior to the meeting.

3. Help set up the online meeting. You will receive a meeting link prior to the Sibshop. Please join on time and have your child enter with the camera and microphone on. Have your child practice muting and unmuting their microphone. Please make sure your child's preferred first name only appears as their screen name.

Thank you again for registering your child for our online Sibshop! We look forward to meeting your child and sharing a fun, meaningful experience together!

Best,
[NAME]

Figure 6.8. Sample welcome email to parents for online Sibshops.

AN ANNOTATED SCHEDULE FOR AN ONLINE SIBSHOP

The following pages contain an annotated sample schedule for a 90-minute online Sibshop, detailed description of Sibshop activities modified for an online setting, and lists of materials to gather that will help your first online Sibshop be as successful as possible. One nice thing about online Sibshops is they require few materials and your biggest consideration for most activities will be who will lead them. Additional recreational, discussion, information, and food activities for subsequent Sibshops can be found in Chapters 7–10 and in the online Sibshop Facilitator Forum, which can be found through www.siblingsupport.org.

ANNOTATED SAMPLE ONLINE SIBSHOP SCHEDULE

It is a good idea for all facilitators to log in at least 15 minutes before kids are scheduled to arrive. This provides time for staff to troubleshoot technology, practice transitions, and set up videos/links to online games, screens to share, and so forth. To set the tone as kids trickle in, stream music (jazz, world beat, or any kid-friendly tunes) to welcome them and build excitement.

Welcome	5 min
Self-Portraits	10 min
Strengths & Weaknesses	10 min
Feelings-on-a-Screen	15 min
Stretch It Out	5 min
Suitcase Race	15 min
Time Capsules	15 min
Sound-Off	10 min
Closure	5 min

Once everyone is in the meeting, introduce yourself and your organization, and have fun explaining what your Sibshop is all about! For a first Sibshop, your welcome activity may be longer and is a good time to ask the group to set and agree on some basic ground rules for communication and confidentiality.

Preparations/Materials: Technology setup, music, links to games/videos

Who will set up the technology?

Who will find/prepare music/game links?

Who will welcome siblings and how will you transition between facilitators for activities?

Trickle-In/Introductory Activity: Self-Portraits

The online version of the Face Tags activity is a fun way to invite siblings to focus on themselves before the Sibshop. They decide what unique attributes they will draw and bring to the meeting. Before the Sibshop starts, ask each participant to draw a self-portrait to share with the group. The drawing can be as creative or realistic as the artist wishes! Ask each participant to briefly introduce themselves (name, age, where they live) and say one thing about their picture. Model this by drawing and sharing your own self-portrait. This can also be a trickle-in activity, with kids drawing as soon as they join, if you expect it to take more than 10 minutes to get everyone logged into the meeting. If done as a trickle-in, communicate to parents in advance the need for participants to bring markers/crayons/paper to the meeting.

Materials: Siblings should have markers/crayons/pens and paper

Introductory Activity: Strengths & Weaknesses

For the online version of this classic Sibshop activity (see pp. 114–116), the facilitator asks each participant to share one thing they do well, one thing they do not-so-well (or would like to do better), and the same about their siblings with support needs. This can also be a good time to ask participants if they know the name of their siblings' disability, especially if you have new participants in your group.

Materials: Screen share p. 116

Feelings-on-a-Screen

This activity is an online version of "Feelings-on-a-Rope" (see pp. 140–141). It provides participants with opportunities to rate, on a scale of 1 to 10, how they feel about different topics. A rating of 1 is a major dislike, a rating of 10 is the best, and the other numbers are somewhere in between. Prior to the Sibshop, ask each sibling to create a set of cards numbered 1–10 or to print and cut out cards from a page you email to them. Or, keep it simple and ask participants to hold up the number of fingers that represent their rating. Facilitators then pose a series of questions that each participant can "rate" by holding up the card or number of fingers that represents their feelings. You may start with a general question such as, "Your feelings about rollercoasters," and transition to more sib-related questions such as, "Your feelings about having friends over when your sibling with support needs is home." Ask participants why they chose the number they did. You can play this game over and over with different questions.

Materials: Small cards numbered 1–10 (or print and cut; p. 141)

Warm-Up/Low-Energy Activity: Stretch It Out

In Sibshops, we never sit around for very long—especially when we are looking at screens! By now participants will be more than ready to get moving! Stretching is a great way to warm up before moving on to more physical activities—or at any time during your Sibshops when you sense participants need a movement break. Start by choosing your favorite stretch and invite everyone to stretch with you for 10 seconds. Then, invite each participant to pick their favorite stretch, and count to 10 (or 5 and 5 if you switch sides) as the group holds it. Don't be surprised if some energetic sibs choose more rigorous exercises! Be prepared to do jumping jacks, push-ups, burpees, and sit-ups!

High-Energy Activity: Suitcase Race

Destination: imagination! This activity will take us around the corner or around the world, depending on where our minds lead! Invite participants to think about—but not share just yet—a special place that they would like to visit. Their special place could be anywhere in the world, as near or far as they wish. It might be a place they have always wanted to go or one they have visited and loved.

Once they have their special place in mind, ask participants to think about what they would pack in their suitcase to bring on their trip. What three must-have things would they not leave home without?

Before participants share where they are going and what they will bring, we will add another twist! Rather than just *tell* us about their must-have items, they will *show* us what they are. Participants will find three essential items in their home and have *3 minutes* to bring them back to their screens. Set a timer and get ready to have some fun!

Materials: Have your own special place in mind, and have three essential items from your home or workplace nearby. Also, a timer (add to the urgency by doing a screen share of an online timer). Screen share p. 184 of this document as you finish describing the activity.

Discussion Activity: Time Capsules

To prepare for the online version of this activity from p. 134, write the "times when," in the following list, on individual pieces of paper (or print and cut the list into strips with one bullet on each). Then place the papers in individual "time capsules" (colorful plastic eggs or envelopes) numbered 1–11. Place the time capsules in a colorful basket, bag, or a shoebox that is made to look like a time capsule. Participants then take turns selecting a number from 1 to 11, and answering the question from the corresponding capsule, which the facilitator pulls from the container dramatically and reads. Other participants can then answer the question if they wish. You can repeat this activity at different meetings and add "times" that are relevant to the current environment/priorities for your participants.

Examples of times could include the following:

- A time when I was really proud of my sibling

- A time when I was really proud of something I did

- A time when I was really embarrassed by my sibling

- A time when my sibling caused problems with a friend

- A time when I helped my sibling in a special way

- A time when my sibling helped me in a special way

- A time when my sibling really made me mad

- A time when my sibling made me laugh

- A time when I was confused about my sibling's support needs

- A time when I embarrassed my family!

- A time with my sib that I always want to remember

Materials: Slips of paper (as described previously), numbered "capsules" (e.g., bathroom tissue tubes, plastic eggs, envelopes), a small box or colorful gift bag

Who will prepare the time capsules?

Who will lead the activity?

Discussion Activity: Sound-Off

This open-ended activity adapts well to an online format and gives participants permission to air their feelings about life with a sib who has support needs. To begin, screen share the Sound-Off sheet and announce, "During Sound-Off we'll have a chance to tell others how we feel about having a sib with support needs. Everyone will probably fill this out differently. For instance, someone might write, 'If I could tell the *whole world* just one *great* thing about having a sibling with support needs it would be: *he's a really neat guy even though he has a hard time learning.*' Someone else might write, 'If I could tell *the kids on the school bus* just one *bad* thing about having a sibling with support needs, it would be: *I hate it when they pick on my brother.*'"

Give participants a couple of minutes to complete their sentence, and afterward encourage participants to read their Sound-Off. There is frequently a wide range of responses, including some very personal comments. Finally, respect the wishes of those who do not wish to share.

Materials: Sound-Off screen share, pencils

Who will lead Sound-Off?

Closure

This is a great time to thank everyone for joining, share the date of your next Sibshop, and conduct a poll on favorite activities to plan for it!

Debriefing and Planning for Subsequent Sibshops

After you say goodbye to the participants, this is an opportunity to discuss what went on while it is still fresh in your minds. You will also spend a few minutes planning for the next Sibshop. Again, if you spend a few minutes at this time, your group may not need to meet again until the next Sibshop. The Activity Planning Form can help you plan your next Sibshop.

EVALUATING YOUR PROGRAM

After you have held two or three Sibshops, whether in-person or online, seek out feedback from participants and their parents. Contributed anonymously, this feedback will provide you with invaluable information and allow you to adjust and improve your program. At the end of a session, distribute pencils and a consumer evaluation sheet, such as the official Sibshop feedback form (see Figure 6.9). For online Sibshops, consider adding a poll at the end of your meeting, or linking to a short survey. As parents pick up their children, hand them a consumer satisfaction survey, such as the parent feedback form (see Figure 6.10). To increase your chances of having the questionnaires returned, also

The Official Sibshop Feedback Form

Date: _____

Your age: _____

Name of Sibshop leaders: _____

Your name (optional): _____

1. What do you like most about Sibshops? _____

   _____

   _____

2. What don't you like about Sibshops? _____

   _____

   _____

3. Please tell us what you think about the Sibshop activities. _____

   _____

	Good	So-so	Not-so-good	Don't remember
a. Warm-up activities (_____)	1	2	3	4
b. Games (_____)	1	2	3	4
c. Discussion activities (_____)	1	2	3	4
d. Cooking activities (_____)	1	2	3	4
e. Information activities (_____)	1	2	3	4
f. Guest speakers (_____)	1	2	3	4

4. Are the Sibshop leaders (circle one):

   Helpful?   Interesting?   Boring?   Other? _____

Figure 6.9. Sibshop feedback form.

(continued)

5. Is there something you want to know that we could learn during a Sibshop? _____

_____

_____

_____

6. Is there something you would like to talk about with the other kids? _____

_____

_____

_____

7. How can we make these Sibshops better? _____

_____

_____

_____

8. Do you think other kids whose siblings have support needs would like to go to a group like this?

☐ Yes ☐ No   Why? _____

_____

_____

_____

9. Do Sibshops make you think of your sibling? How? _____

_____

_____

_____

10. Is there anything else that you want to say about Sibshops? _____

_____

_____

_____

Parent Feedback Form

Please take some time to answer each of the following questions about your child's participation in the Sibshop series. Be as honest and open in your answers as possible. Thank you for your time and attention.

Date: _____

Sibshop leaders: _____

Meeting time and location: _____

Your name (optional): _____

Rate your satisfaction with the following aspects of the group on a scale from 1 (very dissatisfied) to 5 (very satisfied). If you have no opinion or the item is not applicable, circle N.

1.	Meeting time	1	2	3	4	5	N
2.	Location	1	2	3	4	5	N
3.	Length of Sibshop	1	2	3	4	5	N
4.	Group composition	1	2	3	4	5	N
5.	Communication and contact with Sibshop leader	1	2	3	4	5	N
6.	Sibshop format	1	2	3	4	5	N
7.	Sibshop activities/content	1	2	3	4	5	N
8.	Opportunities for parent input	1	2	3	4	5	N
9.	Impact on your child's knowledge of disabilities or illness	1	2	3	4	5	N
10.	Impact on your child's feelings toward their brother or sister	1	2	3	4	5	N
11.	Impact on your child's feelings toward other family members	1	2	3	4	5	N
12.	Impact on your child's self-image	1	2	3	4	5	N
13.	Impact on your concerns about your child	1	2	3	4	5	N
14.	Impact on your knowledge/awareness of your child's needs	1	2	3	4	5	N
15.	Quality of the Sibshop series, overall	1	2	3	4	5	N

16. Comments regarding above items (please note item number) _____

_____

17. Has your child talked about what has happened during the Sibshops? ☐ Yes ☐ No

Comments: _____

_____

_____

18. Has your child seemed to enjoy the Sibshops? ☐ Yes ☐ No

Comments: _____

_____

_____

Figure 6.10. Parent feedback form. *(continued)*

19. Was there any particular activity that your child seemed to have really enjoyed? ☐ Yes ☐ No

    Comments: _____

    _____

20. Has your child seemed upset by any meeting? ☐ Yes ☐ No

    Comments: _____

    _____

21. Has any activity made a strong impression on your child? ☐ Yes ☐ No

    Comments: _____

    _____

22. What do you think your child has learned from the Sibshops? How have they benefited so far?

    Comments: _____

    _____

23. Is there any way in which you feel your child may have been harmed by the Sibshop activities? ☐ Yes ☐ No

    Comments: _____

    _____

24. Overall, are you glad your child participated in the Sibshop series? ☐ Yes ☐ No

    Comments: _____

    _____

25. Is there anything we should consider for future Sibshops to make them more enjoyable or informative? ☐ Yes ☐ No

    Comments: _____

    _____

26. Any other comments?_____

    _____

    _____

Please return this questionnaire to:_____

provide a self-addressed, stamped envelope. The survey can also be emailed to parents to complete online or returned to you by email, and we suggest sending it soon after the event while Sibshops are fresh in parents' minds.

CONCLUSION

In the chapters that follow, we provide detailed descriptions of favorite Sibshop introductory, discussion, recreational, food, and informational activities. As you plan your first Sibshop, be sure to read the introductions to each of these chapters. They contain more information that will help you plan and present Sibshop activities for the first time.

7

Introductory and Trickle-In Activities

When we help start a new Sibshop, one question we often ask participants is, "Not counting your own brothers and sisters, how many of you have ever met other siblings of kids with support needs?" It still surprises us to find out that usually only 20% or so have ever met another sibling. When participants first arrive, they may feel eager, curious, or wary. Some may not even fully understand why they are there. This is a new experience, and they are not sure how to learn about other siblings, how to share things about themselves, or why doing so might be helpful. Introductory activities help break the ice, establish common ground, and reassure participants that this could be fun. The introductory activities presented in this chapter will help you and your colleagues accomplish the first Sibshop goal:

 Goal 1: Sibshops provide siblings of children with support needs an opportunity to meet other siblings in a relaxed, recreational setting.

This seemingly simple opportunity—to meet their peers—may be the most important experience that Sibshops provide to the young sibs we serve. How you introduce yourselves to the participants, and the participants to each other, will set the tone for the day. Be prepared for the day's events so that you can attend to participants as they arrive. Remember that for many first-time participants, attending your Sibshop was their parents' idea, not theirs. Some participants may not even fully understand what a Sibshop is and why they are there. Consequently, from the moment they walk through the Sibshop door, you want to make the young participants feel that you are happy to see them, interested in who they are, and ready to have fun.

One simple but effective way to set the stage is to play world-beat music as kids arrive. The infectious music welcomes kids, prevents stuffy silences, and creates an atmosphere that says, "Something's going to happen here!" If you are new to world-beat music, visit the Putumayo website. Putumayo specializes in world-beat music, and they have a terrific selection of irresistible music available in a variety of formats, including Apple Music and Spotify playlists linked on their website. You might also consider searching "Putumayo world beat" on your favorite music streaming service to discover new songs to set the tone at your Sibshop.

The activities you offer at the very beginning of a Sibshop can help break the ice and introduce participants to the facilitators and each other. "Trickle-in" activities are good to use as participants are arriving. These activities can be as simple as a craft, an art activity, or inviting participants to join a pick-up basketball or volleyball game. Or you can enlist their help in making water balloons or grating cheese to prepare for an activity later that day. Many of these activities, such as Face Tags, begin as soon as the participants walk through the door. Once most participants arrive, it will be time for slightly more organized introductions. Some of the activities described in this chapter, such as Strengths & Weaknesses, will introduce participants to one another. Others, such as Knots, will warm up a group by putting them in close physical proximity.

Face Tags

Materials: Standard sticky-back name tags, a good selection of fine-point felt-tip pens, a few pairs of scissors to share, copies of the Face Tags sheet

Name tags are standard issue at most Sibshops, so why not make them fun to design and wear?

As participants arrive, give each a Face Tags sheet (see Figure 7.1), a sticky-back name tag, and access to a wide array of colorful markers. Facilitators can model artistic license by creating and wearing their own outrageously designed Face Tag.

Face Tags allow participants to draw a self-portrait as a part of their name tags. These self-portraits can be as realistic or as outlandish as the artist desires! As participants arrive, they select a face shape that most looks like their own face from the Face Tags sheet. They then fill in and color the faces to resemble themselves. Once completed, they cut out the Face Tag, leaving a bit of room at the top or bottom. Next, they write their names on the sticky-back name tag. They attach the "extra room" they left on their Face Tag to the bottom of the sticky back of the name tag. There will still be lots of sticky surface left, so have them use this to attach the completed Face Tag to their shirts. For subsequent Sibshops, consider using thematic or seasonal name tags. Instead of a face, they can decorate an image of a bird, Valentine, snowperson, leaf, snowflake, turkey, and so forth.

Facilitators hosting online Sibshops may find Self-Portraits, a Face Tag variation, to be a more effective activity for a virtual setting.

Self-Portraits

Materials: Markers/crayons/pens, paper

Great for online Sibshops, Self-Portraits are a fun way for participants to introduce themselves to their fellow Sibshoppers.

In Version 1, ask each participant to draw a self-portrait to share with the group before the Sibshop starts. As with Face Tags, let participants know that their self-portraits can be as realistic or as outlandish as they wish! Once online, ask each participant to briefly introduce themselves and say one thing about their picture. Model this by drawing and sharing your own self-portrait.

For Version 2, have kids draw their Self-Portraits as soon as they join the call. Be sure to let parents know in advance that Sibshoppers will need to bring markers/crayons/paper to the meeting.

Figure 7.1. Face Tags.

Group Juggling

Materials: (In order of preference) beanbags, stuffed animals, and/or rolled-up socks. Balls are not a great choice because they roll away too easily. For a summer Sibshop (outdoors), consider water balloons!

Although it can be difficult to juggle three balls by yourself, it is easier with a little help from your friends. Or is it?

A group of five or six participants, standing in a circle, gently toss a ball back and forth, establishing a pattern: Madison throws to Sam, Sam throws to Jorge, Jorge throws to Gina, and Gina throws to Madison. You can suggest two helpful strategies: Call the name of the person to whom you are throwing as you throw the ball, and always keep your eyes on the person who tosses you the ball. Once this pattern is perfected with one ball, another ball is added. And then another ball. And then another.

For younger children, try the Useless Machine variation of Group Juggling. To play, create a pattern just like Group Juggling, but instead of throwing the beanbags, you pass them, preferably at a rapid clip. Useless Machine is wonderfully pointless and appeals to both kids and adults. An outrageously fun wonderful warm-weather Group Juggling variation is to use softball-size water balloons! Pro tip: Save this variation for the very last activity of the day, and play it in the parking lot where parents will be ready to pick up their somewhat soggy kids!

Human Bingo

Materials: Human Bingo sheet, pencils. *Optional:* Three small, silly prizes (e.g., glow-in-the-dark slugs)

This is a great introductory activity for a group of school-age siblings. It is guaranteed to warm things up in a hurry!

To begin, ask which participants know how to play Bingo. Have these participants describe the rules—that you win by completing a horizontal, vertical, or diagonal row of boxes. Distribute Human Bingo sheets (see Figure 7.2) but not pencils. Ask the participants how they think Human Bingo is played. Using hypothetical examples, let the participants know that a box is completed by filling in the name of a person in the group who meets the conditions or can perform the actions specified in the box. For example: "If I asked Maurice if he likes blue cheese, and he answers yes, I would write his name in the blue cheese box." Explain that, like regular Bingo, the first person to complete a horizontal, vertical, or diagonal row is the winner. When that person wins, they yell "Bingo!" Pass out pencils, say "Ready, Set, Go!" and stand back! Kids asking questions, wiggling ears, imitating elephants, and writing simultaneously create a funny and friendly, if chaotic, scene. You can stretch out this activity by having three winners: one who wins by the rules described previously, another who fills in the four corners first, and a third who is able to assign names to all 16 boxes.

HUMAN BINGO

Find someone (besides yourself) who . . . .

Has a bird for a pet.	Can name the last four U.S. Presidents	Has four kids in their family	Can imitate an elephant
NAME_____	NAME_____	NAME_____	NAME_____
Likes anchovies on their pizza	Has been to the Statue of Liberty	Has a dog for a pet	Can do the splits
NAME_____	NAME_____	NAME_____	NAME_____
Has visited their special sib's school	Can wiggle their ears	Can roll their tongue	Likes blue cheese
NAME_____	NAME_____	NAME_____	NAME_____
Was born in another state	Has been to Disney World or Disneyland	Knows why their sib has a disability	Can pat their head and rub their tummy for 10 seconds
NAME_____	NAME_____	NAME_____	NAME_____

Sibling Support Project · Seattle, Washington

Figure 7.2. Human Bingo.

"I Am" Poems

Materials: Photocopies of "I Am" poem sheet, pencils

In this easy icebreaker—good for both in-person and online Sibshops—participants complete sentences that end up being a poem about themselves.

Following is one version of the "I am" poem format, but feel free to tweak it any way you wish. To begin, distribute papers and share how you completed an "I am" poem about yourself. Be sure to emphasize that everyone's poem will be different and that is what makes these poems special. (And, in case they're worried, no rhyming is necessary!) Once completed, have the participants share their poems. If a participant is reluctant to read their poem, offer to read it for them (often, this does the trick with shy participants). If the participant remains reluctant, no worries! The poem may be too private to share.

I Am

I am (something that is special about you)

I wonder (something you are curious about)

Sometimes I hear (an imaginary sound)

Or I see (an imaginary sight)

I want (something you really want)

I am (the first line of the poem restated)

I pretend (something you pretend to do)

I feel (a feeling you have)

Sometimes I worry (something that really bothers you)

But I laugh (something that you find funny)

I am (the first line of the poem repeated)

I understand (something you know is true)

I say (something you believe in)

I dream (something you actually dream about)

I try (something you really make an effort about)

I hope (something you actually hope for)

I am (the first line of the poem repeated)

Favorites I

Materials: A slip of paper as described, pencils

Even though the participants will share the common denominator of having a sibling who has support needs, they will be different from one another in many ways. One small way of celebrating these differences is to try an activity such as Favorites I or II. Favorites II is especially good for younger participants.

Favorites I creates a flurry of activity and warms up a crowd quickly. At the very beginning of the Sibshop, participants are instructed to fill in a slip of paper providing the following information:

- What is your favorite food?

- What is your favorite hobby?

- What is your favorite television show?

Collect the completed slips, mix them up, and redistribute them at the beginning of the activity. Participants then must find the person who wrote on their piece of paper by asking others what their favorites are (e.g., "Is your favorite hobby skateboarding?"). Because participants are simultaneously seeking the writer of the paper they are holding and are being sought, the activity creates mild confusion. But don't worry—it is a pleasant, constructive commotion. Once everyone finds the person they are seeking, participants introduce their "partners" to the group and announce their favorites.

What is your favorite food?

What is your favorite hobby?

What is your favorite TV show?

DON'T WRITE YOUR NAME ON THIS PAPER!

Favorites II

Materials: 5″ × 7″ index cards, felt-tip pens, safety pins

Favorites II is especially fun with younger groups (6- to 8-year-olds) and is easily adapted for online Sibshops.

At the beginning of the Sibshop, instead of name tags, give each participant a 5″ × 7″ index card and a felt-tip pen. Have available as a model two posters illustrating index cards. One poster will describe the information you wish to elicit:

- Favorite TV program
- What I like to do for fun
- Name
- Word that describes me
- Favorite food
- Favorite color

The second poster will have an illustration of the card as it might be completed by a participant:

- Adventure Time
- Jump rope
- Belinda
- Silly
- Pizza!
- Purple

Help the participants fill out a card that describes their favorites. At the beginning of the Sibshop, ask the participants and facilitators to share the information on their tags. This is a variation of Favorites II worth considering: Have siblings fill out the cards and place them in a hat. Then, a facilitator or participant picks out a card and the group guesses whose card it is.

Strengths & Weaknesses

Materials: Strengths & Weaknesses activity sheet, pencils

Strengths & Weaknesses (or Strengths & Areas for Growth, as one savvy young sib suggested!) helps participants begin to think in terms of their sibling with support needs.

Strengths & Weaknesses serves two purposes: First, it acknowledges that everyone has strengths and weaknesses, and second, it provides participants permission—from the start—to say flattering and (should they wish) not-so-flattering things about their sib with support needs.

Introduce the activity by asking the group if they believe that everyone has strengths—things that they do well. The answer, of course, will be yes. Ask them about people who have disabilities or illnesses: Do they also have strengths? Then, ask them whether most people also have weaknesses, or "areas for growth"—things they wish they could do better. As you introduce this activity, model the sharing you would like to see from the participants. If you are a good cook but a truly awful singer, describe, with gusto and detail, how good and bad you are at these activities.

Have the participants pair off with someone they have not met before and, using the Strengths & Weaknesses activity sheet shown in Figure 7.3, have them interview each other about their strengths and weaknesses and the strengths and weaknesses of their siblings with support needs. Distribute pencils and the activity sheet and dispatch the participants to various corners of the room. Allow approximately 5 minutes for the interviews.

When the interviews are completed, regroup in a circle and have the participants introduce their partners and describe their partners' strengths and weaknesses as well as the strengths and weaknesses of their partners' siblings. This can be a good time to ask the person being introduced if they know the name of their siblings' disability. It can also be a good time to explore common experiences (e.g., "Does anyone else have a brother or sister who can't talk?" or "Sounds like we have a few musicians here. Who else is good at music?" or "How many other people do we have here who have a hard time keeping their room clean?" [Then, in mock horror] "Oh, no, not you too!").

For an online version, the facilitator asks each participant to share one thing they do well, one thing they do not-so-well (or would like to do better), and the same about their siblings with support needs.

Two Truths and a Lie

Materials: None

This slightly sneaky way to learn more about one another is probably best for older kids who understand the concept of "playfully fibbing." It is good for both in-person and online Sibshops.

To begin, have the participants sit in a circle. Ask each player to think of two interesting facts that are true and to create one "fact" that is false. One at a time, the players share their facts about themselves with the group. Other players ask questions to determine which two facts are true and which one is false. For example, one player might say, "I have two sisters," "My family lives on a big farm," and "I play on a baseball team." Participants then guess which of the three facts is not true, asking questions ("What position do you play?") if they wish. Once everyone has made their choice, the player reveals the lie ("Living on the farm is the lie! I live in the city in an apartment!").

Knots and Giant Knots

Materials: None

In Knots, a group of five to eight players tie themselves together into one big knot.

To begin this activity, players stand shoulder to shoulder in a circle, facing inward. The players extend their hands and grab two other hands, observing two rules: 1) Do not take both hands of the same person, and 2) Do not take the hands of the person next to you. Once knotted, players gently try to untie the knot, stepping over and under arms and pivoting handholds without breaking their grip. Can it be untied? There is only one way to find out! This game is guaranteed to get participants close in a hurry!

STRENGTHS & WEAKNESSES

Everybody has strengths — that is, things they do well.

Everybody has weaknesses — things they don't do so well.

Turn to the person next to you, interview him or her, and find out ONE strength they have and ONE weakness.

Also, find out ONE strength and ONE weakness for their sibling with support needs.

Take good notes. You'll introduce the person you interviewed!

Name of person you interviewed:
_____

One strength: _____
_____

One weakness: _____
_____

Name of person's brother or sister with support needs: _____

His or her strength: _____
_____

His or her weakness: _____
_____

Your Name: _____

who to forgot water me?

Figure 7.3. Strengths & Weaknesses.

After playing Knots, consider playing Giant Knot. Have everyone stand in a circle and say:

- *When playing Knots, is untying the knot easier or harder when there are more people? (The correct answer is harder!)*

- *Do you think all of us could tie ourselves into one, big gnarly knot and successfully untie it? (Expect some doubts!)*

- *We can, but we'll have to cheat just a little bit. Go ahead and hold the hand of the person next to you. At the end of a regular round of Knots, some people face the inside of the circle and some people face the outside of the circle, and that's okay. If you want to face outside of the circle at the end of the game, go ahead and turn around now.*

- *Now, pretend that we're at the end of the game. Let's travel back in time to the beginning of the game when we were tied up into a Giant, Gnarly, Incredibly Tangled Knot!*

As you say this, start twisting toward the middle of the circle, taking others with you. Encourage others to do this also until all are tied in a giant "knot." Then say:

- *Can we untie ourselves? Of course, we can!*

As the knot unravels, complement players for being geniuses!

Pass the Moves

Materials: None

Looking for a game that is fun and features social distancing? Look no further! Pass the Moves is like the old game of Telephone, but with moves!

Have all participants line up behind a facilitator with everyone spread 6 feet apart. Ask all players to close their eyes and let them know that they can only open their eyes when their name is called.

The facilitator calls on the player behind her and silently shows this person two or three simple movements, such as jazz hands, twirl, jump on one foot, and so on. Following this, the facilitator turns around and faces forward. Next, the second player turns to the third person in line, says his name, and shows the third player the moves that she learned from the facilitator. The second player turns around and faces forward. Continue with all remaining players.

When the moves get to the last player, everyone opens their eyes to see if the last player's movements match the moves created by the facilitator. To learn how the movements evolved during the game, have each player show the movements they passed along. If playing multiple rounds, have a Sibshopper be first in line and create the movements in the following round.

Snowball Fight

Materials: One piece of 8.5″ × 11″ paper (rescued from recycling is fine!) per player, pencils

Have each participant write one fact that other Sibshop participants might not know (but is not some family or personal secret!). You can decide if you wish this to be a "generic" fact (e.g., "I used to live in Alaska," "There are 12 kids in my family," "I broke my leg when I was 4") or "sibling related" (e.g., "My sister knows the movie *Shrek* so well that she can act out the entire movie," "Doctors say they have never seen a child with the same disability that my brother has," or "Once, my little sister asked this lady why she talks so much"). *Note:* Sibshoppers should NOT write their names on their piece of paper!

Tell the participants to crumple the papers into balls. On your cue, have them toss the "snowballs" to the center of the room, creating a snowball-like chaos. Have each participant find a snowball, uncrumple it, and read the fact written on it. Have the participants search out the author of the fact written on their snowball. Because they will be searching for their snowball's original owner while simultaneously being asked questions, there will be some additional—albeit mild—chaos.

Once all the original authors have been found, have the participants introduce the authors to the group by reading their fact—for example, "This is Liam. He wrote that the school band he plays in will be going to New York next year."

One way to change up this activity is to provide participants with a serious or not-so-serious question or prompt on a piece of paper. Participants write their answers on the paper and crumple it up into a snowball. Prompts could include:

- What is your favorite color?
- What do you like about yourself?
- What do you like about your sib?
- What do you like to do with your sib?
- What is your favorite thing to do?
- Share about a time you helped your brother or sister in a special way.
- Share about a time when your brother or sister helped you in a special way.
- What do you want people to know about your sib?
- Share about a time you were mad at or frustrated with your sib.
- Share about a time your sib was mad at or frustrated with you.
- What is hard about having a sibling with support needs?
- What makes you happy?
- What makes your sib happy?
- What is something positive about having a sibling with support needs?
- If you had a wish for your sib, what would it be?
- What is a wish you have for yourself?
- Share about a time when you had fun with your sib.
- What is your favorite animal?
- What is your favorite restaurant?

Go Stand in the Corner!

Materials: Sheets of large 8″ × 14″ paper and markers, or two chalkboards/white boards, chalk/dry erase markers, erasers

In Go Stand in the Corner! we vote with our feet.

To prepare, have two facilitators stand in opposite corners of the room or gym. One facilitator will have a stack of paper with the words from Column A (e.g., Baseball, Orange Juice, Burger King) with one word or phrase per sheet of paper written in large letters. The other facilitator will do the same with words from Column B (e.g., Football, Apple Juice, McDonalds). (Alternatively, both assistants can write the choices on chalkboards/white boards for each round.) Have the participants join you in the center of the room.

To play, ask the participants: "Which describes you best?" The facilitators then hold up their piece of paper with great flourish and encourage Sibshoppers to run to their choice.

Column A	or	Column B
Baseball		Football
Orange juice		Apple juice
Burger King		McDonalds
Cereal		Bacon and eggs
Spiderman		*Guardians of the Galaxy*
Potato chips		Tortilla chips
Get up early		Sleep in
School, thumbs up		School, thumbs down
Pizza, pepperoni		Pizza, extra cheese

Once your Sibshoppers have raced to the corners to let you know whether they are an Oreos or chocolate chip cookies person, shoo them back to the center of the room to prepare for another round of "voting."

Have several pieces of blank paper on hand so the participants can privately suggest other choices. For an online version, create a poll where participants can vote for their favorites.

SibTree

Materials: Kraft paper, markers, tape, scissors, construction paper

Besides being a wonderful autumn trickle-in activity, SibTree can also be a great way to publicize your Sibshop.

To prepare, draw the trunk and branches of a tree, approximately 5 feet high, on kraft paper. At the bottom of the tree, write in large letters, "SibTree." On brightly colored construction paper, draw leaves—or hands—and cut them out. On these leaves (or hands), put a variety of questions such as the following:

- What do you like about yourself and why?

- What do you like to do with your sib?

- What is one thing you would change in your life and why?

- What is one thing that is really great about your sib?

- What is one thing that is a little difficult about having a sib with support needs?

Put the leaves into a box and have the kids pick one and answer the question on it. When finished, the participants affix their leaf to the SibTree. Continue to add new leaves to the tree throughout the day, perhaps during snack or lunch or even at subsequent meetings. At the end of the day, call the kids' attention to the SibTree. Remind them that, when they arrived, the tree was "barren" with no leaves, hands, and so forth, and that they gave it "life," just the way their ideas, energy, and sharing brought the Sibshop to life. One Sibshop moved the tree to one of the main halls in the center they use and left it up as an autumn decoration. They found that their SibTree generated much interest and was good public relations for their Sibshop!

The Big Wind Blows

Materials: One chair (or paper plate) for each participant, minus one

A variation of musical chairs, The Big Wind Blows can be an introductory activity, recreational activity, or even a discussion activity!

To begin, arrange chairs in a circle, facing inward, with some space between chairs (handy for social distancing). There should be one chair for each player, minus one. One player agrees to be the "Big Wind" and stands in the center of the circle, with everyone else seated.

The Big Wind then announces, "The Big Wind blows on those who _____," where the blank would be filled with a true statement about themselves. By way of example, it could be "The Big Wind blows on those who have a dog."

At this point, all players who have a dog—including the current Big Wind—stand up and quickly try to find a new seat. There is a catch, however: players may not take seats directly adjacent to them. One person will be left without a seat. This person becomes the new "Big Wind" for the next round. As you might imagine, there are many directions to go with this game, including the following:

The Big Wind blows on those who _____:

- Have sibs who have _____.

- Have sibs who get physical therapy.

- Have sibs who get speech therapy.

- Have sibs who make them laugh.

- Have sibs who bother them.

- Have attended Sibshops for more than 1 year.

- Love pizza!

- Hate broccoli!

- Love broccoli!

- Have read a *Harry Potter* book.

- Can't get out of bed in the morning.

- Have more than one brother or sister.

- Play a musical instrument.

Variations: Have a box with suggestions (e.g., the ones mentioned in the previous list) written on slips of paper. Or have the Big Wind select a slip of paper. Or make the box available only if the Big Wind can't think of a topic. If you don't have chairs, just use paper plates taped to the floor (or simply placed on the ground if you are outside) instead.

Sibshop Action Art

Materials: White or light-colored mural kraft paper (2–3 yards), scissors, crayons or markers

Sibshop Action Art is a great warm-up activity that gives each kid a chance to "fit" their individuality into the group!

Prior to the Sibshop, decide on a word or phrase applicable to the group (e.g., "Sibshop") and draw it in big bubble letters on the kraft paper. Then, cut the paper into puzzle-like pieces, one for each member of the group. Remember to cut through the letters so that each piece has just a part of one or two letters.

As the participants arrive, give each one a piece of the puzzle and explain that it may be decorated however they wish. Colors, shapes, and tones will vary with each child's emotions and feelings. When each participant is finished, or the time is up, explain that it is now time to fit all of the individual pieces together into a whole. Guesses are welcome as to what the finished word or phrase will be! Tape the pieces together as they are fitted correctly and hang the puzzle on the wall for all to see as you begin your group circle or full-group activity.

Sib Roll

Materials: Regular or oversize dice. For online Sibshops, try an online dice roller.

Created by Michelle Ellison McDaniel, Sib Roll uses dice and a simple sheet to get kids talking.

To prepare, create a poster or handout with content similar to the model:

SIB ROLL!	
⚀	Tell us something you're good at:
⚁	Tell us something your sib is good at:
⚂	Tell us what you like to do for fun:
⚃	Tell us one thing you are looking forward to in the next year:
⚄	Tell us one wish you have for your sib:
⚅	Tell us what you like about Sibshops:

To play, have participants roll the dice. The number on the face of the dice will determine which statement they will respond to.

True Facts!

Materials: True Facts! sheet, pencils

Have the participants find someone they have not met before and interview this person using the True Facts! sheet (see Figure 7.4). Then, have the participants reverse roles. Finally, have each participant introduce the person they interviewed to the group. This activity is good with older Sibshop participants. For online Sibshops, consider splitting the sibs up into breakout rooms to complete their surveys.

The Web

Materials: A ball of heavy yarn

Build cohesiveness in your group by spinning a web of shared thoughts and experiences.

To begin, have the participants sit in a circle. Hold a ball of yarn in your hands and state, "If I were an animal, I would like to be a _____." Hold the end of the yarn and gently toss the yarn ball to a participant. Ask this participant, "If you could be an animal, what would it be?" Once this player answers, they hold onto the string but gently toss the ball to someone else. This continues until everyone has shared and players have created a web. Other possible questions include the following:

- What do you enjoy doing in your spare time?

- What is your favorite color, song, place, or food?

- Who is someone important to you and why?

- What is one thing you always wanted to do?

When You're Hot, You're Hot!

Materials: One "When You're Hot, You're Hot" activity sheet for each participant, pencils

Like Strengths & Weaknesses, this activity acknowledges that we all have different talents and limitations.

With this activity, participants fill out the sheet shown in Figure 7.5 and share a sample of their findings with the group. As the participants share their results, celebrate the diversity of the responses and acknowledge similarities.

An adaptation for both in-person and online Sibshops is to give each child four cards reading *Easy, Hard, Impossible,* and *Never Tried It.* Facilitators then ask questions found on the When Your Hot sheet (e.g., "For you, how hard is it to do a cartwheel?"). Sibshoppers then raise the card most appropriate for them.

True Facts!

Ladies and gentlemen, we want the dirt, the scoop, the hard cold facts about the person you are interviewing. Please find out the following:

- This person's name: _____

- This person's school and grade: _____

- Favorite animal: _____

- Favorite TV show: _____

- Least favorite TV show: _____

This person's response to the following question:

If I could rule the world for a day, the first thing I would do is _____

_____

_____

_____

Name and age of sib with support needs: _____

Name of sibling's support needs (if it has a name, that is!): _____

What is this sibling doing today? _____

Finally, describe this person's ideal weekend: _____

_____

_____

_____

_____

_____

_____

_____

Figure 7.4. True Facts!

When You're Hot, You're Hot

And when you're not, you're not! Nobody does everything well. Things that are easy for some folks are difficult or even impossible for others. That's okay! Life would be pretty boring if all of us did the same things well—and pretty tough if we all had problems doing the same thing! Let us know how well you can do each of these things by putting an *X* in one of the boxes beside it.

For me, it is				
	Easy	Hard	Impossible	Never tried it
Adding numbers "in your head"				
Ballet				
Braiding hair				
Chin-ups				
Climbing a rope				
Cooking a whole meal				
Dancing				
Doing a headstand				
Doing a magic trick				
Doing cartwheels				
Doing science projects				
Drawing				
Flying a kite				
Jumping rope				
Memorizing a part for a play				
Painting				

Figure 7.5. When You're Hot, You're Hot. Adapted from *We All Come in Different Packages* (Konczal and Petetski, 1983, p. 13). *(continued)*

Playing a musical instrument				
Playing chess				
Riding a horse				
Rollerblading				
Saving money				
Shooting baskets				
Singing				
Skateboarding				
Skipping				
Sleeping in				
Spelling				
Swimming				
Swinging on monkey bars				
Telling a joke				
Tossing a football				
Typing				
Using a computer				
Using a yo-yo				
Whistling				
Writing a story				

Sibling Spotlight

Materials: None

Suggested by longtime Sibshop provider Bobbi Beck, Sibling Spotlight is a great way to make participants feel important and recognized.

A week prior to your Sibshop, ask one participant if they would be the Spotlight Sibshopper for the next meeting. At the start of the Sibshop, interview them about them and their sib. Be sure to allow time for questions from other participants! This activity is also good for online Sibshops.

Hi-Five

Materials: None

Hi-Five, created by Ursala Schwenn, gets all participants interacting quickly to see what they have in common.

To begin, have participants stand in a circle (or jellybean or amoeba, based on your space and your group's circle-up skills). Introduce the activity by noting that even though they are a big group—with some kids who have been coming "forever" and others who are brand new—they also have a lot in common! Tell participants that you will read a list of statements. If that statement is true for them, ask that they please come to the middle of the circle and give a high-five to anyone else for whom that is also true. Have participants return to their spot when ready for a new statement. Pick 10–15 statements that you think will speak best to your group, starting with the most basic questions first.

School

- I am in kindergarten or first grade.
- I am in second or third grade.
- I am in fourth, fifth, or sixth grade.
- I am in middle school or high school.

Sibshops

- This is my first or second time at Sibshops.
- I have been coming to Sibshops for 1 or 2 years.
- I have been coming to Sibshops for 3 or more years.
- I don't know how long I have been coming!
- I am super excited about being at Sibshops.
- I am a little nervous about Sibshops.

Family

- I have two kids in my family.

- I have three kids in my family.

- I have four or more kids in my family.

- I have a sibling with a support need.

- I have more than one sibling with a support need.

Sibling

- I have a sibling with Down syndrome.

- I have a sibling with autism or Asperger's.

- I have a sibling with a condition that is rare, and not many people know about it.

- My sibling's support need does not have a name, or doctors don't know.

- I don't know what my sibling's support need is.

- My sibling has more than one support need.

- My sibling learns differently than other children their age.

- My sibling communicates or talks differently than I do.

- My sibling behaves and acts differently than other children their age.

- My sibling eats differently than other children (e.g., tube, allergies).

- My sibling moves or gets around differently than I do.

- My sibling sometimes gets more attention than I do.

- My sibling sometimes has different rules than I do

- I play differently with my sibling than I do with other kids.

- My sibling goes to the same school as I do.

- Sometimes, it upsets me how other kids treat my sibling.

- Sometimes, it upsets me how other adults treat my sibling.

- Sometimes, it upsets me how I treat my sibling.

- Sometimes, I get mad or frustrated at my sibling.

- Sometimes, I do special things to help my sibling.

- Sometimes, my sibling does special things to help me or show they care.

- Sometimes, I wish I knew more kids who also had a sibling with a support need.

- Sometimes, I need a break or special activities without my sibling.

- I know I can come to Sibshops to talk about all these things AND have special time for just me AND have a ton of fun!

My Wish

Materials: Sheets of paper with a heart drawn on both sides, felt-tip pens

Suggested by Sibshop provider Bobbi Beck, My Wish is a great trickle-in activity.

Provide sibs with a sheet of paper with a heart drawn on both sides. Ask participants to write a wish they have for themselves on one side and a wish they have for their sib on the other side and decorate it with drawings should they wish. It is helpful to have one or two facilitators share a completed My Wish sheet while explaining the activity. As with many Sibshop introductory and discussion activities, some sibs may choose not to share their wishes. This activity is good for online Sibshops, too!

M&M Game

Materials: M&M candies, tablespoon, small disposable cups

As you will see in the next chapter, the M&M game can be a great discussion activity, but it makes an excellent introductory activity as well.

To play, have the participants sit in a circle. Distribute cups and give each player a heaping tablespoon of M&Ms—but instruct them NOT to eat them—not yet anyway!

Assign something to each M&M color that you would like the participants to share (e.g., "If you have a red M&M, tell us your favorite movie"). After hearing about everyone's favorite movie, all the red M&Ms can be eaten. Here are a few other things that you could assign to an M&M color:

- What is your favorite hobby?

- What is your favorite book?

- What is your favorite food?

- What was your proudest moment?

- What is your sibling's name?

- What is the name of your sibling's support need (if there is a name for it!)?

- What do you want to be when you get older?

- Where in the world would you most like to live?

- Who is your role model?

After the player answers the question, they can eat the M&M color associated with the question. If parents or Sibshop providers can arrange to have the heaping tablespoon of M&Ms available, this activity can be easily done online.

Would You Rather . . .

Materials: A list of questions such as those found below. Many more questions can be found by searching the internet for "would you rather questions kids."

Suggested by Suzanne Salmo, Would You Rather asks participants to choose one of two (sometimes perplexing, sometimes outrageous) options.

To begin, have Sibshoppers stand in a large circle. With great drama, pose one question and have participants move to a designated area depending on their answer. Alternatively, participants can sit in a circle and simply raise their hands. This activity is good for online Sibshops!

- Would you rather live in a theme park or in a zoo?

- Would you rather eat a bowl of spaghetti noodles without sauce or a bowl of spaghetti sauce without noodles?

- Would you rather be the smartest person in the world or the best athlete in the world?

- Would you rather eat broccoli-flavored ice cream or meat-flavored cookies?

- Would you rather have the power to be invisible or be able to fly?

- Would you rather kiss a frog or hug a snake?

- Would you rather have super strength or super speed?

- Would you rather have four arms or four legs?

- Would you rather have a pool or a trampoline?

- Would you rather be a professional athlete or an actor in the movies?

- Would you rather be able to live 100 years in the past or 100 years in the future?

- Would you rather work alone on a school project or work with others on a school project?

- Would you rather ride a roller coaster or see a movie?

Find Someone Who . . .

Materials: None

To begin, have participants stand. Tell them that they will find someone with whom they have something in common. Begin with the following:

In a minute, I want you to find someone who was born in the same month as you. When you do find someone born in the same month as you, link arms. If there are two or three in your group, you're good! Hang tight until everyone else gets in a group. If there are more than three, break up into smaller groups. And if you can't find anyone born in the same month as you, link up with someone who also can't find a partner. Ready? Go!

In subsequent rounds, you might say, "Find someone who has the same favorite color," "Find someone who as the same number of brothers and sisters," and so forth. Once everyone is in a group of two or three, have participants share a little information about themselves with the other members of their group—for example, "Now, I want you to tell the other members of your group what magical power you would like to have—and why!" "What is your favorite pizza topping?" or "What animal would you like to be?" In later rounds, when group members are more comfortable with each other, you can ask members to share: the name of their sibling's disability (if there is one, of course!), what services their sibling receives, and so on.

Marble Mazes

Materials: Paper plates (preferably plates with high edges), marbles, construction paper, tape and/or glue sticks, colorful straws, scissors, wax craft sticks (e.g., Wikki Stix)

A great Trickle-In activity, Marble Mazes transforms paper plates, marbles, and a few other items into mazes.

Prepare by making three marble mazes of increasing complexity: On one, make simple arches by taping down 1″ × 3″ strips of construction paper. On a second, glue down straws of various lengths to make a simple maze. On a third, use Wikki Stix to make a curved maze. Demonstrate how to navigate a marble through the mazes you've created. Allow the participants to choose which materials they want to use to create their own mazes.

One Thing Hard, One Thing Easy

From Hayley Menges of Easter Seals Midwest in St. Louis, this simple activity is perfect for online and in-person Sibshops.

To play, tell participants that during One Thing Hard, One Thing Easy, you will be sharing one thing that has been hard since the last time they met and one thing that has been pretty good. When they are ready, they can make a peace sign with their fingers.

Have one facilitator go first to model the sharing you would like. Let participants know that if they feel a connection to what someone is saying, they can give the group a "hang loose" hand sign. Along the way, they may share interactions they have had with their sibs or new things they have tried, and share in general how they are doing.

Draw It Out

Materials: Paper, markers

Whether in person or online, Draw It Out is a fun way to keep hands busy while waiting for everyone to arrive.

Pick a topic from the following list and have participants use paper and markers to draw their responses.

- What makes you happy today?
- What is your favorite meal?
- What is your favorite movie?
- Who is your favorite character from a book, movie, or TV show?
- Where would you like to travel to?
- What would you do if you had a magic wand?

Have participants share their drawings.

By the end of the first 30 minutes of your Sibshop, the young participants will have properly greeted and been introduced to one another and, with some of the more physical activities, may even be "warmed up" to the point of a light sweat! Now, you are ready to try other Sibshop activities, such as those described in the following chapters.

8

Sibshop Discussion and Peer Support Activities

Peer support and discussion among participants occur throughout a Sibshop, often in a variety of formats. Sometimes, discussion is incidental to another activity, such as the introductory activities described in Chapter 7. Often, the discussion and peer support opportunities are informal. One of the reasons we like cooking and craft activities is because of the sharing that takes place while Sibshoppers grate cheese for pizza or create masterpieces with pipe cleaners, Popsicle sticks, and paint. Sometimes, the support offered is unspoken, with participants taking comfort in the knowledge that they are among kindred spirits.

Participants also experience support through more formal discussion. For instance, several Sibshop activities are designed to encourage them to reflect on their experiences with their siblings who have support needs. These activities offer a counterpoint to the lively recreational activities. Whether it is formal or informal, planned or incidental, the peer support and discussion offered at a Sibshop seek to accomplish two of our five Sibshop goals:

 Goal 2: Sibshops provide siblings with opportunities to discuss common joys and concerns with other siblings of children with support needs.

 Goal 3: Sibshops provide siblings with an opportunity to learn how others handle situations commonly experienced by siblings of children with support needs.

Most activities presented in this chapter are designed to allow siblings—perhaps for the first time—a chance to discuss their lives with others who share similar experiences. They also provide participants an opportunity to explore strategies to address situations that siblings sometimes face, such as feeling invisible or not knowing what to say to classmates who make fun of their siblings. Other activities are designed to encourage discussion on a variety of topics—some personal and some disability related. These activities may refer to the sibling with support needs, but sibling issues are not always the sole focus. Providing discussion activities on other topics acknowledges that participants are whole, multifaceted people and not only "a sibling-of-a-person-with-support-needs."

Although they may be therapeutic for some siblings, Sibshop peer support and discussion activities are **not a form of group therapy**, nor are they an adequate substitute for a child who needs intensive counseling. Children who may need to be referred for other services include

- Children showing signs of depression as demonstrated by reports of decreased appetite, sleep disturbance, chronic fatigue, apathy, loss of interest in previously enjoyed activities, changes in behavior or personality, or preoccupation with the subject of death

- Children who display outbursts of anger or emotional lability

- Children who demonstrate low self-concept or describe themselves as worthless or not appreciated by anyone

- Children who are extremely withdrawn or noncommunicative

- Children who act out in the group or are markedly defiant

- Children who report a lot of stress symptoms or physical complaints (Usdane & Melmed, 1988, p. 13)

When in doubt, facilitators should always err in the direction of safety and consult the child's parents about their possible need for further assistance.

The following sample Sibshop discussion activities will help get you started.

Time Capsules

Materials: Slips of paper (as described below), aluminum foil, "capsules" (e.g., film canisters, paper tubes, plastic eggs), a small box

In Time Capsules, siblings get to talk about various times in their lives. To prepare, write the times, listed below, on individual pieces of paper. Then, place the papers in individual "time capsules," listed previously, wrapped in aluminum foil to give them a futuristic look. An alternate method is to place the slips of paper in a shoebox made to look like a time capsule. Participants then select a capsule or a piece of paper from the capsule for the group to discuss. Examples of times could include the following:

- A time when I was really proud of my sibling

- A time when I was really proud of something I did

- A time when I really was embarrassed by my sibling

- A time when my sibling caused problems with a friend

- A time when I helped my sibling in a special way

- A time when my sibling helped me in a special way

- A time when my sibling really made me mad

- A time when my sibling made me laugh

- A time when I was confused about my sibling's support needs

To adapt this for an online Sibshop, tell the participants that there are (for example) nine time capsules in the box. Ask who wants to pick a number between 1 and 9. If, say, 4 is chosen, randomly pick four capsules out of the shoebox and read the fourth. Put the remaining capsules back in the box.

Pair Share

Materials: Paper plates (or piece of paper); trinkets/candy/beads (optional)

Pair Share, submitted by Beth Mix, is an easy way to guide pairs of kids in one-to-one conversations.

To prepare, write discussion questions on paper plates, one question per plate. Include some funny questions (e.g., "If you invented a candy bar, what would be in it and what would you call it?") as well as some serious questions (e.g., "Has your sib ever embarrassed you? How?"). Should you wish, you can place a handful of candies or trinkets (e.g., pencils, temporary tattoos, erasers, beads) on each plate.

To play, disperse the plates throughout the room and divide the group into pairs. Have participants circulate through the room, talking with each other to answer the questions. If you use candies or trinkets, the kids can take one for each question they answer. Debrief with the full group. (If the kids collected beads, they can string them on a lanyard afterward.)

Walk a Mile in My Shoes

Materials: None

Walk a Mile in My Shoes asks participants to see the world from their siblings' point of view. It can easily be played online and is best with sibs older than 10 years. Share with the group the proverb "Don't judge someone until you've walked a mile in their shoes." Discuss what this means. Each member of the group then gets to "try on the shoes" of their siblings. Acknowledge that although no one can really speak for another person, siblings are as qualified as anyone to imagine what their brothers and sisters who have disabilities might say. Discuss questions such as the following:

- What would your sibling say about having a disability?
- What would your sibling say about having you as a sibling?
- What would your sibling say about their life?
- What would your sibling say about school?
- What would your sibling say about their friends?

Sound-Off

Materials: Sound-Off activity sheet, pencils

Sound-Off is an open-ended activity that gives participants permission to air their feelings about life with a sibling who has support needs. To begin, hold up the Sound-Off sheet (see Figure 8.1) and announce that "During Sound-Off, we'll have a chance to tell others how we feel about having a sibling with support needs." Everyone will probably fill out the sheet differently. For instance, someone might write, "If I could tell the whole world just one great thing about having a sibling with support needs, it would be: 'He's a really neat guy even though he has a hard time learning.'" Someone else might write, "If I could tell the kids on the school bus just one bad thing about having a brother or sister with support needs, it would be: 'I hate it when they pick on my brother.'"

Figure 8.1. Sound-Off.

Distribute the workshop sheets and pencils and give the participants 5 minutes to complete the worksheets and illustrate them if they wish. If you have sufficient staff and kids who may balk at paper-and-pencil activities, offer to be their secretary or scribe for the day. Kids love the opportunity to have someone take dictation! At the end of 5 minutes, encourage the participants to read their Sound-Off sheet. There is frequently a wide range of responses, including some very personal comments. Respect the wishes of those who do not wish to share.

To play online, let participants and parents know that all Sibshoppers will need a blank piece of paper and a pen or pencil. After you introduce the activity, share the following via your screen:

Sound-Off!

Fill in the blanks with your own word choices!

If I could tell (Who would you tell?): _____

one thing that is (What kind of thing?): _____

about having a sibling with support needs (What would it be?): _____

Tanabata

Materials: Strips of brightly colored paper; markers; bamboo poles or bamboo, willow, or other branches

Yasuko Arima, a Sibshops pioneer in Japan, tells us that Japanese children love Sibshop recreational activities but can be reticent about discussing their families. She gets around the shyness by creating a Sibshop activity from a traditional Japanese activity done during Tanabata, or the Japanese star festival. During Tanabata, it is traditional for people to write their wishes on small strips of colorful paper and hang them on bamboo branches. Yasuko asks her Sibshoppers to write wishes they have for themselves, their siblings, and their families on small strips of paper and hang them on the bamboo branches (you could use bamboo poles or a nearby tree branch). She gives them a chance to share their wishes but does not require them to do so.

Superheroes

Materials: Paper, crayons or markers

If your Sibshop has a plethora of very active children, you know how challenging discussion activities can be. Many children prefer action, and sitting down to talk is not their idea of a good time. If this is the case, let Superheroes come to the rescue! With Superheroes, siblings reinvent themselves—or their sibs—as superheroes. Superheroes is easy to adapt for online Sibshops.

Provide the participants with paper and markers and ask them to create drawings of themselves as a superhero. Have them annotate their drawings with comments about their super strengths (e.g., My super sense of smell allows me to locate French fries from miles away), super accessories (e.g., laser-guided atomic flying wheelchair), and any Kryptonite-like weaknesses they may have (e.g., Teletubby dolls, school-cafeteria tuna noodle casseroles).

While their hands are busy, engage the participants in a discussion about how superheroes use their powers for the cause of justice. Ask them what their superheroes fight for. The participants may want to share a story about the hero and their adventures. If time permits, have them create more superheroes—this time featuring their sibs who have support needs.

Other variations could include making a mural of superheroes on a long sheet of kraft paper, or using clay or playdough to make three-dimensional superheroes. Suzanne Salmo, who runs Sibshops at the United Services for Children in St. Peters, Missouri, suggested this activity.

Discussion Gift

Materials: Small gift or bag of candy, wrapping paper

Discussion Gift is a decidedly rewarding activity! To prepare, select a gift that can be shared with the group, such as a bag of candy. Wrap the candy in multiple layers of wrapping paper, making a few more layers than players. On each layer, write or tape a question related to having a sibling with support needs. Especially for older sibs, you may wish to use the Slam Book questions (see pp. 150–152). Sitting in a circle, each participant takes a turn opening a layer and answering the question that is revealed. The last question can be: "If you get the gift, will you share it with the group? Why or why not?" If all goes well, this person will share the bounty with fellow Sibshoppers!

Dear Aunt Blabby

Materials: Letters to Aunt Blabby in individual envelopes addressed to "Dear Aunt Blabby"

Since it was first presented in the early 1980s, Dear Aunt Blabby has been the most durable of Sibshop discussion activities. Aunt Blabby, an advice columnist, receives letters from siblings who have concerns similar to those the participants may experience. Because she is not a sibling herself, Aunt Blabby needs help from experts to answer questions posed by her correspondents. The letters are read, and Sibshop participants—who are experts on the subject of being a sibling of a person with support needs—provide the letter writer with advice, drawing from their own experiences.

Typically, some of the advice provided by the participants is thoughtful and helpful, although some—kids being kids—is less so. Facilitators will want to accept each participant's solution to the problem and reinforce suggestions and strategies that are especially useful. Actual advice and strategies, while useful, are secondary to the experiences shared by the participants. If participants have had experiences similar to the letter writer's experience, they share them with the group. In doing so, participants learn that there are others who have faced similar situations and that there are a variety of possible solutions.

To introduce the activity, ask the group questions such as the following:

- "Who knows what an advice columnist is?" (Consider updating Aunt Blabby to a blogger.)

- "They may be smart and wise, but do advice columnists/bloggers know everything?" "Can they answer any question?" (You're looking for "no" here.)

- "What do they do when they can't answer a question?" (You're hoping for "they ask an expert.")

- "What do you think **all** the kids in this group are experts on?"

Once siblings establish their expertise on being the sibling of a person with support needs, hold out letters (which have been placed in envelopes marked "Dear Aunt Blabby") and allow the participants to select a letter and read it to the group. After the participant has read the letter, you may wish to reread it, pausing now and then to inquire whether anything like this has ever happened to any of the participants. Then, ask their advice: "What should Perplexed do?" "Who has also felt like Perplexed?" "What are some strategies that Perplexed might try?" End the discussion of each letter by restating the helpful strategies offered by the group.

As with other discussion activities, Dear Aunt Blabby works best in groups of five to eight. A group this size encourages a variety of responses yet allows each participant a chance to talk. Although it is a good idea to have six or seven letters in reserve, you may respond to only three or four letters in each session. To keep the interest level high, be sure to move on to a new letter before participants become bored.

Dear Aunt Blabby is easily adapted for online Sibshops. Some Sibshops recruit friends who dress up as Aunt Blabby and pop onto their screens with a purse full of letters for the group to answer. Other Sibshops begin the activity by asking the participants if they have a question for Dear Aunt Blabby.

See Appendix E for sample letters to Dear Aunt Blabby to use or adapt. When selecting, adapting, or creating letters, make sure that you present problems that are sufficiently common to generate discussion among participants.

M&M Game

Materials: Small paper cups (one per participant), each filled with approximately 10 M&Ms of various colors; large sheets of paper with questions written in red, orange, yellow, brown, blue, and green

This is an effective way to get young sibs to talk! As you will see, there are many ways you can vary this simple game.

Have the participants sit in a circle and hand each child a paper cup containing M&Ms. Tell the participants that they can't eat them—not yet, anyway. Ask the group which M&M colors they have in their cups and, with the group, establish that there are usually red, orange, yellow, brown, blue, and green candies. Ask someone to pick one of these colors. If, for instance, someone suggests red, ask that all kids who have red M&Ms in their cups stand up. Tell them they may eat their red M&Ms once they have answered the "red question." Then, tape the red question (which you have written with a red felt-tip pen) to the wall. Go around the circle and have each sibling answer the red question before eating their red M&Ms. Continue with the remaining colors. The questions for each color can be about anything—sibling related or not; the following are some ideas:

- If you were a Popsicle, which flavor would you be?

- What makes you happy about your sib?

- What makes you mad about life with your sib?

- What is your favorite thing to do with your sibling?

- Has your sib ever had a temper tantrum in public?

- What was the funniest thing your brother or sister with a disability has ever said?

- If you were an animal, what would you be?

- What is your favorite movie of all time?

- As a variation, have participants come up with questions for each color before playing.

Feelings-on-a-Rope

Materials: One rope, approximately 20 feet long

Not to be confused with soap-on-a-rope, Feelings-on-a-Rope transforms two participants and one rope into a human Likert scale. To begin, the participants sit on the floor facing two facilitators (or participants) who are holding a rope stretched between them. The facilitators describe the activity something like this:

Has anyone ever been asked to rate something on a 1-to-10 scale, such as "What do you think about the new school lunches?" or "What do you think about this new TV show?" When you rate things like this, "1" usually means that you don't like it at all and "10" means that you like it a lot! A "3" would mean that you don't really like it, but you don't hate it. A "7" would mean that it's pretty good but you don't love it. A "5" rating would mean that it's just okay.

We're going to do some ratings here. Julie (who is at the other end of the rope) is going to represent number 1. I'm going to represent number 10. We're going to ask for your ratings of different things. First, we'd like your feelings about The Extremely Important Pepperoni Issue. Julie, being on the low end of the scale, feels that pepperoni is the worst possible thing you could put on a pizza. I, being on the high end of the scale, think that pizza is not pizza without pepperoni! It's the best stuff in the world! Now, what do you think about pepperoni on pizza? When I call on you, I want you to come up and rate how you feel about pepperoni by placing your hand on the rope. If you hate it as much as Julie does, hold the rope near her end of the scale. If you love it as much as I do, hold the rope near my end of the scale. If you are some-where in between in your feelings about pepperoni, hold the rope somewhere in between. Mike, come up and show us how you feel about pepperoni!

Have the participants come up, one by one, and place themselves on the scale. Keep going until everyone is standing, holding some part of the rope. Ask participants why they rated pepperoni the way they did. After a brief discussion, ask all participants to sit down. Tell them that you want to know what they feel about other things. Present issues for the participants to come up and rate. These issues could include sibling-related issues such as the following:

- Family outings with your sibling who has support needs (1 = I hate going out with my sib and 10 = I love going out with my sib)

- Having friends come over (1 = don't like it when my sib is around and 10 = no problem at all when my sib is around)

- Going to the same school as your sibling with support needs (1 = never in a million years! and 10 = It's great to have my sib there)

- Playing with your sibling (1 = I can't stand playing with my sib! and 10 = We get along great!)

- Sharing a room with your sib who has support needs (1 = I hate it! and 10 = I wouldn't have it any other way)

You can intersperse sib issues with non-sib issues, such as school, local sport teams, TV shows, and so forth. Allow participants to come up with their own issues they would like the group to rate.

Note: After each child has come up and chosen a place on the scale, discuss the reasons behind their ratings before going on to the next issue.

Feelings-on-a-Rope can easily be played online as Feelings-on-a-Screen! Instead of coming up to a rope, they can signal their "rating" by holding up fingers to the screen, typing their number in a chat box, or holding up one of 10 previously made index cards displaying numerals 1–10. During Feelings-on-a-Screen, consider adding the scenario "going to school with your sibling in the next room."

Three Wishes

Materials: Small boxes with lids, felt-tip pens, glue, glitter, colored sand, shells, and so forth. Also: tub(s) of cake frosting, pretzel rods, candy sprinkles

A fantasy art project/discussion complete with edible magic wands—does it get better than this? This activity, submitted by Sheila Swann-Guerrero of Chicago's Advocate Illinois Masonic Medical Center, works great with younger Sibshop participants.

Provide participants with small cardboard boxes to decorate with colored sand, shells, felt-tip pens, glitter—almost anything will do. While the decorated boxes are drying, give sibs three strips of paper each and instruct them to write down three wishes. The first is a wish for themselves, the second is a wish for their sibling, and the third is a wish for their family. After completing their wishes, the participants will place the "wish slips" in their box for safekeeping, and each sib is given an opportunity to share their wishes with the group.

Sheila and colleagues do Three Wishes as part of a fantasy-themed Sibshop. They conclude this activity with edible magic wands. To make the wands, simply have the participants dip pretzel rods into frosting and then roll the frosted tip in sprinkles. Sheila notes: "The original recipe called for placing the pretzel wands on wax paper to set up in the fridge. We don't bother doing that. The sibs just eat them right away. They've been a big hit."

I Am/We Are

Materials: Pre-made posters, handout, sticky notes; markers, pencils, or pens

Submitted by Jess Kruger, who runs Sibshops in New York, I AM/WE ARE provides Sibshop participants an opportunity to develop positive perceptions of themselves, their families, their communities, and others who share common interests.

To prepare, create two large posters, one with "I AM" and one with "WE ARE" written in large block letters such as:

| I AM | WE ARE |

Next, prepare a handout for each participant:

I AM

WE ARE

To begin, distribute the handouts and writing utensils and explain that everyone will start with the I AM section. Encourage participants to write words that define themselves as an individual, such as *a daughter, a son, a brother, a sister, a friend, a basketball player, an artist,* and so forth. These, you can tell them, are "identity" words. Next, focus on "affirmation" words that describe participants' positive attributes or characteristics, such as *kind, a good cook, a good listener, a loyal friend, can make people laugh, a good singer,* and so forth.

After they record their answers on their handouts, have participants share their responses with the group and facilitate an informal discussion about their word choices as you do so. Next, distribute sticky notes and have participants transfer their top answers on the notes and affix the notes to the large I AM poster.

Next, turn the group's attention to WE ARE by noting that, even though the group members are different in many, many ways, they are alike in one important way. Ask them what that way might be. Someone will eventually say, "We're all sibs" and acknowledge that this unites them as a community. Ask, "What are some common experiences among siblings?"

Participants will likely bring up challenges sibs face, so be sure to acknowledge that all the challenges mentioned are valid. Also, explain to the participants that challenges can help make us *resilient*—able to withstand or recover quickly from difficult situations. Other attributes that can be discussed include *strong, nonjudgmental, insightful, knowledgeable about disabilities, tolerant of and kind to people who are seen as being different,* or other attributes mentioned in Chapter 4, Unique Opportunities.

Facilitate a discussion about the "sibling community" by asking questions such as these:

- How do these experiences shape who we are and our personalities?

- How does being a sib affect how we view the world?

- What do we all share as "sibs"?

- What makes Sibshops so special?

- Thinking about affirmations (those words that speak to the sibs' positive attributes), what do you hope for the sibling community?

- What do you deserve to feel because of your sibling experience?

Have kids brainstorm and record their thoughts on the WE ARE section of their handout and encourage them to share their WE ARE responses should they wish. Distribute more sticky notes and have participants transfer their top answers to the notes and affix the notes to the large WE ARE poster. Allow some time for participants to look at the posters and review the sticky notes. Facilitate a reflection discussion with questions such as these:

- What happened?

- How did it make you feel?

- Do you feel that you related to this activity or that it affected you? Why or why not?

- Why is talking about our experiences as sibs important?

- What do you think are some of the benefits of an activity like this?

If you have a group of older sibs (12+) and a group of younger kids (5–11) in your Sibshop, you can do this activity first with the older group and then have them facilitate it with the younger sibs. This helps develop mentoring skills in the older kids, enables the younger kids to see older versions of themselves, and enables everyone to gain a new perspective on their sib experiences!

Wheel of Feelings Beanbag Toss

Materials: One beanbag and a sheet of poster board on which to draw a "feelings" wheel. When completed, the wheel should be at least 2 feet in diameter. Divide the wheel into pie-shaped sections and label them with feelings such as *proud, confused, excited, worried, embarrassed, happy, irritated,* and so forth. If you are offering an online Sibshop, find a customizable online spinner and share the spinner with participants.

Have the group sit in a circle on the floor with the feelings wheel in the center, several feet from the participants. Explain what will happen in the first round and demonstrate by taking the first turn. During Round 1, each player takes a turn tossing the beanbag onto the wheel. The feelings word on which the beanbag falls determines the feeling the player will describe. The player then shares an example of when they felt that way. Thank each person in turn for sharing their feelings. Complete the first round before explaining Round 2.

During Round 2, each player again tosses the beanbag. Wherever the beanbag lands, the player describes a time they had that feeling about their sibling with a disability. If a facilitator has a sibling with a disability, they may wish to go first, modeling the type of response they wish from the participants. This round frequently sparks discussion, as participants tend to share similar experiences. Facilitators may wish to prompt participants with comments such as, "I wonder if anyone else ever felt that way?" At the end of each turn, be sure to return to the comment of the "tosser" and thank them for sharing before passing the beanbag.

Tammy Besser of the JCFS of Chicago created a variation on Wheel of Feelings, which you can call "Tubs of Feelings" or "Buckets of Feelings" if you wish! She uses plastic buckets or tubs and asks the participants to choose a feeling. They then decorate their bucket with their "feelings" word and any objects they like, such as feathers, puzzle pieces, foam pieces, stickers, and so forth. While the participants decorate their tubs, facilitators lead an informal discussion on the feelings the participants chose and how their decorations portray those feelings. When completed, participants line their buckets up against a wall. The participants take turns tossing a beanbag into the buckets and talk about the feeling written on the bucket. During the first round, the participants talk about a time when they experienced the feeling described on the bucket where their beanbag landed. During the second round, they describe when they felt that emotion toward their sib with support needs. During the third round, they describe a time when their sibling felt that emotion. During the final round, they share any stories they may have about the feeling represented by the tub in which their beanbag landed.

Same and Different

Materials: Photos of the participants and their siblings with support needs (as described below), kraft paper and markers, or a whiteboard and dry-erase markers. For online Sibshops, have siblings/parents send you digital photos that you can share on-screen.

Especially good with younger children, this activity reinforces what many brothers and sisters know intuitively—people with disabilities are more like their family members than they are different from them. Consider it a pre-advocacy activity! This is also easily adapted for an online Sibshop.

Prior to the Sibshop, send a note home requesting that the participants bring two photos (e.g., school pictures) to the next Sibshop: one photo of the child with support needs and one of the child who attends the Sibshop. Having children show up with the two photos can be the biggest challenge for this activity, so consider sending a second reminder to parents.

To begin, select one pair of photos and post them where the participants can see them. On a piece of paper or whiteboard, make two columns, one marked Same and the other Different. Say to the participants, "Here are Elena and Mateo. How are they the same?" Have the group brainstorm as many ways as possible that Elena and Mateo are the same (e.g., same hair color, same family) before asking Elena. Then, ask Elena to help the group out by telling other ways that she is the same as Mateo (e.g., both like same television shows, both like the color blue). Record the ways that they are the same in the appropriate column. Repeat this for differences.

Finally, ask, "Is one of these kids better than the other?" Briefly discuss how different does not mean better. Ask the group, "Who would like to go next?"

Gratitude Sticks

Materials: A set of pick-up sticks and a poster describing things to be thankful for

Thanks and gratitude to Donna Heim for suggesting this activity!

From time to time, we need to remind ourselves of people, things, and experiences we are thankful for. This activity is a great way to explore gratitude at a Sibshop. To prepare, create a poster like this:

- **Yellow:** A <u>food</u> you are thankful for

- **Green:** A <u>person</u> you are thankful for

- **Black:** An <u>experience</u> you are thankful for

- **Pink:** A <u>place</u> you are thankful for

- **Orange:** A <u>sense</u> (e.g., sight) you are thankful for

- **White:** An <u>animal</u> (real or stuffed!) you are thankful for

- **Red:** A <u>thing</u> you are thankful for

Other possibilities could include a kind act, a sweet gesture (e.g., a spontaneous hug from a baby), song, book, movie, and so on, you are thankful for.

To play, have players sit in a circle. With gusto, tell players something you are grateful for. It can be something big (you got to go to Hawaii) or small (your husband made you coffee and toast that morning). Ask the group, "Are there things in your life—big or small—that you are grateful for?" After one or two responses, tell the group that you will all be talking about things you are thankful for with the game of Gratitude Sticks. Review the rules of Gratitude Sticks, which are the following:

- The facilitator holds all the sticks in a bundle and holds them vertically on the surface of a floor or table.

- The facilitator releases their hand and lets the sticks scatter.

- The person to the left of the facilitator then picks up the top-most stick without disturbing the sticks below.

- *Optional rule:* If sticks get disturbed, the player loses their turn, and the facilitator bundles the sticks and drops them again.

- Players who pick up a stick look at the color and the poster to learn what topic they will talk about.

Sibshop Jenga

Materials: Jenga game set

Almost everyone knows how to play Jenga, right? Players remove one block at a time from the tower, and then stack it on top. The last player to stack a block without making the tower fall wins the game! This version of Jenga gets kids talking.

To prepare, use a permanent marker (e.g., Sharpie) to write numbers on Jenga blocks 1 to 54, because a standard Jenga has 54 blocks. Create a numbered list of 54 questions from the questions list found in the Sibling Slam Book activity (pp. 150–152) or questions you or your Sibshoppers create.

My Sib & Me

Materials: Legal-size paper (one sheet per child), crayons or colored pencils

Longtime Sibshop provider Tina Prochaska says that her Sibshoppers love this variation on Same and Different and Favorites.

To begin, have the participants fold a piece of paper in half, making a "book." Next, have them open the book and write "My Sib" on the top of one side and "Me" on the top of the other. On the "My Sib" side, have the participants write or draw their sibs' favorite (or least favorite!) foods, games, toys, and so forth. Then, have the participants repeat the activity on the "Me" side, making sure to match the categories. When everyone is finished, ask the kids to compare the sides, discussing how many things are similar or different.

My Sib & Me can be adapted for online Sibshops.

Rainbow of Wishes

Materials: A large paper cloud of your own making; strips of paper of all colors of the rainbow; pens, pencils, or markers; tape

This discussion activity would be great for a March Sibshop because it has a St. Patrick's Day theme—but it is good anytime! What would you do if you found a pot of gold at the end of a rainbow? Many thanks to Jessica Nix of Sibshops of Utah County for sharing this activity!

To prepare, create a large cloud out of white paper. On it, write "Rainbow of Wishes for Our Siblings" and tape the cloud to a wall or another flat surface. Also, cut strips (approximately 4″ × 1″) of construction paper in various colors.

To begin the activity, share the Irish lore about finding a pot of gold at the end of a rainbow. Have each participant think of what they would purchase for themselves if they found a pot of gold, and share this with the group.

Next, ask each participant to think of and share what they would purchase for their sibling with support needs. Give each participant a marker and a strip of colored paper on which they will write their idea. Tape these strips of paper to your large paper cloud.

Finally, ask each participant to think about what they would wish for their sibling with support needs. This is to be something that money can't buy. Have them write these wishes on another piece of colored paper, share their ideas with the group, and attach them to the paper cloud.

Variation: Before creating a "Rainbow of Wishes for Our Siblings," create a "Rainbow of Wishes for Ourselves." Besides asking participants what they would purchase with their pot of gold, you can also ask them what nonmonetary wishes they have for themselves.

Strengths & Weaknesses, Jr.

Materials: Chalkboard and chalk, or whiteboard and dry-erase markers

Try this activity with younger siblings who may not have the writing skills to easily accomplish the Strengths & Weaknesses activity found in Chapter 7.

Divide a long chalkboard/whiteboard as shown in Figure 8.2 with the participants' names on the top and their siblings' names on the bottom. Announce to the group: "Everybody has strengths—that is, something they do well. And everybody has weaknesses—areas for growth—things they wish they could do better." Provide dramatic examples of abilities of which you are proud and equally dramatic examples of things at which you are truly awful. Then, ask the group, "Do you think that people who have support needs have strengths—things they do really well? How about weaknesses—things they don't do so well?"

Tell the group that they will now have a chance to share their own strengths and weaknesses as well as the strengths and weaknesses of their siblings with support needs. Let them know that you will list these on the board and that they can add to their lists of strengths and weaknesses as you go along. Frequently, participants will be "inspired" to add another strength or weakness after hearing another participant's contribution.

To play online, create a table with as many columns as you have kids and switch the page layout from portrait to landscape. Have the first row filled out with participants' names and strengths in bold (e.g., **Emilio's Strengths; Danielle's Strengths**). Share your screen with participants and ask them to share their strengths and type in their responses in the cells beneath. Following the discussion of strengths, continue with their weaknesses before finishing with their siblings' strengths and weaknesses.

Two Bug Activities: That Bugs Me! And the Love Bug

Materials: Paper plates, construction paper, scissors, stapler, writing implement (crayons, markers, pens, or colored pencils). Optional: Jiggly eyes, pipe cleaners, foam shapes, glitter

These activities, suggested by Tammy Besser of the Sibshop at the JCSF of Chicago, offer siblings opportunities to talk about what bugs them—and what they love—all while constructing a bug!

Emilio's strengths	Xavier's strengths	Jayla's strengths	Danielle's strengths
Basketball	Soccer	Jumping rope	Keeping my room clean
Video games	Math	Science	Spelling
	Pizza making	Singing	

Emilio's weaknesses	Xavier's weaknesses	Jayla's weaknesses	Danielle's weaknesses
Making his bed	Jumping rope	Spelling	Cooking
Spelling	Saving money	Homework	Telling jokes

Our Sibs Who Have Support Needs!

Mia's strengths	Aniyah's strengths	Tracy's strengths	Kelly's strengths
Funny	Soccer	Can't think of any	Very curious
Learning to walk	Likes to cook		Learning to sign

Mia's weaknesses	Aniyah's weaknesses	Tracy's weaknesses	Kelly's weaknesses
Has temper tantrums	Math	Embarrasses me	Gets into Danielle's stuff
	Gets into Xavier's stuff		Can't talk

Figure 8.2. Sample chart for Strengths & Weaknesses, Jr.

Frequently, children are more open to talking about their feelings when engaged in an activity. For That Bugs Me, the paper plate (or two paper plates stapled together, plate surface side toward the middle) is the body of the bug. To prepare, cut out shapes and legs on construction paper. Have the participants write down something that bugs them on a leg or shape to attach to the plate. Here are some example questions:

- "What bugs you about school?"

- "What bugs you about relatives?"

- "What bugs you about your sibling?"

- "What bugs you about your parents?"

- "What bugs you about yourself?"

Ask the participants to share what they have written as they attach the legs to their bugs. The Love Bug is the same activity, only the questions are about love.

- "What do you love about school?"

- "What do you love about your sibling?"

- "What do you love about your home?"

Variations: Do not limit yourself to the materials listed in the previous lists—other materials (e.g., wallpaper remnants, fabric samples) can be used to decorate the bugs. Also, the two types of bugs can be combined into one bug; one side is the bothersome part of the bug and the other is the love bug.

Graffiti Wall

Materials: A long sheet of kraft paper, markers and crayons

Graffiti Wall provides participants with a chance to express and discuss in a novel way a wide range of feelings they may have toward their brothers, sisters, and parents.

To prepare, line a long wall (e.g., a hallway) with kraft paper and make vertical lines with a marker to create columns 2 feet wide. At the top of each column, print in large letters a word from the array of ambivalent feelings your participants may have for their siblings (e.g., *proud, angry, left out, inspired, embarrassed, amazed, confused*). Leave two columns blank. The number of columns you have will depend in part on the number of participants in your Sibshop. You should have at least one column for every two participants, with a minimum of eight columns.

In an area or room away from the wall, ask the participants to close their eyes and think of their sibling for a short while, perhaps 30–45 seconds. Then, with their eyes still closed, ask them to volunteer a "feelings word" that describes how they feel when they think about their sibling. After this, have them open their eyes. Explain to the group that most brothers and sisters have mixed feelings about their siblings, regardless of whether or not they have support needs. Tell the group that in Graffiti Wall, they will have a chance to express this mixed bag of feelings in a new way. Hand the participants one felt-tip pen each (preferably each a different color) and lead them to the wall that you have prepared. Review the feelings listed on the wall, noting that these are feelings that siblings sometimes have about one another. Ask if they have any other feelings that should go into the two blank columns. Ask them to choose a column and, in that column, write about or illustrate a time when they had that feeling about their sibling with support needs. For participants who have poor writing skills, facilitators can help by serving as scribes. After the participants have finished one column, they can move to another column and contribute an additional story or picture. At the end, review the stories and pictures in each column with the group.

Inside/Outside Bags or Masks

Materials for bags: Paper bags, glue, family and kid magazines, internet photos, markers, scissors

Materials for masks: Poster board or paper plates, markers, scissors, elastic string

How we feel on the inside does not always match what we show on the outside. Inside/Outside allows participants to represent artistically how they feel and what they choose to share with others.

To begin, share with your participants an example—preferably a humorous example—of when you felt one way but acted another way. Perhaps you were really irritated by someone but had to smile anyway. Or perhaps you were embarrassed by something your child did but needed to pretend that nothing happened. Point out to the kids that most of us do that now and then, and for some people, much of their life is like that: The outside is different from the inside.

Tell them that with this activity, they will be able to represent the inside/outside feelings they sometimes have. Although this can be about feelings the kids have about their siblings, it doesn't have to be. It can represent feelings they had at a certain time or how they feel all the time.

For the bag activity, set up a table with paper bags, kid and family magazines, glue, markers, and scissors. Have the kids rummage through magazines or photos and cut out pictures that represent their feelings. Have them glue the "outside" feelings to the outside of the bag and have them either glue or place the "inside" feelings inside the bag.

For the mask version, have them draw their inside feelings on one side of the mask and their outside feelings on the other side. Cut out holes for the eyes and for string. Thread strings through the holes.

Have the kids share their artwork with the group. Ask them who they have with which to share their inside. It might be a parent, a favorite aunt or uncle, a friend, fellow Sibshoppers, a pet, or even a stuffed animal.

Sibling Slam Book

Numerous Sibshop facilitators have used the questions posed in *The Sibling Slam Book: What It's Really Like to Have a Brother or Sister With Special Needs* (Meyer, 2005). In *The Sibling Slam Book*, 80 teenage brothers and sisters were asked to respond to 54 questions, and their responses are formatted in a casual style that calls to mind a composition notebook that was passed around the back of a classroom.

Cut the questions into fortune-cookie–style strips, place the questions in a hat or bag, and have the participants choose a question for the group to answer. To play online, ask one of the participants to be a "stopper." Place questions in a bag and rummage through the bag until the stopper says, "Stop"!

Alternatively, use the following questions to have your Sibshoppers create their own slam book. Or, if you're really feeling brave, place the whole list on a dartboard and let a dart decide which question the group should answer!

- What should we know about you?

- What should we know about your sib?

- How many kids are in your family?

- Describe yourself to someone who cannot see you.

- How would you describe your relationship with your sib?

- Do you like hanging out with your sib? What do you do?

- How do your friends describe you?

- What do you want people to know about your sib?

- Do you think your sib knows they have a disability? (If so, what does that mean to them?)

- Do you have any good stories about your sib?

- Is your outlook on life different from your friends' outlook on life? How?

- Do you think being a sib has affected your personality? How?

- What makes you proud of your sib?

- When you were younger, did you ever wish you had a disability so your parents would pay more attention to you?

- Do your friends get along with your sib? Do you tend to pick friends who are likely to get along with your sib?

- What do you tell your friends about your sib's disability?

- Do your friends ever ask questions?

- What is your pet peeve?

- What item must you have with you all the time?

- Can you imagine what it would be like if your sibling didn't have a disability?

- Does your sib ever frustrate you? How?

- What are some advantages—good parts—of having a sibling with support needs?

- What are some disadvantages—not-so-good parts—of having a sibling with support needs?

- Describe a perfect day.

- If you could change just one thing about your sib (or your sib's disability), what would it be?

- What do you see for your sibling's future? What part do you think you'll play in that future?

- What annoys you the most about how people treat your sib?

- Do your parents include you in discussions about your sib? How do you feel about that?

- Has your sib ever embarrassed you?

- Do you know lots of other sibs and, if so, how do you know them?

- How is your sib treated by kids in your community?

- What career choices sound good right now?

- What is something you said you'd never do but did anyway?

- What is the hardest thing to do as a sibling of a child with support needs?

- What is the sweetest thing someone has done for (or said to) you?

- Is there something about your sib that just makes you smile?

- Is there anything about your sib that just makes you angry?

- How do the people at your school/church/synagogue/after-school group treat your sibling?

- What are some words or phrases you use the most?

- Has something ever happened to your sib that scared you?

- Do you ever feel invisible?

- If you could meet one person, dead or alive, who would it be?

- If you had a choice, would you get rid of all the disabilities in the world—or just the negative reactions to them?

- What was your most embarrassing moment?

- What is the best advice you've given or been given?

- Where do you see yourself in 10 years?

- What life lesson have you learned from being a sib?

- What is your happiest moment?

- If you could have just one day when your sibling did not have a disability, what would you choose to do on that day?

- What is the toughest thing about being a sib of a child with a disability?

- What is the weirdest question you've ever been asked about your sib?

- If you had one wish for your sibling, what would it be?

- Do you have a favorite quote—or lyric?

- What is the one question we should have asked but didn't? (And what's the answer?)

Sibshop Share

Materials: An assortment of writing utensils and types of paper, one or two laptops opened to a word processing program (optional)

Sibshop Share, another activity submitted by Jess Kruger in New York, asks sibs to share their wisdom with younger and newcomer sibs about what Sibshops mean to them.

To begin, provide participants with a selection of writing utensils and types of paper (e.g., lined, construction paper, blank white sheets). Because some kids type better than they can write, consider making a laptop or two available. For some kids, writing of any kind is a chore, so offer to be their scribe/secretary by announcing that "If anyone isn't in the mood for writing and has ever dreamed of having their own secretary or scribe, please know that today is their lucky day! We'd be happy, privileged, and honored to be your secretary and do the writing for you! All you have to do is let your needs be known!"

Tell participants that they have much to offer young sibs and those who may be nervous about attending a Sibshop, and ask them to write a few sentences on topics such as the following:

- What do you value most about Sibshops?

- What is the best part of Sibshops?

- What would you tell a new sib who is considering joining?

You will likely get some remarkably insightful responses! Ask participants to share their responses and ask if you can use their responses on a poster you've made. Let them know that they can omit their name or choose a pen name should they wish. Here's just one of the responses that Jess's Sibshoppers wrote:

Dear New Sib,

It is great that you are considering Sibshops. In case you are skeptical, I totally understand. You may be worried that it will be boring or a waste of time or your voice won't be heard. Trust me, it is the complete opposite. I'm like a lot of other siblings who look forward to Sibshops every time. It is a great place to connect with others, vent about your life, and have a laugh. It's good for everything! Everyone's voice is heard because everyone's story is different. What you say can help others in ways you don't even realize. Anyway, I hope you join! I have been doing it for 5 years and it is a blast! Hope to see you there.

The comments generated by Sibshoppers are a great way to advertise your Sibshop. In addition to using them on posters, you can send participants' comments to parents once they register their children for the first time. Just be sure you seek participants' and parents' permission before sharing comments with the public.

OPEN DISCUSSIONS

You can use open group discussions successfully with older siblings (especially out in community settings, e.g., pizza parlors and skate parks, where teens like to be) or with articulate younger participants who do not require the more formal structure of a Dear Aunt Blabby or Time Capsule activity to talk about their lives. Open discussions also may be valuable for siblings who have participated in some of the previously listed activities and are ready to participate in a more in-depth or personal discussion. Open discussions follow a facilitated group discussion format. Although participants select the topics for discussion, the discussion is not without structure. Facilitators introduce the activity, establish a few ground rules, probe for topics of common interest or concern, and facilitate and close the discussion when appropriate.

The following example shows how one facilitator introduced a discussion and established ground rules:

All of you are different from one another in hundreds of ways: what you like to eat, the way you look, the clothes you choose, and so on. But there is an important way that you are the same: You are all brothers and sisters of children with support needs.

We have learned a lot about kids with support needs, but very little about their brothers and sisters. We don't know whether having a sib with support needs is a good thing, a bad thing, or a little of both. Today, we will have a chance to switch roles. In a way, you will be the teacher and I will be the student, although we will all be learning from one another. We will have a chance to learn what you think and how you feel about your sib, your parents, your family, your friends, and yourself.

There are a few rules. First, I would like you to talk about yourself and how you feel, rather than guess how others feel. Second, I would like you to feel free to respectfully disagree with one another and me. If someone says something that doesn't ring true to you, speak up!

Third, I would like us to maintain confidentiality. That usually means not telling anyone outside of the group what was said inside the group. I would like it to mean that we are kind to one another. That means not laughing when someone shares something personal. It also means that when we talk about what we say outside the group, we protect one another and do not use names.

Now, I would like you to introduce yourself, and tell us what brings you here today. If there is something you would like the group to talk about, please mention it.

Going around the circle, siblings introduce themselves and share why they came. Facilitators will acknowledge and accept all responses, including the inevitable, "My parents made me come." As participants introduce themselves, facilitators may ask a question or make a comment. Throughout the introductions, participants may need to be reminded that they can ask one another questions, make comments, or suggest topics for discussion.

When a sibling offers a problem or topic for discussion, the facilitator will want to find out if it is a concern that other participants share. The facilitator may wish to check in with the other siblings and say, "I wonder if other siblings have ever experienced anything like this." This will not only give the facilitator an idea of how widespread the concern is, but it will also make the participants reflect on their lives and think about their common experiences. The facilitator should list the topics the siblings suggest and note how many siblings indicate interest in each topic. Look over the topics the siblings mention (we recommend that you write them down) and select a topic for discussion. The topic you choose will depend on the siblings' relative interest in the topic and its appropriateness for discussion. Some topics may not be appropriate—they may be too specific for general discussion, or they may be requests for specific information. Of course, you should not ignore these topics or questions, but rather try to address them individually.

To begin the discussion, ask the participant who suggested the chosen topic to share some further thoughts on the subject, and then open it up to the group for discussion. For instance, if the siblings want to talk about what to do when strangers stare at their sibling, the facilitator may wish to guide the discussion to elicit a wide range of problem-solving strategies for responding to people's stares. Following is an example of questions you can use to facilitate a group discussion of effective strategies. Remember to use questions that begin with *what, why,* and *how,* because those are most likely to elicit discussion.

Step 1. What is the problem?

Ask the person who brought up the topic to expand on it. For example: "Shannon, tell us some more about what happens when people stare at your brother."

Step 2. Who else has the problem?

You probably know from the siblings' introductions who else has experienced this problem. Present the concern to the group. For example: "Other people said that people sometimes stare at their sibs. I'm interested: Has that happened to the rest of you?"

Step 3. Why does the problem exist?

This can help the group explore the issues underlying the problem. For example: "Why do you think people stare at people who have disabilities? Why does this bother you?"

Step 4. What have you tried?

This will help draw out the array of strategies participants have used. "What do you do when people stare at your sib?" The facilitator should acknowledge all responses but give special attention to those that are appropriate, creative, or workable.

Step 5. Has that worked?

This is an important follow-up question to Step 4. For example: "What happens when you do that or say that?"

Step 6. What are some other ways of solving this problem?

Drawing on what the group has learned in Step 3 (Why does the problem exist?) and the strategies that worked in Step 4 (What have you tried?), the group, under the facilitator's guidance, will then begin to search for additional creative solutions. For example, say, "A moment ago, we said that people who stared at people with disabilities did so because they probably do not know anyone who has a disability. What are some other ways that we can help people get to know people with support needs so that they will not stare at them?" (A most creative solution to this problem was volunteered by a sibling whose mother says to staring strangers: "You seem to be interested in my daughter. Would you like to meet her?")

Remember that these are only guidelines for group problem solving; not all discussions will follow this outline exactly. Also, discussion may not always focus on problems that siblings experience. Participants may wish to express their thoughts and opinions on a wide variety of subjects related to their experiences as siblings of a child with support needs.

Mo Langley of California's Sandy Feet Initiative (where she runs a *surfing* Sibshop!) gets open-ended conversations going by asking participants to write letters to their sibs that they can share, throw away, or keep and by asking older sibs for the advice they'd give to their 9-year-old selves.

CONCLUSION

When they are well run, Sibshops discussion activities are among the richest and most memorable experiences facilitators can offer participants. During these activities, participants listen to and learn from one another, share knowing laughs, discuss the good times and the tough spots, and trade war stories and helpful strategies. When they learn that their peers sometimes feel the same way they do, participants experience camaraderie, their feelings are validated, and they feel less alone with their concerns. These activities can be potent experiences for the people who lead them as well. The insights and wisdom expressed by these young participants often stay with facilitators for a long, long time.

9

Sibshop Recreation and Food Activities

When we survey young participants about what they like best about Sibshops, they invariably tell us, "the games and activities." Although Sibshops are intended to provide participants with peer support and education, we could not be more pleased with participants' strong endorsement of our recreational and food events. The spirited games and activities, which account for more than half the time spent at a Sibshop, are an essential element of a successful program and are critical to accomplishing the model's first goal:

 Goal 1: Sibshops provide brothers and sisters of children with support needs an opportunity to meet other siblings in a relaxed, recreational setting.

We are unapologetically enthusiastic about having fun, and we feel that recreational events are key to providing peer support from a kid's-eye view. Recreational activities promote informal sharing and friendships among participants, and the friendships siblings begin during Sibshops frequently grow outside the program, providing ongoing sources of support that may last a lifetime. We recall watching several preteen girls playing in the gym at the close of a Sibshop held in a small New England city. The girls had just met that day but had become fast friends, having spent the previous 4 hours playing, cooking, and talking about their lives, families, and interests. Their parents, who had arrived to pick up their children, were struck by how well the girls were playing and how reluctant they were to leave. One parent noted, "You know, these girls will probably know each other as adults."

Recreational events also make Sibshops appealing to the young participants. We are never surprised to learn that a child is reluctant to attend a Sibshop for the first time. After all, a sibling might think, "Why should I give up a Saturday to hang out with a bunch of kids I don't know just because they have a sibling with a disability?" Recalling Sibshop games and activities often leads a participant to return to the program's discussion and information activities, and benefit from them further. In short, recreation is essential to a Sibshop.

The games, activities, and food projects reflect the model's emphasis on siblings' strengths and wellness. They are an indispensable component in a program that seeks to celebrate the many contributions made by brothers and sisters.

GAMES—NEW AND OTHERWISE

Many of the Sibshop recreational activities have been adapted, with permission, from various sources, most notably the New Games Foundation. If New Games are new to you, you are in for a treat. They are offbeat, fun, and sometimes silly games designed to appeal to a wide range of ages and abilities. (New Games, while ideal for school-age children, were originally developed by and for playful adults. Consequently, most of the activities we present will also work well with teenagers.) Some games are competitive, but most are not. In any event, playing, not winning, is what is fun and important. Most New Games require little equipment but a lot of energy.

In the next section, we provide capsule descriptions of some of our favorite games and activities. We have selected activities that have minimal equipment needs. New to this edition are activities that siblings can enjoy during online Sibshops. Should you wish for more ideas, consider searching the internet for "group activities for kids," "online games for groups of kids," "socially distant activities for kids," or even "team-building activities for kids." Still more tried-and-true Sibshop games and activities, for both online and in-person Sibshops, are regularly posted on the Sibshop Facilitator Forum. The forum is a perk reserved just for registered Sibshop facilitators.

Of course, you will want to customize and enrich these games with your own skills and ideas. If you have musical, artistic, or dramatic talents, be sure to share your gifts with the participants. The Sibshop model is sufficiently flexible to allow facilitators to express their own creativity, and we know that when facilitators have fun, kids have fun.

PRESENTING SIBSHOP RECREATIONAL ACTIVITIES

As noted in Chapter 5, Sibshop facilitators will need diverse skills. On the one hand, presenting Sibshop discussion activities requires facilitators to model the thoughtfulness and reflection we desire from the young participants. On the other hand, Sibshop recreational activities call upon the facilitators to be exuberant, dramatic, and "on." The following are some general tips on how to make your games and activities successful:

- Before the Sibshop begins, decide who will "pitch" the activity. This person will be responsible for gathering materials (if any) and deciding what assistance the other facilitators will provide. Will everyone do the activity together, or will the participants break into groups with a facilitator assigned to each group?

- Become familiar with the activity you will present. Sibshops are safe places to try a game or activity that is new to you and the group—and even to make mistakes. In fact, a facilitator responding to a mistake with humor and grace can be an extremely helpful model to siblings who struggle to be "perfect." Be sure to read the directions for an activity before the actual Sibshop. It will be difficult to inspire adventurous, imaginative play if you must read the instructions to the group. As Scouts BSA advises: Be prepared.

- When explaining the activity, place yourself at the edge—not the center—of the circle, so that everyone can see you. For large groups, have participants sit in a semicircle. They can watch you demonstrate the activity with a small group of volunteers before they begin the activity in smaller groups. Regardless, pitch the activity with gusto. This is not the time to be tentative. If you pitch it with enthusiasm, they will love your activity!

- Explain the rules and the structure of the activity as simply and as clearly as possible. After you explain the activity, ask for questions, but do not get involved with needlessly lengthy answers. Often, just playing the game will answer most questions.

- When explaining the activity, first describe it in a general way ("Who knows how to play Tag? Let's play Blob Tag—It's Tag with a twist!"). Demonstrate the game with volunteers as you explain the object of the game: "Let's pretend Sarah is It. She chases Jason and tags him." (Take Sarah's hand and tag Jason.) "Now they're both It!" (Join their hands.) "Holding hands, they chase Michael and tag him, and then all three are It!" (Have one participant tag Michael.) "They keep tagging, and the Blob keeps getting bigger and bigger until there is only one very fast person left! Are there any questions?"

- Present the activity in a way to encourage participation and playfulness. The New Games Foundation recommends inviting participants to play by saying, "Let's try. . ." instead of "You're going to. . ."

- Encourage variations. Sibshop participants and their energetic facilitators can always come up with variations on games and activities. Think of your Sibshop as a game lab: Some of the ideas will work and some will not. Regardless, a Sibshop is an environment where playful invention and experimentation are not just indulged but encouraged.

- Be certain to make all safety issues very clear! Make sure that all participants understand any warnings before proceeding with an activity. If necessary, ask siblings to repeat and explain the reasons for the warnings. You can play most of the in-person activities described in this chapter in a gym or a large multipurpose room. Make sure that the environment is as free as possible of objects that might injure participants or facilitators as they zoom across the room in a spirited round of Sharks and Minnows.

- Make sure that the activity is appropriate for the kids in your Sibshop, and for the time during which it is being held. Some Sibshop games begin with instructions asking participants to "grab the hand of the person next to you." If you have Sibshoppers who, for instance, are from religious communities that prohibit kids from holding hands with someone of the opposite gender, pick another game. Also, consider current events and be sensitive to participants' needs. After a tragic shooting in one community, it was decided that playing Pushpin Soccer—a crowd favorite that entails popping balloons—was not a good idea.

- Be sensitive to moods and energy changes. Like a stand-up comedian who gauges the audience's laughter to know when to move on to the next joke, assess the energy and interest remaining in an activity to determine when to move on to the next one. Provide occasional low-energy activities to allow participants to catch their breath between the high-energy activities.

- Sometimes, you will be able to make a connection between the recreation activity you are presenting and some aspect of having a support need. An example would be Sightless Sculpture and artists who have disabilities. If you can make a connection, great—just don't oversell it!

Have fun! This isn't school! Model your ability to laugh at yourself and forgive yourself for making mistakes, which can be a true gift to the young high achievers who may be in your group. One perk of facilitating a Sibshop is the opportunity to get in touch with your playful self. Your obvious enjoyment of the activities you present will set the tone for your young participants.

Following, in alphabetical order, are recreational activities that we have enjoyed. It is not an exhaustive list by any means. If you are a registered Sibshop provider, you can discover more activities on the Sibshop Facilitator Forum. If you have a favorite that you would like to share with a wider audience, we hope you will let us know.

Airport

Good with younger participants—and a lively exercise in cooperation!

Energy Level: Medium

Environment: Indoors and large open space

Materials: Blindfolds (e.g., bandanas, inexpensive medical facemasks pulled over eyes instead of nose and mouth) and objects to use as safe obstacles, such as pillows, chairs, coats, and shoes

To play, divide the group into pairs. One player will be the pilot; the other will be the air traffic controller. The players currently not selected become the runway and form two lines about 10 feet apart, facing each other. Place items on the runway and then blindfold the pilot. (To make it more challenging with an older group, blindfold the pilot before placing the items.) The controller verbally guides the pilot with statements such as "Walk forward five steps, walk to the right, step to the side." The sideline players can give hints such as "Watch out," "Good job," or "You hit something." The pilot continues until they reach the controller even if they touch an object. The game continues until all pairs have had a turn.

Backlash

This makes for a great variation on the relay race once partners can manage a few steps in their new form!

Energy Level: High

Environment: Gym or other open indoor or outdoor area

Materials: Balloons

To begin this relay-race variation, divide the participants into two (or more) teams, and then divide each team into pairs who are of similar height. Instruct the partners to stand back to back and link arms. Have facilitators place a balloon between the pairs' backs.

To begin the race, one pair from each team runs to the end of the gym and back in the balloon-in-the-middle, back-to-back, linked-arms position. The object—to keep the balloon between them—is not so hard while just standing, but running is something else! Players will likely try push-me/pull-you techniques until they realize that side-stepping is probably the best approach. Once back at the starting position, they unlink and wedge the balloon between the backs of the next pair, and the race continues.

There are at least two variations of Backlash. First, instead of wedging the balloon between their backs, each person can hold a balloon in his or her hands while running in the same linked, back-to-back position. When it comes time to transfer the balloons, the pair may not unlink arms. Second, for a truly wild version, try this variation with water balloons—outside, of course!

Balloon Badminton

WisconSibs' Christiana Yablonowski reports that Balloon Badminton is a hit at her Sibshops!

Energy Level: High

Environment: Gym or other open indoor area

Materials: Balloons, paper plates, 6-inch adult tongue depressors, masking tape, markers

As a trickle-in activity, have participants create a racquet by decorating paper plates. Help them tape two tongue depressors end to end and then tape one end of the "stick" to the middle of the back of the paper plate.

When it is time to play, give each participant a balloon to practice on their own. Next, break the group into pairs and have them volley one balloon with their partner. Finally, have the whole group come together and swat one balloon, then two, then three, and so on. Feel free to add other challenges, such as "no talking," "keep one hand behind your back," and so on.

Balloon Birdseed Beanbags

Or should that be Birdseed Balloon Beanbags? Or maybe Balloon Birdseed Bags? Regard-less, BBBs are multicolored lemon-shaped balls that are easy and fun to make and perfect for individual juggling, Group Juggling (see p. 110), or hacky sack.

Energy Level: Medium

Environment: Indoors, in a cleared, open area

Materials: See below

Blessed is the Sibshop that has "crafty" facilitators. Much informal sharing occurs during the creation of crafts such as Balloon Birdseed Beanbags. Plan for stations for two to four kids. Each station will have the following:

- A medium bowlful of inexpensive birdseed or dry grain

- Balloons (9"–12" round) of various colors. Each ball will require three balloons; conse-quently, if you wish to send your Sibshoppers home with a set of three balloons to juggle, you will need nine balloons for each participant.

- Spoons, one per participant
- Scissors
- At least one funnel made from the cut-off top of a plastic soda bottle

Demonstrate making a BBB as follows:

- Stretch Balloon 1 over the mouth of the soda bottle funnel.
- Spoon birdseed into the funnel until the balloon is filled to its neck (smoosh down a bit if needed).
- Using scissors, cut off most of the neck of Balloon 1.
- Select Balloon 2, which should be a different color than Balloon 1.
- Cut off the neck of Balloon 2.
- Perhaps with the help of a partner, gently stretch the opening of Balloon 2 over the opening of Balloon 1. Your BBB should now be sealed.
- Cut off the neck of Balloon 3 (a different color from 1 and 2).
- Take your scissors and make small slits into Balloon 3.
- Gently stretch the opening of Balloon 3 over Balloon 2 so that the opening of Balloon 2 is sealed by Balloon 3.
- The color of Balloon 2 will peek through the slits you made in Balloon 3, resulting in a very cool effect!

Your BBB is ready to use!

Balloon Duo

This is another cooperative partner balloon race.

Energy Level: High

Environment: Field or gym

Materials: Balloons

To play, partners stand side by side and link arms. The leader gives each team one balloon. After the leader says, "Go," partners bat the balloon forward with their free arms, keeping it in the air while racing toward a finish line. If a balloon hits the ground, players may scoop it up but may not unlink arms.

Balloon Stomp

Does any Sibshop item offer more cheap thrills than balloons? Whether they are filled with water and juggled (see Group Juggling), used in place of a soccer ball (see Pushpin Soccer), or employed as faux muscles (see Muscle Beach), balloons are an indispensable Sibshop item. In this genteel game, they are stomped.

Energy Level: High

Environment: Indoors or outdoors

Materials: At least one large, inflated balloon per player, with a yard of inexpensive yarn tied to the end

Use the yard of yarn to tie a balloon to the ankle of each player. On your signal, players stomp on the balloons of other participants while trying to protect their own balloon.

Beach Ball Bounce

Try this when weather turns your thoughts to the beach—and for many of us, that could be the middle of winter!

Energy Level: Medium

Environment: Indoors

Materials: One lightweight beach ball for each of six players

To begin, divide the group into teams of equal numbers—six is a good amount. Have each team count off 1 through 6. To play, Player 1 hits the ball in the air, shouting, "One!" Player 2 continues, hitting the ball and shouting their number. The goal is to keep the ball in the air and to hit the ball in order. If a team drops the ball or hits it out of order, they begin the round over. Have teams keep track of "perfect" rounds (e.g., 1–6 with no drops). The winner is the team with the most perfect rounds within a predetermined time (e.g., 3 minutes).

Behavior Modification

Here is a crash course in shaping behavior.

Energy Level: Medium

Environment: Indoors

To play, ask two volunteers to leave the room. While they are gone, the rest of the group decides what physical position (not too difficult or detailed) they would like the volunteers to assume when they return. The group also decides how they will let the volunteers know whether they are getting close to the desired pose. Among the signals we have used are clapping loudly or softly, cheering or booing, or humming high or low. The volunteers then reenter the room and attempt to replicate the pose.

Blindfold Sort Out!

After a few exuberant activities, this low-energy yet appealing activity can be just the ticket!

Energy Level: Low

Environment: Indoors or outdoors

Materials: Blindfolds (e.g., bandanas, inexpensive medical facemasks pulled over eyes instead of nose and mouth)

To play, give each player a slip of paper with a unique number and then blindfold each participant. Shuffle the participants around, keeping them in a small group. Ask the group to put themselves into numerical order without using sight or sound. To finish, all players must be holding hands in a straight line in numerical order. Variations include sorting by alphabetical order, age order, tallest to smallest, and birth dates.

Blob Tag

A tag game that grows on you.

Energy Level: High

Environment: Field or gym

Materials: None

This is a great game in an open gym. Choose one person to be "It." When It tags someone, they both become It. Holding hands, they go after a third. The three, holding hands, go after a fourth, and so on until all players are It—except for one very fast-moving individual.

Body-Part Musical Chairs

This is a good activity to try with younger sibs.

Energy Level: Medium

Environment: Indoors or outdoors

Materials: Chairs or mats

To start, have the participants sit in chairs in a big circle with the chairs facing out. Have music ready. When the music starts, remove one chair and have the players jog around the circle. When the music stops, the facilitator calls out a body part. Each person must then touch that body part to a chair—one person per chair. If a participant touches a chair before the body part is called, out they go! And the one person who does not get a chair is out as well. Start simply: knee, hair, left elbow. As appropriate, make it more complicated: bare feet, someone else's left hand (they must grab one of the people who are already out, and so forth).

Cheeto Head

Suggested by longtime Sibshop provider Bobbi Beck, Cheeto Head is a wacky target game where players throw Cheetos at the head of a teammate whose head is covered in shaving cream!

Energy Level: Medium

Environment: Best outdoors; indoors will likely require more cleanup

Materials: Cheetos, inexpensive shower caps, foamy shaving cream, paper towels

To begin, one person sits on a chair and puts on a shower cap. Next, cover the cap in a thick layer of shaving cream. The other team member (or members) stands behind a line opposite the seated player. During a preset period (1–2 minutes), team members throw Cheetos at the seated player and attempt to get them to stick to the shaving cream. The seated player can assist by moving their head to help "catch" the Cheetos. The team with the most Cheetos stuck to the shaving cream wins.

Dance Party

Shake up an online Sibshop with a dance party!

Energy Level: Medium to high

Environment: Indoors

Materials: None

At the end of a Sibshop, announce that at the next Sibshop you will have a dance party to showcase their favorite songs and participants' best dance moves. Have the kids brainstorm songs that they like and think others will like too. Between Sibshops, find these songs online.

At the next Sibshop, you can introduce the activity this way: "Remember the songs we picked at the last Sibshop? Which of you picked 'Uptown Funk'? You're going to show us your best moves and we're going to join you!" Play the cued-up song and model the "dance like no one is watching" exuberance that you wish to see among your Sibshoppers!

Dangling Donut-Eating Contest

As much fun to watch as it is to play, the Dangling Donut-Eating Contest is sure to appeal to all Sibshop gourmands. Like many Sibshop games, DDEC is a great photo-op!

Energy Level: Low

Environment: Indoor hallway with beams or ceiling to which tape will stick; or outside, perhaps under monkey bars on a playground

Materials: Yarn, heavy tape, broom (or drop cloth for the many crumbs), and a cake donut (powdered sugar is even better) for each player

Prepare for this activity by threading a piece of yarn through the middle of each donut and tying it around the donut, making sure that the yarn is long enough so that when taped to the ceiling (or tied to the monkey bars), the donut will dangle at mouth level of the players. To begin, line up the contestants, have them keep their hands behind their backs, and attach their donuts at proper height. At the "Go" signal, the participants race to see who indeed is the most capable dangling-donut eater. There are sure to be crumbs, so have a broom or shakable drop cloth on hand. (If you are in a smaller area, this race can be done in heats.)

Dot's Dot

An opportunity to stretch the imagination, often with impressive results. Easily adapted for online Sibshops.

Energy Level: Low/trickle-in

Environment: Tables and chairs

Materials: Sheets of blank paper, pencils, crayons. Optional: 1/4" circular color-coding dots, available from office supply stores

Have each participant cover a sheet of paper with 20–25 randomly scattered dots. Collect these papers and redistribute them, or have participants simply trade with a neighbor. Have players concentrate on the dots to imagine

a picture, and then connect the lines so that the picture emerges. If some are having difficulties, have participants turn the paper in different directions to imagine other possibilities.

Fingerprint Pictures

It is amazing the amount of art that is available at one's fingertips! This activity can be adapted for online Sibshops.

Energy Level: Low/trickle-in

Environment: Tables and chairs

Materials: Paper, washable ink pads or wide washable markers, thin markers or crayons, wipes or paper towels, soap for cleanup

Place a sheet of paper at each seat and enough ink pads and markers so that materials are within easy reach of each artist. Once the participants roll up their sleeves, they can begin inking their fingers. Show the participants how to press their fingers and thumbs into the ink pad and then firmly onto the paper. If ink pads are not available, use washable markers—but please, no permanent markers (e.g., Sharpies)! Encourage kids to experiment with different forms and different techniques, such as rolling the fingertip or even printing the sides or heels of their hands.

Once the participants have finished making their fingerprints, have them wipe their hands with a paper towel and use markers to draw faces and designs to give their blotches some character.

5-Second Game

Another game shared by Bobbi Beck, 5-Second Game, is perfect for online and in-person Sibshops.

Energy Level: Low

Environment: Online or indoors

Materials: Stopwatch

To play, ask participants to name three things in 5 seconds. Some prompts, such as "Things That You Wish You Could Tell Your Friends About Your Sib," will probably take longer than 5 seconds, but the goal is to keep the game moving along quickly.

Favorites:

- Favorite foods
- Sibling's favorite foods
- Favorite things to play outside
- Favorite things to do with your sibling
- Favorite zoo animals
- Favorite things to wear in the winter
- Favorite summer activities
- Least favorite things to do
- Sibling's least favorite things to do

Types of things:

- Types of playground equipment
- Names of animals
- Names of colors
- Ice cream flavors
- Types of candy
- Colors of eyes or hair
- Disney movies
- Superhero movies
- Video or board games
- Favorite Halloween candy
- TV shows
- Types of disabilities
- Kinds of street signs
- Types of exercise during gym
- Your favorite foods
- Names of songs
- Names of adults you know
- Superheroes
- Foods at McDonald's
- Animal sounds
- Your favorite parts of Christmas or other holidays
- Things you like most about Sibshop

About Your Sib:

- Your sib's favorite toys
- Your sib's favorite things to do
- Foods your sib won't eat
- Things you wish your sib would stop doing
- Things your sib is good at doing
- Things you wish you could tell your friends about your sib
- Your sib's favorite foods
- Your sib's favorite Halloween candy
- Things your sib does every day
- Things that bug your sib

- Things your sib can't live without

- Things you and your sib argue about

- Things that scare your sib

- Games you play with your sib

- Things that make your sib happy

- Things you wish your sib could do

- Things your sib does during a meal

- Things that make your sib laugh

- People who are special to your sib

- Best things about your sib

The Floor Is Lava

The Floor Is Lava is a favorite at many Sibshops. This is how Christiana Yablonowski plays it at her Sibshop in Appleton, Wisconsin.

Energy Level: High

Environment: Indoors or outdoors

Materials: Two each of a variety of items: pool noodles, pillowcases, scooters, spot markers, floor mats, and so on

To prepare, divide materials into two piles of identical items. Set the two piles at one end of the room, spaced approximately 10 feet apart. Divide the group into two teams and have them stand next to one pile of items. Explain that you just learned that the floor is lava, and their job is to use the items to get all their teammates to the other side of the room using the items in the pile to avoid touching the floor. To start the game, announce in a mock-horror tone, "THE FLOOR IS LAVA!!!" During play, if someone "falls into the lava," pause the game and issue a "Revival Task" that the teams complete to continue. This task could be answering a riddle, singing and dancing to a verse of a silly song (e.g., Hokey-Pokey), answering a "Would You Rather" question, and so on.

Fox and Chickens

Never underestimate the ferocity of a Mother Hen protecting her young!

Energy Level: High

Environment: Indoors, in a cleared, open area

Materials: None

To play, line up the group in single file—except for one player. That player is the Fox! Have everyone in line hold the waist of the person in front. These are the Chicks, and the player at the head of the line is the Mother Hen.

At your cue, the Fox attempts to catch the last Chick in line. The Mother Hen flaps her wings and follows the Fox (with her Chicks following her) to prevent the Fox from catching the last Chick. When the last Chick in line is caught, this Chick falls in behind the Fox and holds the Fox's waist as he tries to get more Chicks. As more Chicks are caught, the Fox's line eventually gets longer than the Mother Hen's. The game continues until all Chicks are caught. For full effect, encourage clucking!

High, Low, Surprise Me!

Cassandra Flores shared this great "get-up-and-move" activity where participants choose the energy level. It is perfect for both online and in-person Sibshops!

Energy Levels: High, low, and "surprising"!

Environment: Indoors, in a cleared, open area

Materials: None

To play, ask a participant to choose a movement category. Their choices are High, Low, or Surprise Me. Once chosen, announce an activity in the chosen category for all to do. If needed, demonstrate the activity. A twist on High, Low, Surprise Me! is to have participants take turns choosing the movement category *and* making up the activity!

High-energy choices:

- Jog in place.

- Do five push-ups against the wall or on the floor.

- Do 10 jumping jacks while humming your favorite song.

- Do "head, shoulders, knees, and toes, knees and toes."

- Do five frog jumps.

- Do 10 left-foot hops; switch and do 10 right-foot hops.

- Participants have 15 seconds to find their favorite toy/thing.

- Pretend to play your favorite sport and the group guesses what it is.

Low-energy choices:

- In slow motion, trace your name in the air in front of you; then, trace it backward.

- Stand up on tiptoes with eyes closed. Lift one foot off the ground.

- Assume the Witches Brew pose: Sit cross-legged, arms out in front, hands clasped together and move arms in big horizontal circles like you're stirring a giant pot.

- Stand in tree pose; switch legs.

- Hold your arms above your head in a "V" shape for VICTORY.

- Try 4-7-8 breathing by following this breathing pattern: First, empty your lungs of air. Second, breathe in through your nose for 4 seconds. Third, hold the breath for a count of 7 seconds. Finally, exhale forcefully through your mouth, pursing the lips and making a "whoosh" sound, for 8 seconds. (Have participants repeat the cycle 4 times and note that this is good for relaxing, de-stressing or falling asleep.)

- Name three of your favorite foods.

- Try five-finger breathing by stretching your hand out like a star. Then, starting at the base of your thumb, run your forefinger from your other hand to the top of the thumb while breathing in through your nose. Hold your breath at the top of your thumb and then breathe out slowly through your mouth as you trace your thumb to the base on the other side. Repeat for the remaining fingers.

Surprise Me! choices:

- (Online) Find something BLUE in your house and show the camera. (Repeat with other colors.)

- Do a dance move. (Participants can follow the leader or volunteer or just make up their own move.)

- (Online) Draw your favorite food and show us on the screen.

- Wink your left eye while snapping the fingers of your right hand. Now wink your right eye while snapping fingers on your left hand.

- Pat your head with one hand while making circles on your belly with the other hand. Now reverse hands.

- Make pretzel arms: First, stick your arms out in front with your thumbs up. Second, turn your thumbs down. Third, cross your arms at your wrists. Fourth, lace fingers together. Fifth, bring clasped hands up and tap your forehead. Finally, take your arms back down and stretch out in front.

- Name three Disney movies.

- Make three types of noises for the group to guess.

Hog Call

This is an activity as refined and subtle as its name suggests.

Energy Level: High

Environment: Gym or other large room

Materials: Bandanas if you wish to blindfold players. Alternatively, you can ask players to promise to keep their eyes closed while they play the game. More importantly, you will need slips of paper for the Red Team and the Blue Team.

Each of the Red Team's slips of paper will have a word that somehow "goes with" the words found on the Blue Team's slips of paper. For example, if a member of the Red Team gets a slip of paper that says

Red Team	Blue Team
Batman	Robin
Peanut butter	Jelly
Bacon	Eggs
Homer	Marge
Salt	Pepper
Bagel	Cream cheese
Ball	Glove
Bert	Ernie
Needle	Thread
Cookies	Milk
Nuts	Bolts
Lock	Key
Pen	Paper
Mickey	Minnie
Stars	Stripes
Bread	Butter
Salsa	Chips
Moon	Stars
Spaghetti	Meatballs
Hot chocolate	Marshmallows

"bagel," someone on the Blue Team will get a slip of paper that reads, "cream cheese." The following are other examples to consider of things that go together. When you create the slips of paper, you can avoid confusion by writing the Red Team's slips in red and the Blue Team's slips in blue.

To play, clear the room of all furniture, making a wide-open area that is free of obstacles. Divide the group into two teams of equal numbers and have each team go to opposing walls. Distribute the slips of paper carefully so that for every "Batman" you have a "Robin." It helps to stack the decks of slips in order. Consequently, if the order of the Red Team's deck is "Batman, Peanut Butter, Bacon," the order of the Blue Team should be "Robin, Jelly, Eggs." Dealing the deck from the top will ensure that everyone has a match.

Explain to the group that a member of the other team has a slip of paper with a word that some-how goes with the word on the slip of paper they now have. Say, "For instance, if someone on the Red Team has 'Superman,' someone on the Blue Team probably has 'Lois Lane.'" Further explain that to play the game, they must find their match with the other team by walking toward the middle of the room—with their eyes closed—and shouting whatever is on their slip of paper and listening for the word that goes with it. Once they find their match (by using only sound), players can open their eyes and go to the side of the room. Demonstrate with a fellow facilitator using Superman and Lois Lane. There is one more catch, however, and this is what makes this game special: All players search for their matches simultaneously! Consequently, while Salt is looking for Pepper, Bert is also looking for Ernie, and Spaghetti is looking for Meatballs. Hog Call is over when the last pair has been matched.

Human Spring

Human Spring is a counterpart game to Stand-Off (see p. 183). In this game, players cooperate to keep each other balanced upright.

Energy Level: Medium

Environment: Grassy area or indoors on mats

Materials: None

Two players stand with feet spread, facing each other at an arm's distance, holding their arms up in front, palms forward. Keeping their bodies as rigid as possible, partners gently lean forward, catch each other with their palms, and rebound to a standing position. Too easy? Take a short step back and try again. This works best on a soft surface!

Instant Replay

Try this decidedly silly name-learning game after a warm-up activity such as Knots, Group Juggling, or Human Bingo (see p. 115, p. 110, and p. 110, respectively). This activity is easily adapted for online Sibshops.

Energy Level: Medium

Environment: Indoors

Materials: None

Standing in a circle, each group member announces their name while making an extravagant motion. For instance, Kai may hop into the circle on one foot (or turn circles with his hands raised or slap his knees) and then shout his name. After Kai demonstrates, everyone else does an "instant replay." That is, they simultaneously perform the same motion and say, "Kai!" Going around the circle, encourage the participants to introduce themselves with dramatic gestures.

Islands

This game is akin to Musical Chairs, but if you make contact in this game, you are out!

Energy Level: High

Environment: Field or gym

Materials: Paper plates (one for every three or four participants); recorded music (optional)

To play, scatter plates on the ground. Instruct the participants to begin wandering around the "islands." When the referee calls "Islands," everyone runs to touch a plate. Although more than one person can touch a plate, the last person to get to a plate is "out." In a departure from many Sibshop activities, Islands does not promote contact—in fact, if any two people touch at all while scrambling for the plates, they are out! Continue to reduce the number of plates as the group grows smaller, until there are just a few people ready to pounce on a single island. A variation is to play music while the participants wander about the islands, stopping the music to signal that the land rush is on.

Joke of the Day

Energy Level: Low

Environment: Online or in-person Sibshop

Materials: None

At the end of a Sibshop, tell participants to bring a joke to the next Sibshop. In an email to parents, have them remind their kids to select a joke they would like to share with Sibshop friends. During the next Sibshop, ask participants to share their joke. Some will likely forget, and others might be too shy. No worries!

Keep the Balloon in the Air

This is a good game for young Sibshoppers; it was suggested by Tammy Besser of JCFS Chicago. It can easily be adapted for online Sibshops.

Energy Level: Medium

Environment: Indoors, in a cleared, open area

Materials: Balloons

Give each child an inflated balloon. Tell the children that they can hit the balloons into the air, but they can't let them touch the ground. The only other rule is that the same person cannot touch the same balloon twice in a row. This encourages them to interact in creative ways as well as to engage in group problem solving.

The Lap Game

What is the one thing that disappears every time you stand up? Your lap, of course! In the Lap Game, participants attempt to sit on each other's laps—everyone, at the same time. Can it be done?

Energy Level: Medium

Environment: Indoors or outdoors

Materials: None

Have all the participants stand shoulder to shoulder, elbow to elbow, and ankle to ankle in a tight circle. Each player then turns to the right and places their hands on the waist (or shoulders) of the players directly in front. When signaled by the leader, all players simultaneously guide the players in front of them to sit on their knees. If done correctly, all players are sitting in the laps (or, more correctly, on the knees) of the person behind them. If not done correctly, the players create a human—if ridiculous—representation of the domino theory. If all goes well and everyone has a lap to sit on, the group may try to lift their arms in the air and applaud themselves. If players are feeling especially brave, they may try to walk in this seated position, with someone signaling "Right!" "Left!" and so on.

Last Details

Try this one in person or online when the group needs a breather from some of the more raucous activities.

Energy Level: Low

Environment: Indoors

Materials: Optional: wearable props such as glasses, hats, scarves, gloves, buttons

Have the group divide into pairs. If you are using props (this can be done successfully without them), let each person select one or two at this time. Each person then faces their partner, carefully observing the other's details. When signaled by the leader, players turn their backs to each other and, within a minute, rearrange four details. Both players face each other again and try to see if they can identify what has been changed. To play online, select one participant at a time to rearrange details while their camera is off.

Last Kid Standing

Our favorite Sibshop activities require few materials, are easy to "pitch," and feature a healthy dose of barely contained chaos. Last Kid Standing meets these requirements handily! One warning: The materials required—spring-style clothespins—are living antiques and may be a challenge to find!

Energy Level: High

Environment: Indoors or outdoors

Materials: One clothespin for each player

To begin, give each participant a clothespin. With the help of friends, pin clothespins to the back of each player's shirt. To play, all players simultaneously attempt to remove the clothespins from the back of other players while not allowing other players to remove their own. Once a player's clothespin has been taken, that player moves to the side. Continue until you have only one player left. One Sibshop facilitator adapts the game by coloring half of the clothespins red and the other half blue to create two teams. The last team standing wins!

Look Up, Look Down

This activity, suggested by longtime Sibshop provider Diana Rovetti, is a simple, fast, and fun game that needs zero equipment!

Energy Level: Medium

Environment: Indoors or outdoors

Materials: None

To begin, have players stand in a circle with their heads bent forward and looking down at their feet. The facilitator then shouts, "Look up!"

All players look up at someone else. (Looking at the ceiling or into the distance is not allowed!) If two people make eye contact, they leave the group. Should you wish, you could have these players scream upon making eye contact!

The facilitator then says, "Look down," and everyone looks down again. The facilitator again says, "Look up," and the process continues. The game continues until there are only two players left. When there are only two people left, you can determine the ultimate winner with rock-paper-scissors or a coin toss.

Marshmallow Battleship

A favorite at the Sibshop facilitated by Suzanne Muench, this game uses large marshmallows to play a life-size game of Battleship.

Energy Level: High

Environment: Indoors or outdoors

Materials: Jumbo marshmallows and large room dividers (or sheets hung from a clothesline to create a divider)

Optimal Number of Participants for This Activity: 10+

To begin, create two large spaces using room dividers or sheets, blankets, and ropes to create a large divider. You will want something tall that will not allow kids to see through. If possible, set up the divider so there is a wall on one side. This helps contain the marshmallows as they are thrown.

Split the group in two. Ideally, there will be five to seven participants on each side, depending on how much space you have.

Have participants sit on the floor in random places on their side of the divider. Once they are seated, they cannot move. Each team then takes a turn throwing over one large marshmallow, with a goal of hitting one of the participants on the other side. Once hit, that person is out of the game. Participants cannot move or duck to avoid being hit. Once a person is hit with a marshmallow, they are "out," must leave the playing area, and can watch how close the others come to hitting someone on either side. Remind "out" players that they cannot give hints to teammates about where to throw a marshmallow. The team to have all their participants "sunk" loses the game.

Mouse Trap

Who is more cunning, the sneaky mice or the cat that is just pretending to sleep?

Energy Level: High

Environment: Open area

Materials: None

Optimal Number of Participants for This Activity: Minimum of 10 players

To begin, four or five players become The Dreaded Trap by standing in a circle with hands joined and raised in the air to create entrances and exits for the Mice. One player is chosen to be the Fearsome Cat. The Cat, who pretends to sleep, faces away from the trap with eyes closed. The remaining players become the Cunning and Clever Mice who dart quietly in and out of the Trap past the sleepy Cat.

To capture the Mice, the Cat suddenly opens their eyes and yells, "Snap!" The players who are the Trap immediately bring their arms down, snaring the rascally rodents. Captured Mice now become part of the Trap. The game continues with the Trap becoming larger and larger until there is only one victorious Mouse.

Mummy

Hardly original but always fun, Mummy is another great crowd-pleasing activity for late October!

Energy Level: Medium

Environment: Indoors

Materials: Toilet paper, masking tape

To play, divide the group into teams and have the team decide who will be the mummy. Give each team two rolls of toilet paper and, optionally, a roll of tape. Tell your participants that the goal of the game is to wrap the mummy completely so that all that is showing are the mummy's eyes and nose—no clothing and no skin should show. Have teams race to see who will finish their mummy first. If you wish to make it a bit harder, you can tell them that they must wrap their mummy in one continuous strand of toilet paper. If their strand of toilet paper breaks (and it will), they must connect the broken strand with masking tape. Variations include having nonplaying players vote on their favorite mummy or having the fully wrapped mummies compete in a race or competition of your invention.

Muscle Beach

This is a game sure to "pump you up"!

Energy Level: Medium

Materials: For each group of five participants: one oversized sweatshirt (purchased, if needed, from a thrift store) and 10 balloons of assorted sizes. Handy to have: pictures of Dwayne "The Rock" Johnson, Arnold Schwarzenegger in his prime, Kevin Nealon and Dana Carvey as "Hans and Franz," or any body builder, including women such as Iris Kyle (obtained from the internet, perhaps).

To begin, have each group of five select a representative. The representatives come to the front of the room and are given oversized sweatshirts. You will acknowledge that these kids indeed look strong, but not nearly as strong as (whipping out your pictures) The Rock, Arnold, or Hans and Franz. Tell them that's perfectly fine because you (and your fellow facilitators) are there to (wait for it) Pump Them Up!

Explain that their teammates will have 4 (or fewer—your choice) minutes and 10 balloons to blow up, tie, and stuff in the sweatshirt to make their teammate the most muscled rock star there. Hand out the balloons and start the timer. Once the time is up, have facilitators (or kids) judge which balloon-enhanced kid is indeed "Most Buffalicious."

Mutual Monsters

Step aside, Dr. Frankenstein; here come the real monster makers!

Energy Level: Low

Environment: Tables and chairs

Materials: A sheet of letter-size paper and pencil/crayons/markers for each person

To begin, distribute paper and pencils and have the participants fold their sheet of paper in thirds. On the top third, everyone draws the head of a monster, person, animal, or creature. As they draw, have all the artists extend the neck of their creation a little past the first crease in the paper. When completed, have the participants fold back the top third so that it is hidden and pass their papers to neighbors. Now, *without looking at the head,* everyone draws a torso and arms in the middle section of the page connecting to the neck lines. This time, have them extend the waist a little past the second crease. Now, fold the paper again and pass it to a different neighbor. Everyone now, *without looking at the other sections,* draws legs and feet on the bottom third of the paper. When all players are finished, they unfold their papers and share their masterpieces with the whole group. It helps to have a completed drawing to show participants as you describe the activity.

Pass the Sponge

This is a great game for a hot day! Contributed by Donna Heim.

Energy Level: High

Environment: Outdoors

Materials: Two large sponges, four buckets (two large buckets filled with water, and two smaller buckets of equal size), towels

To begin, divide participants into two teams and have them form lines. Place the full bucket at the front of each line and the empty buckets at the end of each line. To play, the first person in each line dunks the sponge in the water and then passes the sponge overhead to the person behind them. Passing continues to the last person in line who then squeezes water out of the sponge into the empty bucket, runs to the front of the line, dunks the sponge in the bucket of water, and begins passing it overhead down the line once more. The first team to fill their bucket wins!

Psychic Shake

How can you find your comrades if you can't talk?

Energy Level: Low

Environment: Field or gym

Materials: None

Have all participants silently select a number—either *one, two,* or *three.* Once they decide, people quietly circulate, giving each other handshakes of one, two, or three shakes. When players meet someone with the same number, they hold hands and search for others of their number. When all is done, for curiosity, see if there are three equal groups. Once you try it this way, ask your participants how they could change the game. Instead of shaking hands, you might find yourself winking, hopping, stomping, or snapping your fingers!

Pushpin Soccer

Caution: This game mixes kids and pushpins!

Energy Level: High

Environment: Gym or large indoor space

Materials: Inflated balloons (about three per player), 8″ or larger (dollar stores can be a good source for inexpensive balloons); two pushpins (one red, one blue); two large rectangular tables; large lawn-and-leaf bags to contain the inflated balloons. *Optional but recommended:* electric balloon inflator (inexpensive and easily found online).

To prepare for this activity, clear the room and put two large rectangular tables at opposite ends of the room. These will be your goals. To begin, have players line up along a wall and arrange themselves according to height. Starting with the tallest player, have players count off "red," "blue," "red," "blue," and so on. This will ensure two teams—a Red Team and Blue Team—of approximately equal heights.

Have the teams meet at their goals. Explain that in Pushpin Soccer, they will compete with the other team for possession of the balloon. Their job is to use their hands to swat the balloon to their own goal. To score, they must get their balloon across the goal (the table) so that their team's popper can pop the balloon with a pushpin. (At this point, select a person to be the teams' poppers.)

Review—in great detail—the rule that will help ensure that the game is played safely: Players may never, *ever* place their hands over the table. Similarly, the popper may not reach their hands over the table for any reason. This makes the entire table area a "zone of safety" and keeps hands and pushpins apart. Adults stationed near each goal can monitor poppers' and players' adherence to safety rules.

After the warning, hand the poppers their pushpins and bring a balloon onto the court. Toss the balloon into the air and the game begins. Each team swats the balloon toward its popper, who attempts to pop the balloon. Players may swat the balloon with their hands only. For fun, try introducing more than one balloon at a time toward the end of the activity.

If the group has participants of very different heights, consider alternating sets for taller and not-so-tall players.

The Rain Game

Good with young Sibshoppers, this game simulates a rainstorm.

Energy Level: Low

Environment: Indoors

Materials: None

To begin, have all players sit on the floor in a circle. Demonstrate the following actions and have all players copy your actions in the following order:

1. Rub your fingers together and have all players do the same.

2. Rub your hands together, creating a soft sound.

3. Softly clap your hands.

4. Snap your fingers.

5. Clap your hands again, this time a little bit louder.

6. Clap your hands again, even louder.

7. Stomp your feet.

8. Stomp your feet and clap.

9. Reverse actions, returning to quiet.

In an alternate version, all players sit or stand in a circle and do the following:

1. Snap your fingers and have the first person on your left make the same sound. Continue to snap your fingers. The second person to your left then starts snapping his fingers. Then, the third person to your left starts snapping his fingers. And so on. Eventually, everyone in the circle is snapping fingers.

2. Instruct the group to continue snapping fingers as you introduce the next sound, thigh slapping. The person to your left then stops finger snapping and begins thigh slapping. Eventually, the entire group is thigh slapping.

3. Continue to introduce other sounds, such as foot stamping, clapping, tongue clucking, chest thumping, shushing, and so forth.

Red-Handed

Keep passing, 'cause you wouldn't want to be caught red-handed!

Energy Level: Low

Environment: Open area

Materials: One small object (e.g., a marble)

With eyes closed, one player stands in the middle of a circle of players who continuously circulate a small object such as a key or marble. Whether they have the object or not, all players simultaneously pretend to be passing the object. When ready, the center player opens his or her eyes and has three guesses to determine which player actually has the marble. The player caught "red-handed" (or whoever has the marble after the third unsuccessful guess) becomes the new person in the center.

Scavenger Hunt

This is an online Sibshop favorite!

Energy Level: Medium

Environment: Home

Materials: Items found in participants' homes

Select a few items that you think your Sibshoppers might have in their homes. Following are some suggestions, but feel free to add your own. Tell participants that, in this version of Scavenger Hunt, you want them to find objects in their homes and that they will have 2 minutes to find each item. Set a timer for 2 minutes; if 2 minutes seems too long or too short, adjust accordingly. Give participants an opportunity to explain the item they chose.

•   A picture of you when you were a baby

•   One thing you can't live without

•   One thing you never want to see again

•   Someone else's toothbrush

•   Something clean

•   Something from nature

•   Something healthy

•   Something purple

•   Something sparkly

- Something sticky

- Something that makes a noise

- Something that makes you happy

- Something that makes you smile

- Something that moves

- Something that smells good

- Something that starts with the same letter your name starts with

- Something with a face on it

- Something with wheels

- Something you made

- Your oldest toy

- Your sibling

Scrabble Scramble

Spelling tests should be so much fun! Adults have as much fun with this as the kids do!

Energy Level: Medium

Environment: Open indoor area

Materials: 62 sheets of plain, inexpensive 8.5″ × 11″ white paper, wide felt-tip markers (one red, one blue), two large tables placed approximately 20 feet apart

To prepare, use the markers to make two sets of "alphabets"—one red and one blue. Each set will have one letter per page, drawn to fill the page. In addition to the usual 26 letters, each set will also have an extra *A, E, I, O,* and *U.* Consequently, the blue and red sets will use 31 pieces of paper each.

Divide the group into two teams—a red team and a blue team. As older kids and adults will likely have a few advantages in this game, try to make sure that each team has a mix of young and not-so-young players. Place the sets of letters on the teams' tables and tell the participants the goal of Scrabble Scramble: to create a word or phrase on a topic you will give them using only the letters found on their table.

Furthermore, explain that there are three ways to score in Scrabble Scramble: One point is awarded to the team that "builds" their word first. ("Building" a word means that the team has created a word and holds their word up—one letter sheet per player—for the other team to see.) Another point is awarded for the team that builds the longest word or phrase. Finally, 1 point is given to a team that spells their word or phrase correctly! Consequently, a team may score up to 3 points per round, and both teams can score a point for correct spelling.

Before play, remind players that they have two of each vowel but only one of each consonant, so no words with double *R*s, double *S*s, and so forth. Here are some Scrabble Scramble categories you may wish to try: "Anything Disney," "Anything [name of your state]," "Anything Summer," "Anything Food." The team with the most points after a set number of rounds wins.

Scrabble Scramble Score Sheet

Team:	Team:
Round 1 ❑ Best time (1 point) ❑ Most letters (1 point) ❑ Correct spelling (1 point) ❑ Total: _____	**Round 1** ❑ Best time (1 point) ❑ Most letters (1 point) ❑ Correct spelling (1 point) ❑ Total: _____
Round 2 ❑ Best time (1 point) ❑ Most letters (1 point) ❑ Correct spelling (1 point) ❑ Total: _____	**Round 2** ❑ Best time (1 point) ❑ Most letters (1 point) ❑ Correct spelling (1 point) ❑ Total: _____
Round 3 ❑ Best time (1 point) ❑ Most letters (1 point) ❑ Correct spelling (1 point) ❑ Total: _____	**Round 3** ❑ Best time (1 point) ❑ Most letters (1 point) ❑ Correct spelling (1 point) ❑ Total: _____
Round 4 ❑ Best time (1 point) ❑ Most letters (1 point) ❑ Correct spelling (1 point) ❑ Total: _____	**Round 4** ❑ Best time (1 point) ❑ Most letters (1 point) ❑ Correct spelling (1 point) ❑ Total: _____
Round 5 ❑ Best time (1 point) ❑ Most letters (1 point) ❑ Correct spelling (1 point) ❑ Total: _____	**Round 5** ❑ Best time (1 point) ❑ Most letters (1 point) ❑ Correct spelling (1 point) ❑ Total: _____

Sharks and Minnows

Do sharks really bother to eat something as small as minnows? Who knows and who really cares? Sharks and Minnows is an especially lively, easy, and materials-free game that Sibshoppers enjoy!

Energy Level: High

Environment: Gym, large indoor space, or yard

Materials: None

Have participants line up at one end of the wall; they are the minnows. Ask one participant to be the shark. This player stands in the middle of the room. The minnows' job is to get to the other side of the room without being tagged by the shark. Players who get tagged become sharks! Play continues from one side of the room to the other. The last minnow left is the winner!

Sightless Sculpture

Can a person who no longer hears write music? Of course! Beethoven did. Can a person who no longer sees still make sculptures of her friends? Sure! Sightless Sculpture, a great low-energy activity, can also be an opportunity to talk about the intersection of disability and art.

Energy Level: Low

Environment: Indoors

Materials: Bandanas, a long table, two chairs

Place the table at one end of the room and have the participants sit on the floor facing the table. Ask the participants, "Do you think people who have disabilities can be artists?" They will surely answer in the affirmative, so ask them, "Who can give me an example of an artist—famous or not so famous—who had a disability?" You may hear about Van Gogh, Chuck Close, Beethoven, Stevie Wonder, Ray Charles, or a participant's talented sib. Then ask them, "Imagine this scenario: You're a sculptor. More than anything else in the world, you love to make sculptures. But something happened and you lost your vision. Could you continue to do what you so love to do?" They will likely say "yes."

Help the participants brainstorm how they would sculpt without being able to see. Then, introduce the game by telling them that to play Sightless Sculpture, you will need three participants.

To begin, one of the three participants will volunteer to be the Sightless Sculptor, another to be the Blob of Clay, and still another to be the Model (a.k.a. the Model Child). Blindfold the Sculptor and have them stand in front of the table. The Model, sitting in a chair behind the table, arranges their arms, hands, torso, and head in any position they can maintain for up to 5 minutes. The Blob of Clay sits in a chair behind the table next to the Model.

The Sculptor then uses their hands to determine the Model's position and manipulates the Blob of Clay to create an identical statue. Leaders may need to help the Sculptor locate the Model and the Blob of Clay. When the Sculptor feels that the creation is complete, they open their eyes to assess their work. This activity can be done in groups of three or with three people at a time in front of a group.

Snowball Fight

This simple game is loved by Sibshoppers of all ages at any time of the year!

Energy Level: Medium

Environment: Indoors

Materials: Masking tape and 8.5″ × 11″ paper (rescued from recycling is fine!), one piece per player

To get ready, divide the room in half by making a dividing line on the floor with masking tape. Divide the participants into two equal groups and have the groups stand on either side of the masking tape line. Distribute one piece of paper per participant. Have them crumple their piece of paper into a "snowball."

To play, have teams throw snowballs found on their side of the masking tape to their opponent's side as quickly as they can and as far as they can. During play, teams may not put any parts of their bodies over the masking tape lines—only snowballs.

At a time known only to you (and a minute is about right), shout "Stop!" Play should come to a screeching halt. Have each team collect all the snowballs on their side and compare the two piles. The team with the fewest snowballs wins. Repeat as desired!

A variation suggested by longtime Sibshop facilitator Tammy Besser: Before playing, have participants write a fact about themselves on their piece of paper. After the snowball fight, players open the piece of paper and the group tries to guess who the fact is about.

Stand-Off

Be careful how you throw your weight around in this game. It is easy to lose your balance!

Energy Level: Medium

Environment: Open area

Materials: None

Each player stands with feet together, one arm's length away from their partner. To begin, players make palm-to-palm contact and attempt to unbalance their partners by moving their hands and shifting their weight. Award points for when a partner moves a foot, loses balance, or makes contact with any part of the body other than palms. No points are given if both partners lose their balance.

Stand Up!

Included here are variations on this Sibshop classic. Can you and your participants think of others?

Energy Level: Medium

Environment: Outdoors or soft surface

Materials: None

To begin, have pairs of equal height sit back to back, bend their knees, put their feet flat on the ground, and then reach back and lock elbows. On the count of 3, everyone yells, "Stand Up!" and players push back, digging their heels into the ground. If done right, the pair will pop up into a standing position. Can this be done with three or even four people? How about three people facing one another, feet to feet, and holding hands?

Stretch It Out

Stretching is great during any Sibshop, but it's especially useful during online meetings.

Energy Level: Low to medium

Environment: Anywhere!

Materials: None

In Sibshops, we never sit around for very long, even if we have been connecting online. Stretching keeps things moving and can be a great way to warm up before moving on to more physical activities. Start by choosing your favorite stretch and invite everyone to stretch with you for 10 seconds. Then, invite each participant to pick their favorite stretch, and count to 10 (or 5 and 5 if you switch sides) as the group holds it. Don't be surprised if some energetic sibs choose more rigorous exercises! Be prepared to do jumping jacks, karate moves, and even burpees and sit-ups!

Suitcase Race

This is the perfect online activity for when you want to "get out of Dodge!"

Energy Level: Medium

Environment: Online platform (e.g., Zoom)

Materials: Three "essential" items from your home nearby. A timer—consider using an online timer—adds to the sense of urgency.

Destination: imagination! This activity will take us around the corner or around the world, depending on where our minds lead! Invite participants to think about—but not share just yet—a special place that they would like to visit. Their special place could be anywhere in the world, as near or far as they wish. It might be a place they have always wanted to go or a place they have already visited and loved.

To begin, ask the participants, "Who would love to just hop on a plane or a train or car and go somewhere?" Explain that "with Suitcase Race, everyone will use their imagination to go someplace. It could be any place you wish—your grandparents' house, the beach, the South Pole, Disneyland, Italy, whatever you wish!"

Further explain: "I want you to think about what you would pack. What would you put in your suitcase? Specifically, I want you to think about three must-have things you want to put in your suitcase. If you could only bring three things, what would those things be?"

"And now, I want you to find those three things! Don't worry about a suitcase! You'll have 3 minutes to find those three things." Consider posting a slide such as the following:

Let participants know you are starting a timer, and remind them once again that they have 3 minutes (although they may need less). Once everyone is back with their must-haves, share where you want to go, what you have chosen, and why. Have each participant share their destination and items, and explain why they made their choices.

Suitcase Race!
A **special** place
3 items
3 minutes!!

Tough Choices!

This lively game is a favorite at the Sibshops run by Fairfax County (Virginia) Public Schools' school social workers.

Energy Level: Medium

Environment: Online platform such as Zoom

Materials: None

In Tough Choices, participants are asked to pick a preference by performing an assigned movement. It can easily be played online. Depending on your group, you can ask about items individually or as a choice.

To play, assemble participants in a circle and announce, "At Sibshops, we always want to learn more about the kids who attend. During Tough Choices, we're going to find out what *you* like, what floats *your* boat, what bakes *your* cake, what rocks *your* socks, and what sizzles *your* bacon!"

For individual items you might say, "If you like cats, do five jumping jacks!"

Or, if giving a choice, you might say, "If you like cats better, do five jumping jacks! If you like dogs better, raise the roof!"

Movement suggestions:

- Jazz hands
- Jumping jacks
- Dab
- Raise the roof
- Wave your hands in the air
- Peace signs
- Nod your head
- Shrug your shoulders
- Reach for the sky
- Spin in a circle
- Jump up and down
- Jog in place

Prompts:

- Cats vs. dogs

- Pizza vs. tacos

- In-person school vs. virtual school

- [Currently popular video game] vs. [another currently popular video game]

- Soccer vs. basketball

- [One popular sports team] vs. [rival sports team]

- Winter break vs. summer break

- Xbox vs. PlayStation

- Math vs. science

- Arts vs. STEM

- Koala bears vs. pandas

- Beach vs. mountains

- Being invisible vs. being able to fly

- Giving up your cell phone vs. giving up TV

- Living in space vs. living under water

- Cake vs. ice cream

- Waffles vs. pancakes

- Be in the Olympics vs. be in the Super Bowl

- Live in a cartoon vs. live in the ocean

- Grow a tail vs. grow a horn

- Be the president vs. be the NBA MVP

- Travel back in time vs. travel to the future

- Have a pet giraffe vs. have a pet elephant

- Waterpark vs. amusement park

- Be a superhero vs. be a movie star

- Snowboarding vs. surfing

- Zoo vs. aquarium

- Be 5 years older vs. be 5 years younger

Triangle Tag

A geometric twist on tag. Also, an excellent demonstration of how exhausting running around in circles can be!

Energy Level: High

Environment: Field or gym

Materials: Bandanas or wristbands (one per group of four)

To play, divide Sibshoppers into groups of four. Three of the players hold hands to make a triangle. One wears a wristband or a bandana around their wrist and is the "target." A fourth player is the "tagger" and attempts to tag the target while the triangle maneuvers around to protect the target. There is really only one other rule: The "tagger" cannot reach over the arms of triangle members to reach the target. Once tagged, each group selects a new tagger and a new target. If, after dividing into groups of four, you discover that you have a kid or two left over, no worries! Just add them to an existing triangle.

Tug-of-War

This game is simple as can be and great fun for Sibshop participants of all sizes.

Energy Level: Medium

Environment: Field or gym

Materials: Stout rope

To begin, have players line up along a wall and arrange themselves according to height. Starting with the tallest player, have players count off "red," "blue," "red," "blue," and so on. This will ensure two teams—a Red Team and Blue Team—of approximately equal heights and (presumably!) strength.

Beyond this, Tug-of-War needs little explanation: grab a rope and pull! However, do try some variations, including having players wait 10 feet away and, on signal, run to the rope and commence pulling; or stretching the rope over a sprinkler or small filled plastic swimming pool.

Undercover Leader

Wherein leaders exert a very subtle leadership style! This can be used at online Sibshops.

Energy Level: Low

Environment: Open space

Materials: None

To begin, have players sit in a circle on the floor. Choose one person to be "It" and have this person leave the room. Choose another player in the circle to be the Undercover Leader, who will start various body movements—such as head nodding, foot tapping, elbow scratching, or chicken wings—during the game. The rest of the group will follow their lead. Throughout the game, it is important that players not look directly at the Leader for movement changes, or they might blow the Leader's cover!

Once a movement has started, the person who is It is invited back into the room. It watches closely to determine who the Leader is. The Leader, meanwhile, continues to change the movements. When It discovers the Leader's identity, two other players are chosen to become It and the new Undercover Leader, and the play resumes.

Unknot the Knot!

Knots is a Sibshop classic. This is a different—but equally fun—knot activity!

Energy Level: Medium

Environment: Open space

Materials: A long climbing or other rope

Optimal number of participants: 5 to 15, depending on the length of the rope

To begin, tie simple loose overhand knots in the rope—one knot for each player. Space the knots approximately 2 feet apart. Have players select a knot on the rope and stand by the knot on either side of the rope. Instruct players to grab the rope with their nondominant hand on either side of "their" knot. To play, participants must untie all the knots without letting go of the rope, using their free hands to untie the knots.

Virtual Talent Show

Invite your Sibshoppers to show off a special talent—virtually!

Energy Level: Medium

Environment: Online—or possibly in person!

Materials: None

At the end of an online Sibshop, say something like this:

"Most of us are not so good at some things, but most of us are also pretty darn good at something else! We all have talents—some hidden and some not so hidden. Some of us can draw, some can sing, some can twist their bodies in ways that the rest of us can only imagine!

"At our next Sibshop, we will showcase our talents. These could be a painting or sculpture you made, one of your favorite dance moves, a card or magic trick, a joke, a song, a story you wrote, jumping on a pogo stick, Hula Hoops, a cooking project—whatever you like!"

It helps to email parents to remind them of the talent show. Of course, some Sibshoppers will be reluctant and that's okay. Every entertainer needs an audience!

Whispers!

Not all Sibshop games are boisterous—just most of them! Whispers is a great, slightly quieter game for young Sibshoppers.

Energy Level: Medium

Environment: Indoors

Materials: Slips of papers with instructions such as "Tell the next person your name and age," "Tell the next person what your favorite color is and why."

To play, divide the group into two teams and have each team stand in a line. The person at the front of the line reads aloud the instruction on the slip of paper and whispers her answer to the second person in line and so on down the line. The last person in line yells out the final message and runs to the front of the line collecting a new question and starting the process again.

Word Chain

This is good for both online and in-person Sibshops. Two versions of Word Chain follow.

Energy Level: Low

Environment: Indoors

Materials: None

Best for younger Sibshoppers: Choose a topic, such as food, school, vacation, and so forth. Tell players that the first player will say a word ("A..."), the second player says the first word plus their own ("A giant..."), the third person says the first two words plus their own ("A giant hamburger..."), and so forth. The first time you play, start by being Player 1, perhaps offering "A" or "The" as your word. Continue until someone can no longer remember the word chain.

Best for older Sibshoppers: "First Letter, Last Letter" Word Chains can be a fun challenge for kids who can spell. To play, pick a topic such as food. The first player picks a food word such as *taco.* The next player must pick a food word that starts with *o*—the last letter in *taco.* They may pick *orange.* The following player might pick *eggs, espresso, enchiladas,* and so on. If a player can't come up with an appropriate answer, then they are "out." The game continues until only one player remains.

SAMPLE SIBSHOP FOOD ACTIVITIES

Food activities are among the most rewarding Sibshop activities. When we make and eat food together, we are nourished, we express our creativity, and we derive enjoyment from eating the kid-friendly meal we have prepared together. As we cook and eat, we also laugh, tell bad jokes, learn about our likes and dislikes, and talk about our schools, friends, and families. Never underestimate the sharing and informal support that occurs during the breaking of bread. If you have never organized a group cooking activity, these are a few thoughts to keep in mind:

1. **Be prepared.** Locate and set up your materials before your participants arrive. If you are not familiar with the kitchen, plan to visit it well before your Sibshop to take an inventory of the tools you need (and prepare a list of tools you will need to bring) and to be sure that necessary equipment (e.g., oven) works. Even a simple cooking activity such as Super Nachos (a good first-time activity) can be difficult if you forget an important ingredient or tool.

2. **Keep it simple—especially the first few times.** If you cannot remember back that far, kids can be picky eaters. We know that more than 50% of Sibshop participants think that tomatoes (much less green peppers, pineapple, black olives, and so forth) are just "too weird" to go on nachos. Ditto for mushrooms in pasta sauce. That does not mean that you cannot have some on hand for adults and kids who like them, but do not assume that everyone will want them.

3. **Identify as many jobs as possible.** We have found that participants would rather be doing something than watching. They frequently display enthusiasm for even the less-glamorous chores like pot scrubbing, which has amazed us and shocked their parents. As you plan your food activity, consider the number of hands you will want to keep busy. If space permits, consider dividing the kitchen into stations, each responsible for a specific chore. When shopping, purchase food that can be readied by your young participants. For instance, buy blocks of cheese for grating rather than pre-grated cheese or canned cheese sauce.

4. **Think about how much time you will need for the project.** Select or adapt projects to accommodate the time you have available.

To get you started, we have listed some food activities that we and others have enjoyed. Share the foods you love with your young participants, whether it is egg rolls, stir fries, giant chocolate chip cookies, tacos, Belgian waffles, or fruit kabobs!

Super Nachos

The jobs here are grating cheese; chopping tomatoes, green peppers, olives, and maybe onions; spreading the mixture on tortilla chips; and assembling the dish before running it under the broiler. Good with sour cream, beans, and, of course, salsa. This is a good project for when time is limited.

Pizza

For this perennial favorite, try using small pizza rounds and let the young chefs customize their pizzas with a variety of toppings.

Popcorn Candy Mix

Courtesy of Traci Hopper, a Sibshop facilitator at Sharing Hands a Respite Experience (SHARE) in Midland, Texas, Popcorn Candy Mix is not only a sure-to-please cooking project, but it can even be a trickle-in activity! Make the mix early in the Sibshop and let it rest in the fridge until it's time to eat. It will surely give your Sibshoppers something to look forward to! This recipe is enough for four to five people, depending on how many goodies you add. This can also be an online Sibshop food activity if you send the recipe and/or ingredients home to participants before the meeting.

Ingredients:

- 1 bag of unflavored and unpopped microwave popcorn
- 1 cup of white chocolate chips
- 2 handfuls of M&M's
- 2 handfuls of pretzels, either minis or sticks
- 1 handful of mixed nuts or peanuts (optional)

Materials:

- Microwave
- Food prep gloves
- Large heat-proof bowl
- Medium heat-proof bowl
- Large metal spoon
- Sheet pan lined with parchment paper

To prepare, microwave the popcorn as directed on the package; once popped, place it in a large bowl. Using gloved hands, pick through popcorn to remove unpopped kernels.

In the medium bowl, melt the white chocolate chips for 1 minute. Stir until melted and microwave 10 seconds longer if not fully melted.

Pour melted chocolate over the popcorn and add remaining ingredients. Stir gently until everything is coated with the chocolate.

Using a spoon, gently spread mixture onto the parchment paper–lined sheet pan.

Refrigerate for 5–10 minutes for the chocolate to set. If not eating it soon thereafter, transfer it to large plastic zipper bags.

Pro tip: Practice Popcorn Candy Mix at home before making it at your Sibshop. Your family will love you!

Sibshop Subshop

A 6-foot-long submarine sandwich roll sold at some bakeries can add an extra dollop of fun to this activity. You can, of course, pile almost anything on a sub, but we think the sprinkling of Italian dressing is what puts it "over the top." Subs can be a good choice when kitchen space and equipment are minimal.

Homemade Pasta

If you have a pasta machine, know how to use it, and have some ready-made sauce, a group of siblings can turn flour and eggs into homemade linguine or fettuccine in less than an hour. It cooks in seconds. Don't forget the candles, the Italian bread, and maybe some Frank Sinatra music!

Homemade Ice Cream

A time-honored method of channeling youthful excess energy is to crank an ice cream freezer. If you can find an old-fashioned, hand-powered ice cream freezer, by all means, use it! Making ice cream is as educational as it is rewarding. We are always surprised at the number of children who have never had homemade ice cream or made it themselves before. Sometimes, we will churn the ice cream early in the program, pack it in ice to harden, and enjoy it at the end of the Sibshop when participants serve it to their parents, their siblings, and themselves!

No-Bake Energy Bites

The internet abounds with recipes for no-bake energy bites and bars, including peanut-free versions. Start these at the beginning of your Sibshop so you can enjoy them at the end of your gathering. Here is one simple recipe to get you started.

Instructions:
Combine the following in a bowl:

- 1 cup crunchy peanut or almond butter
- 2 teaspoons vanilla extract
- 2/3 cup honey

Add the following to the mixture:

- 2 cups rolled oats
- 1 cup mini semisweet chocolate chips or mini-M&M's
- 1 cup sunflower seeds, ground flax seeds, or chopped nuts

If time permits, chill mixture before rolling into balls by using a small spring scoop or Sibshoppers' gloved hands. Place on a baking sheet and freeze until set up, about 1 hour.

DIY Snack Mix

All you will need for this activity are sealable sandwich bags, gloved hands, and any of the ingredients found in the following list. Our favorite snack mixes include both sweet and salty items.

- Oat cereal (e.g., Cheerios)
- Corn/rice squares cereal (e.g., Chex)
- Chocolate- or yogurt-covered raisins
- Dried apples
- Goldfish crackers (e.g., Pepperidge Farm)
- Granola
- M&M's
- Mini chocolate chips
- Mini marshmallows
- Mini pretzels or pretzel sticks
- Nuts
- Popcorn
- Raisins
- Sliced dried apricots
- Sunflower seeds
- Graham cookies (e.g., Teddy Grahams)

CONCLUSION

Please remember that recreational and food activities are indispensable to create an appealing, memorable, and even magical Sibshop. As noted at the beginning of this chapter, recreational and food activities provide participants with informal opportunities for support and help keep the program's focus on the participants' many strengths. Select, plan, and present these activities with the same care and attention that you would give to other activities. The energy, joy, and imagination that you and your colleagues bring to these activities will be reflected in the faces of the children you are there to serve. Have fun—and they will too!

10

Information Activities, Guest Speakers, and Special Events

As noted in Chapter 4, numerous authors, researchers, and siblings have observed that brothers and sisters have a lifelong and ever-changing need for information on the specifics and implications of their sibling's disability or illness. As with many sibling issues, this need for information is similar to parents' need for information. Compared with parents, however, siblings usually have far fewer opportunities to acquire this information.

Because of their changing needs as they mature, brothers and sisters will need to have their sibling's condition and the implications of the condition reinterpreted as they grow. This need is best addressed when parents and service providers are aware of the concerns of the siblings and regularly share information with them throughout their lives. (If you have not done so already, read Chapter 3 for implications for parents and service providers.) Activities for parents and service providers, such as workshops and sibling panels (see Chapter 11), can be an important step in creating readily available sources of information for siblings as they grow.

WRITTEN SOURCES OF INFORMATION

When available, written information can help brothers and sisters as well. A few agencies (e.g., Epilepsy Foundation of America) have prepared materials for children, including some specifically for siblings. Books such as *Living With a Brother or Sister With Special Needs* (Meyer & Vadasy, 1996) or those listed on the Sibling Support website (www.sibling-support.org) can provide siblings with information on disabilities, therapies, future concerns, and even emotions they may experience. If children cannot read these books on their own, parents can read them to their children—a practice that can be a wonderful method for keeping the lines of communication open.

SIBSHOPS AS INFORMATION SOURCES

In addition to providing recreation and discussion, Sibshops can also be places to learn, as stated in the fourth Sibshop goal:

 Goal 4: Sibshops will provide siblings with an opportunity to learn more about the implications of the support needs of their siblings.

There are, however, limits to the type and amount of information that can be conveyed at a Sibshop. Sibshops for siblings of children with a specific condition (e.g., autism, hearing impairment, cancer) can be a valuable opportunity to convey information about the nature of a sibling's support needs. These Sibshops are generally held as a part of a state, national, or regional conference. However, it can be challenging, if not impossible, to attract sufficient numbers of siblings of people with a specific condition to make a viable local program, except perhaps in large urban communities. Consequently, most community-based Sibshops support siblings of children with various disabilities or illnesses, which can make an in-depth or ongoing discussion about any one disability or illness impractical. Sibshops that include siblings of children who have different developmental and health concerns can be a fine place for participants to learn about unfamiliar disabilities and gain information about, and appreciation for, topics of common interest, such as those described in the following sections.

Services for People With Support Needs

Many participants have siblings who receive services from a wide range of professionals, including adapted physical education teachers; audiologists; interpreters; mobility teachers; nurses; feeding specialists; occupational, speech, and physical therapists; physicians; psychologists; recreational therapists; respite care providers; social workers; and special education teachers. Often, however, brothers and sisters have only a vague idea of what these service providers do with their siblings on a daily basis. Consider inviting a therapist or teacher to your next Sibshop, whether it is in person or online, as a guest speaker. Ask the guest to briefly describe what they do with kids with support needs and, if possible, demonstrate using the "tools of the trade," such as adaptive spoons, augmentative communication devices, or therapy balls. Be sure to leave ample time for questions and listen carefully to the questions, because they will help you determine the participants' knowledge of disabilities, illnesses, and services, and this can help you plan future informational activities.

Information About Disabilities

Often, siblings are interested in learning more about many disabilities, even disabilities other than those that their brothers and sisters have. If your participants seem to have such an interest, consider inviting guest speakers who can provide an overview of a disability and answer the participants' questions. Many disability-related organizations provide community education, often delivered by people who have the disability themselves.

Learning about different disabilities can be helpful in at least two ways. First, it provides participants with a fresh, broadened perspective as they listen and compare and contrast their siblings' disabilities with the one presented. Second, as guests speak, common themes (e.g., self-advocacy, inclusion) frequently emerge, providing siblings with a growing understanding of issues facing all people with disabilities.

Technology for People With Disabilities

Technology is an integral part of everyday life for many of us, and today's children do not know life without it. However, have your Sibshoppers had the opportunity to learn how technology can help minimize or even eliminate daily communication, mobility, and other functional barriers for people with disabilities? Some will be very familiar with assistive technology that is used by their sibs, and others may be fascinated to learn how computers and other devices can help make the world more accessible for people with disabilities. If you are not aware of a local expert on technology for people with support needs, search the internet for "assistive technology state office" and then state-by-state lists such as the one currently found on the website of the Association of Assistive Technology Act Programs. Most colleges, universities, and school districts have departments that facilitate assistive learning technology for students with disabilities, and staff who are knowledgeable about how to use it.

Artists With Disabilities

As discussed in Sightless Sculpture, many well-known artists and musicians have—or had—disabilities. Some of your Sibshop participants may have siblings who have artistic skills. Consider exploring the intersection of art, music, and disability by inviting an artist or local musician with a disability to be a guest speaker. This could be one of your participants' siblings or an artist with a disability from your state. Most states and provinces have programs for artists with disabilities. These programs, like Sibshops, celebrate strengths and diversity. To learn where they are, simply search the internet for "disability arts [state or province]." Also consider searching for "dance disability," "autism arts," and the organization MFPA (Mouth and Foot Painting Artists).

Service Dogs

There is nothing quite like having a friendly yellow lab show up at a Sibshop! Trained service dogs (and not all of them are yellow labs!) perform a remarkable service to people with visual impairments, autism, and epilepsy as well as to veterans and others. Sibshop participants love learning about what service dogs do and how they are trained. Consider inviting a service dog trainer or owner and a dog to your Sibshop. To find resources in your community, search the internet for "service dogs," "guide dogs," and your state or province.

Future Issues

As the research literature suggests, siblings often have unasked questions about the future. Questions that could be addressed during a Sibshop may include "What will happen to my sibling when we grow up?" and "Will my sibling live with me someday?" Survey your group to determine which issues are of greatest interest.

To lead an informational discussion on the suggested topics, a Sibshop facilitator will need to be aware of the range of housing and vocational opportunities available for adults with disabilities, or you will need to invite others who are familiar with the range of services in the community to participate. You may also wish to invite as a guest speaker an adult sibling (or a panel of adult siblings) who has navigated the future planning process with their family, and/or an adult with a disability who can talk about where they live, work, and play. If you need help finding appropriate resources or speakers on adult services, a good place to start is your local chapter of The Arc or your state's Developmental Disabilities Council. Alternatively, you may wish to sponsor a field trip to supported employment sites and meet adults with disabilities who are working and living in the community.

Parents of Children With Support Needs

Perhaps because of parents' desire to protect their typically developing children, many siblings have never heard parents candidly discuss the impact their child's disability can have on them and their families and the unique concerns and rewards parents experience. Siblings who have an opportunity to hear parents discuss their families' situations can gain insights into the workings of their own parents and families.

When inviting two or three parents to share their families' stories and answer participants' questions, for confidentiality reasons, make sure that the parents you invite have more than one child and are not parents of Sibshop participants. It will also help if these presenters have previously spoken to groups about their children and families.

Topics the parents could briefly address are the family's reaction to the child's diagnosis, the special joys and concerns they have regarding their child and family, and the effect that the child with support needs has had on their family, especially siblings. We have found that children often find it easier to talk to other children's parents, so leave plenty of time for questions.

Older Siblings

Listening to the experiences of adult siblings can be instructive and validating for Sibshop participants. Hearing adults talk about growing up as a sibling of a person with support needs will encourage your participants to talk about their lives and it will stimulate conversation among the entire group. Consider inviting Sibshop graduates to share what Sibshops meant to them when they were younger.

On the day of the panel, prepare your Sibshop participants by announcing the panel at the beginning of the program and encourage the participants to think of questions for the panel. To help prepare the panel, you may wish to send panelists guidelines and questions prior to the Sibshop. A sample letter is shown in Figure 10.1.

Special Guests

When a project seemed to be finished, Walt Disney always encouraged his staff to look at it one more time and "plus it." In other words, how can we make this good experience even better? You will want to "plus" your Sibshop frequently to be sure that it stays fresh and exciting for participants.

Special guests can help keep a Sibshop lively and especially rewarding to attend. As with many Sibshop activities, you are limited only by your imagination when choosing a special guest. Examples of special guests you can invite to help ensure that your Sibshops are truly memorable include chefs who can show participants how to make a special dish or dessert, clog or tap dancers who are willing to perform and teach a step or two, jugglers who share the basics of their craft, folk singers who can create songs based on participants' suggestions, a representative from a school for the Deaf and Blind who can lead a Deaf-Blind simulation, actors adept at improvisational theater, teachers of the Deaf who can share American Sign Language signs in an engaging way, gymnasts, martial arts instructors, a yoga teacher who can teach calming techniques and breathing and meditation, or even a local football hero who would enjoy playing touch football with admiring participants.

As you plan your Sibshop, please do not forget informational activities and guest speakers. After all, we promote Sibshops as opportunities to provide siblings with peer support and information with a recreational context. Experience has taught us that arranging informational activities is not difficult and that the rewards are great. Your young participants will be eager to learn!

Dear Panelist,

Thanks for agreeing to be on our adult sibling panel at our upcoming Sibshop. You and the other panelists will have a chance to meet with our 8- to 13-year-old Sibshop participants and informally discuss your experiences growing up with a brother or sister who has support needs. We will ask you to share information about

- **Yourself.** We'll want to know what you do, whether you have a family of your own, where you grew up and went to school, and anything else you wish to share.

- **Your brother or sister with support needs.** We'll want to know what kind of disability your sibling has, how old your sibling is, where they went to school, what your sibling currently does during the day, where they live, and so on.

- **Your family.** We'll be interested in how many children there are in the family you grew up in. If you are older than your sibling, we'll want to know how old you were when you learned that your sibling had support needs. If you are younger than your sibling, we'll want to know how much younger and whether you remember when you realized that your older brother or sister had support needs.

- **What it was like when you were a kid.** Did the support needs of your brother or sister create challenges for you with your parents, friends, schoolmates, or even strangers? Did you come up with solutions to these problems? Growing up, did you have any questions or secret worries about your sibling's support needs? Were there good things that you or your family experienced as a result of having a brother or sister with support needs? Does your family have funny, treasured stories about life with your brother or sister?

A desired outcome of the panel will be the discussion with the younger siblings. Frequently, on hearing "testimony" of the panelists, younger siblings will describe similar experiences that they have had.

Thanks again for being a part of our program!

Sincerely,

Tiana Anderson

Figure 10.1. Sample letter to panel participants.

11

Workshops on Sibling Issues for Parents and Service Providers

One of the most gratifying aspects of providing training on the Sibshops model has been parents' and professionals' keen interest in sibling issues. Parents, who witness the sibling experience daily, tell us that they appreciate an opportunity to discuss and learn about sibling relationships in other families. Teachers, administrators, social workers, physicians, and therapists, who realize that a child's disability has an impact on *all* family members, tell us that they welcome opportunities to expand their understanding of sibling issues. In this chapter, we describe how to present three different types of workshops on sibling issues: a panel of siblings, a workshop for parents and service providers, and an informal meeting for parents of Sibshop participants. All can be easily adapted for an online event, and all are designed to address the fifth Sibshop goal:

 Goal 5: Sibshops provide parents and other professionals with opportunities to learn more about the concerns and opportunities frequently experienced by brothers and sisters of people with support needs.

Because some parents and professionals would rather watch a video, listen to a podcast, or read a book, newsletter, or website than attend workshops, we list alternative resources at the end of the chapter.

SIBLING PANELS

Panels of adult brothers and sisters of people with support needs can be a powerful and valuable method of educating parents and professionals about issues facing siblings. Panelists frequently remark that they, too, leave with an expanded understanding of the sibling experience as a result of listening to the other panelists.

Panel Guidelines

Sibling panels are relatively easy to run, considering the value of the information exchanged. The following guidelines can help ensure that a sibling panel is organized and well attended:

1. **Begin early.** As soon as you decide to host a sibling panel, recruit five to seven panelists using the selection guidelines discussed in this list. Finding appropriate panelists who are available on the dates you select may take longer than you think. Decide on location, time (allowing at least 90 minutes for live events and 60–90 minutes for online panels), and how you will publicize the event to parents and professionals.

2. **Publicize the event.** As noted in Chapter 10, sibling panels are wonderful learning opportunities. Publicizing the panel will ensure that this opportunity is offered to as many parents and professionals as possible. A good turnout will also ensure a rich dialogue between panel and audience.

3. **Seek balance.** Ideally, your sibling panel will be balanced with respect to the following:

   - *Disability or illness type.* Unless the purpose of the panel is to discuss the concerns of siblings with a specific disability or illness, attempt to have several disabilities and/or illnesses represented.

   - *Age relative to the sibling with the disability.* Attempt to balance the panel by inviting brothers and sisters who are older, younger, and very close in age to their siblings with support needs. As you can easily imagine, the experiences of a brother who is 10 years older than a sibling with cerebral palsy will be very different from the experiences of a brother who is 1 year younger than a sibling with cerebral palsy.

   - *Gender.* Brothers and sisters often have different experiences, especially with regard to caregiving expectations and their involvement with the sibling as an adult. Seek to have equal representation of males and females on the panel.

   - *Racial, ethnic, and cultural diversity.* It is important to share a variety of sibling stories and to understand how race, ethnicity, and cultural considerations can impact siblings' experiences.

4. **Invite primarily adult siblings.** Sibling panels benefit from the reflection provided by young adult and older adult brothers and sisters. Although school-age siblings are often more readily available than adult siblings and can comment on issues they currently face, they lack the perspective of older siblings and occasionally suffer from stage fright. If you do include young siblings, invite no more than two panelists between the ages of 8 and 18.

5. **Don't invite panelists' parents.** If possible, ask the panelists' parents not to attend the session. This will help ensure that panelists feel free to talk about their lives and their families.

Two weeks prior to the sibling panel, send each panelist a Sibling Panel Workshop Sheet (see Figure 11.1) outlining questions they may be asked during the program. This "advanced organizer" will reduce the panelists' anxiety and help them prepare their thoughts on the topic prior to the panel. In case they forget to bring these sheets along, have additional copies available to give to the panelists before the program begins.

Sibling Panel Workshop Sheet

Greetings!

Thank you for agreeing to be a member of our sibling panel. During the panel, you will have a chance to discuss what life is like for a brother or sister of a person with support needs—the good parts, the not-so-good parts, and everything in between.

Parents, professionals, and others who have attended sibling panel discussions usually say that they left knowing a lot more about sibling issues than they did before. Panelists have usually learned a lot too.

During the panel discussion, you may be asked to share information on the following:

- Yourself (e.g., where you live, your work or school status, your interests)
- Your sibling with support needs (e.g., age, work or school status, interests)
- Your family (e.g., total number of children, birth order)
- How you learned about your sibling's illness or disability and how it was explained to you
- Whether your sibling's disability or illness ever caused special problems for you (with friends, at school, at home)
- Whether your sibling's disability or illness ever resulted in unusual opportunities
- What comes to mind when you think about your and your sibling's future
- Stories or anecdotes about your sibling, your family, or yourself that you would like to share

We'll leave plenty of time for members of the audience to ask questions. This is often the most informative part of the workshop. At the very end, I may ask the following:

- In retrospect, what do you think your parents did especially well in helping your family accept and adjust to your sibling's support needs?
- What things do you wish they had done differently?
- What advice would you give to a young sibling of a child with support needs? To parents?
- What message would you give to service providers who work with families of people with support needs?

Thanks for your thoughts on this important topic!

Figure 11.1. Sibling panel workshop sheet.

Hosting the Panel

To prepare, arrange chairs behind a rectangular table. If the audience is large, arrange for tabletop microphones. Make sure that water and extra copies of the Sibling Panel Workshop Sheet are available. Have a box of tissues nearby but out of sight. If the panel is online, ensure that only panelists' first names appear on screen and ask audience members to mute their microphones until the question-and-answer time. If audience members have questions during an online panel, encourage them to type them into the meeting chat box and have someone on your team read them at the designated time. Typically, sibling panels are not recorded because panelists may be hesitant to share openly if they are worried about the video later circulating online among an unknown audience.

After all participants have arrived, welcome the panelists and the audience. If time permits and the audience is small, ask audience members to introduce themselves briefly and say what brought them to a sibling panel. Following introductions, let the audience know that they will have an opportunity to ask panel members questions, seek advice from them, and share family experiences.

Then, ask the panelists to introduce themselves and share with the audience information suggested in the first item of the workshop sheet. You may then ask them to respond to subsequent items on the workshop sheet. After asking the panel a few introductory questions, be sure to offer the audience a chance to ask additional questions or make comments. Questions and discussion among parents and panel members will be the most valuable portion of the workshop, so be sure to allow ample time for this. As parents' concerns surface, you may wish to encourage panel members and other parents to share how their families handled a similar situation.

Conclude the program by selecting closing questions from the workshop sheet. *What do you think your parents did especially well? What do you wish they had done differently? What advice would you give to a young sibling of a child with support needs? To parents? What message would you give to service providers who work with families of people with support needs?*

At the very end, be sure to thank the panel members. The questions posed for the panel members will yield valuable insights. Questions also will require panelists to examine and comment on a lifetime of experiences with their siblings, families, and friends that were sometimes happy, sometimes sad, and frequently challenging—no easy task.

A WORKSHOP ON SIBLING ISSUES

During this 1.5- to 2-hour workshop, parent and service provider participants work together to define and discuss sibling concerns, opportunities, and strategies. Discussions are based on participants' observations and experiences. Rather than using an imported "expert" on sibling issues, this workshop utilizes the group's collective expertise.

At the beginning of the workshop, ask the participants to briefly introduce themselves and (if appropriate) their families and share with the group what brings them to a workshop on sibling issues. Following introductions, acknowledge that, for siblings, as for their parents, having a family member with a disability is usually an ambivalent experience. Like parents, siblings may have unique concerns (e.g., need for information about the disability, guilt, resentment) but they may also have unique opportunities (e.g., increased empathy, a special pride, a singular sense of humor).

Suggest to the participants that they, as parents and providers who work with families, are as capable as anyone of defining the concerns and opportunities that their typically developing children experience. In short, let them know of the considerable collective expertise and wisdom of the group. Tell them that, by sharing and discussing their insights with the rest of the group, everyone can leave with an expanded understanding of the sibling experience.

Prior to the meeting, prepare a four-sided worksheet (two pages, printed front to back, stapled) such as the one shown in Figure 11.2. Distribute the pages to the participants and provide pens or pencils. If your workshop is online, either email the worksheet beforehand or make it available (e.g., in the chat) during the meeting. Ask each participant to pair off with another participant (and introduce themselves if they have not met) and take 10 minutes to discuss page 1. If your meeting is online, send each pair into a breakout room to chat. At the end of this time, ask a representative from each pair to share with the larger group the concerns they have observed or identified. Record the general headings on a chalkboard, whiteboard, or, preferably, large sheets of paper. If you are meeting online, you can share your screen and type directly into a document viewed by all.

Next, ask each participant to pair off with a different partner and discuss page 2, strategies to decrease concerns. After 10 minutes, have the participants report back to

Sibshop Issues Worksheet

PAGE 1
(one full page):

SIBLINGS OF
CHILDREN
WITH SUPPORT
NEEDS
UNIQUE
CONCERNS

The goal of this workshop is to define and discuss the unique opportunities and concerns experienced by siblings.

By sharing your observations and experiences, you can help all workshop participants gain a broader understanding of the joys, concerns, and challenges that are a part of being a sibling of a child with support needs.

With your partner, please take a few minutes to discuss any concerns that you feel siblings of children with support needs may experience. Please briefly note the concerns you discuss below:

PAGE 2
(one full page):

STRATEGIES:
CONCERNS

Next, please discuss with your partner ways that parents and other professionals can minimize the concerns of siblings of children with support needs. Please briefly list your strategies below:

PAGE 3
(one full page):

UNIQUE
OPPORTUNITIES

Please discuss benefits or unique opportunities that siblings may experience as a result of growing up with a sibling who has support needs.

Please briefly note these benefits or opportunities below:

PAGE 4
(one full page):

STRATEGIES:
OPPORTUNITIES

Finally, please discuss how we, as parents and service providers, can maximize opportunities experienced by siblings of children with support needs.

Please note these strategies below:

Figure 11.2. Sibling issues worksheet (prepared as a four-sided worksheet, two sheets of paper printed front to back and stapled).

the group. Continue with pages 3 and 4. By the end of the session, the participants will have generated a wide range of issues and have had an opportunity to discuss these issues individually with four different participants as well as with the larger group.

Let the participants know that you (or a participant volunteer) will transcribe the concerns, opportunities, and strategies from the sheets or chalkboard/whiteboard and send each participant a copy.

INFORMAL DISCUSSIONS FOR PARENTS OF SIBSHOP PARTICIPANTS

If you hold your Sibshops as a series of meetings, we suggest that you plan one meeting with a concurrent gathering for parents of participants. This meeting for parents, ideally held midway through the series, does not need to be as long the Sibshop itself—usually 1–2 hours will suffice (30–60 minutes for online meetings). During the meeting, you may wish to utilize the workshop formats described previously, or simply have an open-ended discussion with the participants' parents. To begin, ask parents to introduce themselves, describe their families, and share their reasons for enrolling their children in a Sibshop. This will usually be enough to initiate a lively discussion. Your job is to facilitate conversation and to listen.

This discussion is also an excellent opportunity to seek parents' feedback on your Sibshop. Ask parents what comments their children have made about the program and what suggestions they have to make it better. It is also a good time to discuss the direction of the program, and to seek parents' counsel on how to make Sibshops as responsive and available to families as possible.

This is not, however, a time to share with parents the details of their children's conversations during your Sibshops. Despite some parents' desire to know what their children are saying, the information and opinions shared during Sibshops should be treated as confidential. It can be helpful to share general themes that come up during Sibshops to open doors to conversations at home, but the "golden rule" of Sibshops is that what is said at Sibshops stays at Sibshops. There is, however, an important exception: If a participant shares information that, in your best judgment, parents need to know, it is your responsibility to meet privately with the participant, share your concerns, and discuss strategies for telling their parents. Sometimes, participants will elect to tell their parents themselves, other times they will appreciate your offer to talk to the parents, and still other times they will want your company as you both discuss your concern with the parents.

OTHER RESOURCES FOR PARENTS AND SERVICE PROVIDERS

Not all parents will be able to (or wish to) attend workshops. Many parents prefer to learn about sibling issues through written materials or other media. To learn about sibling-related books, videos, movies, and television shows, visit the Sibling Support Project's website: www.siblingsupport.org.

A

The Sibshop Standards of Practice

Sibshops began in 1982 at the University of Washington. Created by Don Meyer, Founder of the Sibling Support Project, Sibshops now support thousands of young siblings of children with developmental and health concerns in hundreds of locations around the world, with new Sibshops launching every year.

We are truly pleased that there is such interest in Sibshops, and we are committed to ensuring that when parents send their children to a Sibshop, they are sending them to a program that is true to the spirit, strategies, and goals of the model.

To this end, we have worked with longtime Sibshop facilitators to create the following Standards of Practice for programs that wish to be registered Sibshops and use the trademarked Sibshop name, a variation of the name (e.g., "Sib Shop"), and/or the Sibshop logo. We are grateful to the members of the Sibshop Standards of Practice Committee for helping us with this important project.

Please share these Standards of Practice with every facilitator and volunteer for your Sibshop program. Please review the Standards with the other Sibshop facilitators, administrators, and volunteers, and be sure to register your Sibshop online as detailed at the end of this document. If you have questions along the way, please do not hesitate to contact us.

Thank you for taking the time to read these best practices and for understanding the need to uphold the highest standards in our efforts to provide brothers and sisters with information and peer support.

A final note: As a Sibshop facilitator or administrator, you likely offer Sibshops in addition to many other responsibilities. Still, you and your colleagues find time in your busy schedules and lives because you care deeply about siblings and their concerns. Local providers like you, who are making a difference in the lives of sibs daily, are our heroes. We can't thank you enough for supporting the siblings in your community. Please let us know how we may support your important work.

All the best,
Don Meyer, Founder
Emily Holl, Director
Sibling Support Project
www.siblingsupport.org
info@siblingsupport.org

SIBSHOP STANDARDS OF PRACTICE

1. What Sibshops Are—and Are Not

In Chapter 1, page 1, Sibshops are described this way:

> For the adults who plan them and the agencies that sponsor them, Sibshops are best described as opportunities for siblings of children with health, mental health, and developmental needs to obtain peer support and education within a recreational context. They can reflect an agency's commitment to the well-being of the family member most likely to have the longest-lasting relationship with the person who has support needs.
>
> However, for the young people who attend them and the energetic people who run them, Sibshops are better described as *events*. Sibshops are designed to provide siblings with opportunities for peer support. Because Sibshops are designed for school-age children, peer support is provided within a recreational context that emphasizes kids' perspectives.
>
> Sibshops are lively, pedal-to-the-metal celebrations of the many contributions made by siblings of kids with support needs. Sibshops acknowledge that being the sibling of a person with support needs is a good thing for some, a not-so-good thing for others, and, for many, something in between. Sibshops reflect a belief that siblings have much to offer one another—if they are given a chance. The Sibshop model intersperses information and discussion activities with games (designed to be unique, upbeat, and appealing to a wide ability range), cooking and craft activities, and special guests who may teach participants how to mime, how to juggle, or, in the case of one guest artist who has cerebral palsy, how to paint by holding a toothbrush in your mouth. Sibshops are as fun and rewarding for the people who host them as they are for the participants.
>
> Sibshops are not therapy, group or otherwise, although their effect may be therapeutic for some children. Sibshops acknowledge that most siblings of people with support needs, like their parents, are doing well, despite the challenges posed by a family member's illness or disability. Consequently, although Sibshop facilitators always keep an eye open for participants who may need additional services, the Sibshop model takes a wellness approach that encourages children to recognize and build on their skills, talents, and strengths.

Sibshops should never be confused with child care. Sometimes, agencies wish to offer Sibshops concurrently with parent support meetings. While this "two-ring" approach is acceptable, agencies will need to add a "third ring": child care for the children who have support needs as well as for the typically developing siblings who either are not in the target age range or do not wish to be a part of the Sibshop.

Sibshops, therefore,

- Should be decidedly fun to attend

- Provide peer support and information within a recreational context

- May be "therapeutic" to attend but are not therapy, group or otherwise

- Utilize an approach that emphasizes wellness

- Should never be considered child care

2. Endorsing the Goals of Sibshops

As described in Chapter 1 of the Sibshop curriculum, the following are Sibshop goals:

 Goal 1: Sibshops provide siblings of children with support needs an opportunity to meet other siblings in a relaxed, recreational setting.

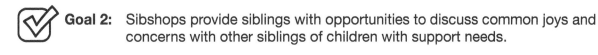

Goal 2: Sibshops provide siblings with opportunities to discuss common joys and concerns with other siblings of children with support needs.

Goal 3: Sibshops provide siblings with an opportunity to learn how others handle situations commonly experienced by siblings of children with support needs.

Goal 4: Sibshops provide siblings with an opportunity to learn more about the implications of their siblings' support needs.

Goal 5: Sibshops provide parents and other professionals with opportunities to learn more about the concerns frequently experienced by siblings of people with support needs.

These goals will drive the activities of your Sibshop. Although most Sibshops do an excellent job with Goals 1–3, Goals 4 and 5 are too often overlooked. Siblings will have a lifelong and ever-changing need for information about their sibs' disabilities and the services they receive. As a peer-support and education model, Sibshops are a marvelous opportunity to provide participants with kid-friendly information about a wide range of topics.

In order for parents to attend to the needs of their typically developing children, they will also need information regarding these lifelong concerns. If we wish to create systemic change that ensures that sibs are on agencies' radars and in their working definition of "family," it will require that we educate our colleagues and advocate for sibs' concerns.

3. Ensuring That Sibshops Are Equitable, Inclusive Spaces

I BELONG. We are committed to ensuring that Sibshops are inclusive, equitable spaces in which every child and facilitator feels a genuine sense of belonging. To this end, we are dedicated to eradicating racial and oppressive barriers so that everyone succeeds. We are devoted to creating a positive, safe, supportive, and comfortable Sibshop environment in which all children and adults can thrive in ways that are helpful and meaningful to them.

4. Referring Children When Sibshops Are Not the Right Approach

Most, but not all, siblings of children with support needs will be well served by Sibshops' lively mix of activities, peer support, and information. For some children, however, Sibshops may not be the right approach. These children may not be comfortable in groups, or they may prefer to receive peer support and information in other ways (e.g., online groups, books, informal opportunities). Other children will have needs that go beyond what a Sibshop can reasonably provide. As mentioned in the previous description of Sibshops, facilitators will need to keep an eye open for participants who may need additional services. Your Sibshop team of facilitators and appropriate administrators should know—in advance of a problematic situation—people and agencies in your community who might be able to help a child (and family) not being well served by your Sibshop effort.

5. Reporting Worrisome Information and Behavior to Parents and Appropriate Agencies

To the extent possible, Sibshops attempt to give participants a safe place where they can openly discuss the "good and not-so-good" aspects of life with a sibling who has support needs. In order to ensure that they can speak freely, facilitators, as a rule, will not specifically divulge what participants discuss during a Sibshop with parents. (Facilitators, however, are encouraged to discuss the general topics that participants discussed during parent meetings.)

On rare occasions, however, children may reveal information that will need to be shared with parents or, in extreme cases, with appropriate agencies. Before such contact is made with either parents or agencies, the concern should be discussed with the entire Sibshop team. Your Sibshop's team should be aware—in advance of a problem—of your state's rules regarding mandated reporting.

6. Making Sibshops Available for Families Who Cannot Afford to Pay

It is reasonable to ask parents to pay a fee for their children to attend a Sibshop. Most Sibshops cost far less than child care would for the same amount of time. Fees can help offset costs associated with running a Sibshop. Perhaps most important, fees help ensure that parents bring their children to the Sibshop that facilitators have worked so hard to make rewarding.

However, a significant effort should be made to ensure that Sibshops are available to families who cannot afford the set fee. On the registration forms of many Sibshops is a statement similar to the following: "A limited number of Sibshop scholarships are available on a first-come, first-served basis. Check here if you'd like your child considered for a Sibshop scholarship." On the same form, other parents who may not have financial concerns can be given an opportunity to contribute to the Sibshops scholarship fund.

7. Family Involvement in Sibshops

Ideally, at least one of your Sibshop's facilitators will be an adult sibling. If this is not possible, seek a parent who can offer advice, provide a family perspective, and help you spread the word about your program. Good word of mouth among families is critical to drawing children to your Sibshop. Family involvement—as well as Goal 5 of the Sibshop curriculum, child–parent connection—will also be achieved by hosting at least one meeting per year for the parents of the children who attend your Sibshop. These meetings may be held concurrently with your Sibshop and can be informal discussions of Sibshop goals and activities, why parents enrolled their children in Sibshops, and general topics discussed by Sibshop participants.

8. Involving Sibs in the Selection of Sibshop Activities

The siblings who attend your Sibshop should be given some say about Sibshop activities. This is especially true for teen Sibshops. Seek their feedback about activities they liked and disliked and ideas that they have for recreation, discussion, and informational activities. The Sibshop curriculum is not so regimented that it cannot accommodate bright ideas from the young people who attend them!

9. Evaluation

At least once per year, your Sibshop should plan on "checking in" with both the young siblings who attend your Sibshop as well as their parents. Use or adapt the feedback forms found on pages 101–104. These evaluations are easy to administer and will provide your team with valuable feedback.

10. Seek Appropriate Facilitators

Based on years of conducting programs for siblings, we believe that Sibshop facilitators should share some varied core skills. As described in detail on pages 72–75 of the

Sibshops curriculum, it is strongly desired that Sibshop facilitators have the following characteristics:

- Have a working knowledge of the unique concerns and opportunities experienced by siblings of children with support needs

- Have personal or professional experience with people who have support needs and their families

- Be familiar with active listening principles

- Have experience leading groups, preferably groups of children

- Convey a sense of joy, wonder, and play

- Be available to meet at the times and dates identified by the planning committee

- Be somewhat physically fit

- Appreciate that the Sibshop participants, not the facilitators, are the experts on living with a sibling with support needs

Review these bullets with members of your team to make sure that your team of facilitators embodies these qualifications. In certain instances, allowances can be made for one team member lacking a particular skill if it is compensated by another team member who possesses that skill. For instance, your Sibshop may have a team member who is gifted at leading group discussions but has a physical disability that makes it impossible to pitch lively recreational activities. This team member's difficulty might be compensated by a team member who may not be especially good at leading group discussions but is highly skilled at leading recreational activities.

11. Training

All programs that use the Sibshops name and logo must have at least one facilitator or administrator who has been certified as a First Generation Sibshop Facilitator (FGSF) by completing the Sibshop Facilitator Training of the Sibling Support Project. All facilitators are strongly encouraged to attend a Sibshop training offered by the Sibling Support Project. It is the single best way to get up to speed on sibling issues and learn what Sibshops are fundamentally about.

These trainings are best when hosted in-person in the community where the new Sibshop is to be created. As training includes a Demonstration Sibshop, these events are a great way to kick off a local Sibshop and educate parents, service providers, and future Sibshop facilitators about siblings' lifelong concerns. When hosting a training is not possible, you may attend a Sibshop training offered elsewhere as an alternative. Although in-person training is the intended and preferred format, online training by the Sibling Support Project is also available. To learn about upcoming Sibshop trainings, visit www.siblingsupport.org.

Although attending training from the Sibling Support Project is preferred, FGSFs may train new staff to assist with Sibshops at their own agencies. Facilitators trained this way are considered Second-Generation Sibshop Facilitators (SGSFs). To ensure that siblings who attend a local Sibshop participate in a program that reflects Sibshops goals and values, SGSFs may not train new Sibshop facilitators, even at their own agency.

To continue offering Sibshops when the only FGSF leaves the organization, at least one person from the host organization must become certified as a FGSF by completing a

Sibling Support Project Sibshop Facilitator Training within 6 months of the departure of the certified facilitator, or with advanced approval by the Sibling Support Project.

As discussed in Standard 2 (Endorsing the Goals of Sibshops), community-based Sibshop facilitators are encouraged to conduct awareness-level workshops on Sibshops. However, they may not train others on how to run a Sibshop model at regional, state, or national venues.

12. Membership in the Sibshop Facilitator Forum

The Sibshop Facilitator Forum (SFF) is an online community just for facilitators from registered Sibshops. SFF is an excellent forum to meet others running Sibshops and share ideas, challenges, and stories of your successes. It is also the easiest way for the Sibling Support Project to communicate with Sibshops across the world. To be a registered Sibshop, at least one member of your Sibshop staff must belong to the SFF. Please note that you must include the name of your registered Sibshop when requesting to join the group at https://www.facebook.com/groups/SibshopFacilitatorForum, or simply search for "Sibshop Facilitator Forum" in the Facebook search bar.

13. Enriching the Sibshop Curriculum

Year-round, Sibshop facilitators come up with novel activities that are not in the pages of the Sibshops curriculum. To encourage sharing the wealth and enriching the Sibshop curriculum, we ask that each Sibshop program submit at least one, and preferably three, activities online at the Sibshop Facilitator Forum on Facebook. These may be recreational (including new games, crafts, art, and cooking projects), discussion topics, or information activities. Sharing will give all Sibshops a rich array of activities to choose from and help all of us provide fun, engaging ways for young sibs to connect! Facilitators are asked to post activities in the discussion section of the SFF page, and save them to the "files" folder. If we use your activity in a future edition of the Sibshop curriculum, we will be sure to give you credit.

14. Appropriate Use of Sibshop Name and Logo

Registered Sibshops may use the Sibshop name and the Sibshop logo, but the name and logo must be used correctly. Please note that it is "Sibshop" and never "SibShop" or "Sib Shop." The Sibshop curriculum is copyrighted and the Sibshop logo is trademarked. Consequently, the Sibshop logo may not be altered in any way without prior permission of the Sibling Support Project.

15. Registering Your Sibshop

To use the Sibshop name and logo, your program must be a registered Sibshop. Luckily, registration is easy, quick, and completed online. ***Please note:*** *All Sibshops must complete this one-time, no-cost online registration.*

To register, do the following:

1. Visit https://siblingsupport.org/sibshops/register-your-sibshop/

2. Enter your information, including completion date of Sibshop Facilitator Training. Consider using a generic email address (e.g., sibshops@myagency.org) in case of staff/ facilitator changes.

3. Look for an email confirmation of your registration (it may land in the spam folder).

4. Save your username and password to log in again to add a profile picture and background photo, and to update information as needed in the future.

Once you register online, we will post key contact information about your Sibshop on our website's online directory. This information will assist countless parents who visit the Project's webpages seeking a local Sibshop for their children. ***Please note:*** *It will be your responsibility to make sure that that your contact information and Sibshop details are up to date.*

B

A Brief Description of the Sibshop Model

For more information on how to start a registered Sibshop, contact the Sibling Support Project at info@siblingsupport.org or www.siblingsupport.org.

WHAT ARE SIBSHOPS?

For the adults who plan them and the agencies that sponsor them, Sibshops are best described as opportunities for siblings of children with health, mental health, and developmental needs to obtain peer support and education within a recreational context. They can reflect an agency's commitment to the well-being of the family member most likely to have the longest-lasting relationship with the person who has support needs.

However, for the young people who attend them and the energetic people who run them, Sibshops are best described as *events*. Sibshops are lively, pedal-to-the-metal celebrations of the many contributions made by brothers and sisters of kids with support needs. Sibshops acknowledge that being the brother or sister of a person with support needs is for some a good thing, for others a not-so-good thing, and for many something in between. They reflect a belief that siblings have much to offer one another—if they are given a chance. The Sibshop model intersperses information and discussion activities with games (designed to be unique, upbeat, and appealing to a wide ability range), cooking and craft activities, and special guests who may teach participants how to mime, how to juggle, or, in the case of one guest artist who has cerebral palsy, how to paint by holding a toothbrush in your mouth. Sibshops are as fun and rewarding for the people who host them as they are for the participants.

Sibshops seek to provide siblings with opportunities for peer support. Because Sibshops are designed (primarily) for school-age children, peer support is provided within a lively, recreational context that emphasizes a kids'-eye view. Sibshops are not therapy, group or otherwise, although their effect may be therapeutic for some children. Sibshops acknowledge that most brothers and sisters of people with support needs, like their parents, are doing well, despite the challenges posed by a family member's illness or disability. Consequently, although Sibshop facilitators always keep an eye open for participants who may need additional services, the Sibshop model takes a wellness approach that encourages children to recognize and build on their skills, talents, and strengths.

WHO ATTENDS SIBSHOPS?

Originally developed for 8- to 13-year-old siblings of children with developmental disabilities, the Sibshop model is easily adapted for slightly younger children and older teens. It has been adapted for siblings of children with other support needs, including cancer and other health impairments, hearing loss, and mental health concerns. Sibshops have also been adapted for use with children who have siblings involved in the foster care or juvenile justice systems, or who have lost a family member. Children who attend Sibshops come from diverse settings including suburban communities (e.g., Bellevue, Washington; Northbrook, Illinois), urban communities (e.g., New York City, St. Louis), rural areas (e.g., Wyoming, Wisconsin), and areas with unique cultural heritages (e.g., Alaska, Hawaii, South Central Los Angeles).

WHO SPONSORS SIBSHOPS?

Any agency serving families of children with support needs can sponsor a Sibshop, provided it can offer financial support, properly staff the program, and attract a sufficient number of participants. We strongly recommend, however, that agencies consider working together to cosponsor a local Sibshop for all the siblings in a given community. (This important topic is further discussed in Chapter 5.) We have found that Sibshops are well within the reach and abilities of most communities. They are not expensive to run and logistically are no more difficult to coordinate than other community-based programs for children, such as Scouts or Camp Fire.

WHO RUNS SIBSHOPS?

We believe that Sibshops are best facilitated by a team that includes service providers (e.g., social workers; special education teachers; physical, occupational, and speech therapists; nurses; child life specialists) and adult siblings of people with support needs. At the very least, the team of facilitators will need to 1) be knowledgeable about the disability or illness represented, 2) possess a sense of humor and play, 3) enjoy the company of children, and 4) respect the young participants' expertise on the topic of life with a sibling with support needs. Qualifications for Sibshop facilitators are further discussed in Chapter 5.

WHAT IS THE OPTIMAL NUMBER OF PARTICIPANTS FOR A SIBSHOP?

Sibshops have been held for as few as five children and as many as 45. Approximately a dozen children, with at least two facilitators, is a comfortable number.

WHEN ARE SIBSHOPS OFFERED?

We encourage you to survey the families you wish to support through Sibshops to identify days and times that work for the majority. Many in-person Sibshops are held on or near weekends, but this may not be ideal for the families you wish to support. Online Sibshops, which are shorter in duration (typically 60–90 minutes) and eliminate commuting time, may be easier to schedule after school or on weekday evenings.

Information to help determine the best day and length for your community's Sibshop can be found in Chapter 5.

HOW OFTEN ARE SIBSHOPS HELD?

Depending on the needs and resources of the community, Sibshops may be offered as frequently as weekly (as with a 1.5-hour in-person after-school program) or as infrequently as yearly (as with an all-day Sibshop that is a part of an annual conference for families from around a state or the nation). Generally, however, Sibshops are presented monthly or bimonthly.

Sibshops may also be offered like a class (e.g., five Sibshops, meeting once a month, with one registration). Offering Sibshops this way can provide a stable group that can form an identity during the months they are together. It can be difficult, however, for some participants and families to commit to a series of dates due to interference with other activities. Sibshops may also be offered as standalone events (e.g., bimonthly meetings with separate registrations). The standalone events offer families flexibility, but participants will vary somewhat from Sibshop to Sibshop.

WHAT ARE THE GOALS OF THE SIBSHOP MODEL?

All Sibshop activities proceed from the following goals:

 Goal 1: Sibshops will provide siblings of children with support needs an opportunity to meet other siblings in a relaxed, recreational setting.

 Goal 2: Sibshops will provide siblings with opportunities to discuss common joys and concerns with other siblings of children with support needs.

 Goal 3: Sibshops will provide siblings with an opportunity to learn how others handle situations commonly experienced by siblings of children with support needs.

 Goal 4: Sibshops will provide siblings with an opportunity to learn more about the implications of their siblings' support needs.

 Goal 5: Sibshops will provide parents and other professionals with opportunities to learn more about the concerns and opportunities frequently experienced by siblings of people with support needs.

SAMPLE SIBSHOP SCHEDULE

10:00 a.m. Trickle-In Activity: Face Tags

10:20 a.m. Introductory/Peer Support Activity: Strengths & Weaknesses

10:45 a.m. Recreational Activity: Knots

10:50 a.m. Recreational Activity: Lap Game

11:00 a.m. Recreational Activity: Last Kid Standing

11:10 a.m. Recreational Activity: Group Juggling

11:30 a.m. Recreational Activity: Triangle Tag

11:40 a.m. Recreational Activity: Sightless Sculpture

11:50 a.m. Lunch Prep

12:00 Noon Lunch: Super Nachos!

12:20 p.m. Lunch Cleanup

12:30 p.m. Peer Support Activity: Dear Aunt Blabby

12:55 p.m. Recreational Activity: Pushpin Soccer

1:15 p.m. Recreational Activity: Hog Call

1:30 p.m. Peer Support Activity: Sound-Off

1:55 p.m. Closure

C

What Siblings Would Like Parents and Service Providers to Know

In the United States, there are millions of people who have health, developmental, and mental health concerns. Most of these people have typically developing brothers and sisters. Siblings are too important to ignore, if for only the following reasons:

- These siblings will be in the lives of family members with support needs longer than anyone else. Brothers and sisters will be there after parents are gone and special education services are a distant memory. If these siblings are provided with support and information, they can help their brothers and sisters live dignified lives from childhood to their senior years.

- Throughout their lives, siblings share many of the concerns that parents of children with support needs experience, including isolation, a need for information, guilt, concerns about the future, and caregiving demands. Siblings also face issues that are uniquely theirs, including resentment, peer issues, embarrassment, and pressure to achieve.

Despite the important and lifelong roles they will play in the lives of their siblings who have support needs, brothers and sisters are often overlooked by even the most family-friendly agencies. Siblings, often left in the literal and figurative waiting rooms of service delivery systems, deserve better. True family-centered care and services can only be achieved when siblings are actively included in agencies' functional definition of "family."

The Sibling Support Project facilitated a discussion in our online community for adult siblings of people with disabilities regarding the considerations that siblings want from parents, other family members, and service providers. The following are themes discussed by members and recommendations from the Sibling Support Project.

THE RIGHT TO ONE'S OWN LIFE

Throughout their lives, siblings may play many different roles in the lives of their brothers and sisters with support needs. Regardless of the contributions they may make, the basic right of siblings to their own lives must always be remembered. Parents and service providers should not make assumptions about responsibilities that typically developing siblings may assume without an open and honest discussion. "Nothing about us without us"—a phrase popular with self-advocates who have disabilities to describe the basic principle behind self-determination—applies to siblings as well. Self-determination, after all, is for everyone—including siblings.

ACKNOWLEDGING SIBLINGS' CONCERNS

Like parents, brothers and sisters will experience a wide array of often ambivalent emotions regarding the effect of their siblings' support needs on them and the family as a whole. These feelings should be both expected and acknowledged by parents, other family members, and service providers. Because most siblings will have the longest-lasting relationship with the family member who has a disability, these concerns will change over time. Parents and providers would be wise to learn more about siblings' lifelong and ever-changing concerns.

EXPECTATIONS FOR TYPICALLY DEVELOPING SIBLINGS

Families need to set high expectations for all their children. Some typically developing brothers and sisters, however, react to their siblings' disability by setting unrealistically high expectations for themselves. Some feel that they must somehow compensate for their siblings' support needs. Parents can help their typically developing children by conveying clear expectations and unconditional support.

EXPECT TYPICAL BEHAVIOR FROM TYPICALLY DEVELOPING SIBLINGS

Although difficult for parents to watch, teasing, name calling, arguing, and other forms of conflict are common among most brothers and sisters—even when one has support needs. Although parents may be appalled at siblings' harshness toward one another, much of this conflict can be a beneficial part of typical social development. A child with Down syndrome who grows up with siblings with whom he sometimes fights will likely be better prepared to face life in the community as an adult than a child with Down syndrome who grows up as an only child. Regardless of how adaptive or developmentally appropriate it might be, however, typical sibling conflict is more likely to result in feelings of guilt when one sibling has health or developmental needs. When conflict arises, the message sent to many brothers and sisters is, "Leave your sibling alone. You are bigger, you are stronger, you should know better. It is your job to compromise." Typically developing siblings deserve a life where they, like other children, sometimes misbehave, get angry, and fight with their siblings.

EXPECTATIONS FOR THE FAMILY MEMBER WITH SUPPORT NEEDS

When families have high expectations for their children with support needs, everyone will benefit. As adults, typically developing brothers and sisters will likely play important roles in the lives of their siblings with disabilities. Parents can help siblings now by helping their children with support needs acquire skills that will allow them to be as independent as possible as adults. To the extent possible, parents should have the same expectations for the child with support needs regarding chores and personal responsibility as they do for the typically developing children. Not only will similar expectations foster independence, they will also minimize the resentment expressed by siblings when there are two sets of rules—one for them and another for their sibs who have support needs.

THE RIGHT TO A SAFE ENVIRONMENT

Some siblings live with brothers and sisters who have challenging behaviors. Other siblings assume responsibilities for themselves and their siblings that go beyond their age level and place all parties in vulnerable situations. Siblings deserve to have their own personal safety given as much importance as the family member with support needs.

OPPORTUNITIES TO MEET PEERS

For most parents, the thought of "going it alone"—raising a child with support needs without the benefit of knowing another parent in a similar situation—would be unthinkable. Yet, this routinely happens to siblings. Sibshops, online sibling communities such as SibTeen, Sib20, and SibNet, state chapters of the national Sibling Leadership Network, and similar efforts offer siblings the common-sense support and validation that parents get from Parent-to-Parent programs and similar programs. Siblings—like parents—like to know that they are not alone with their unique joys and concerns.

OPPORTUNITIES TO OBTAIN INFORMATION

Throughout their lives, brothers and sisters have an ever-changing need for information about their sibling's disability, as well as its treatment and implications. Parents and service providers have an obligation to proactively provide siblings with helpful information. Any agency that represents a specific disability or illness and that provides materials for parents and other adults should offer materials for siblings and young readers as well.

SIBLINGS' CONCERNS ABOUT THE FUTURE

Early in life, many brothers and sisters worry about what obligations they will have toward their sibling in the years to come. Parents can reassure their typically developing children by doing the following:

- Making plans for the future of their children with support needs

- Listening to their typically developing children's ideas, concerns, questions, and suggestions as they make these plans

- Considering backup plans

- Realizing that their typically developing children's availability may change over time

When brothers and sisters are brought "into the loop" and given the message early that they have their parents' support to live their own lives and pursue their own dreams, their future involvement with their sibling who has a disability will become a choice instead of an obligation. For their own good and for the good of their siblings with disabilities, brothers and sisters should be afforded the right to their own lives. This includes having a say in whether and how they will be involved in the lives of their siblings with disabilities as adults and the level, type, and duration of that involvement.

INCLUDING BOTH SONS AND DAUGHTERS

Just as daughters are usually the family members who care for aging parents, adult sisters are usually the family members who look after the family member with support needs when parents no longer can. Serious exploration of sharing responsibilities among siblings—including brothers—should be considered.

COMMUNICATION

Although good communication between parents and children is always important, it is especially important in families where there is a child who has support needs. An evening course in active listening can help improve communication among all family members, and books such as *How to Talk So Kids Will Listen and Listen So Kids Will Talk* (2012a) and *Siblings Without Rivalry* (2012b) (both by Adele Faber and Elaine Mazlish) provide helpful tips on communicating with children.

ONE-TO-ONE TIME WITH PARENTS

Children need to know from their parents' deeds and words that their parents care about them as individuals. When parents carve time out of a busy schedule to take a walk or hike, grab a bite at a local burger joint, or window shop at the mall with their typically developing children, it conveys a message that parents are there for them and provides an excellent opportunity to talk about a wide range of topics. Setting aside a few extra minutes after the child with a disability goes to bed to spend with siblings, exchanging notes in a journal together, or even transforming routine errands, such as grocery shopping, into special one-to-one time for parents and siblings, can go a long way in letting siblings know they are important.

CELEBRATE EVERY CHILD'S ACHIEVEMENTS AND MILESTONES

Over the years, we have met siblings whose parents did not attend their high school graduation—even when their children were valedictorians—because the parents were unable to leave their child with support needs. We have also met siblings whose wedding plans were dictated by the needs of their sibling with a disability. One child's support needs should not overshadow another child's achievements and milestones. Families who seek out respite resources and creative solutions and strive for flexibility can help ensure that the accomplishments of all family members are celebrated.

PARENTS' PERSPECTIVES ARE MORE IMPORTANT THAN THE ACTUAL DISABILITY

Parents would be wise to remember that the parents' interpretation of their child's disability will be a greater influence on the adaptation of their typically developing sibling than the actual disability itself. When parents seek support, information, and respite for themselves, they model resilience and healthy attitudes and behaviors for their typically developing children.

INCLUDE SIBLINGS IN THE DEFINITION OF "FAMILY"

Many educational, health care, and social service agencies profess a desire to offer family-centered services but continue to overlook the family members who will have the longest-lasting relationship with the person who has the support needs—their siblings. When brothers and sisters receive the considerations and services they deserve, agencies can genuinely claim to offer "family-centered"—instead of "parent-centered"—services.

ACTIVELY REACH OUT TO SIBLINGS

Parents and agency staff should consider inviting (but not requiring) siblings to attend planning meetings at every stage of transition in the life of the person with a disability, including informational, individualized education programs, individualized family service plans, and transition-planning meetings and clinic visits. Siblings frequently have legitimate questions that service providers can answer. Brothers and sisters also have informed opinions and unique perspectives on the abilities and strengths of their siblings with disabilities and can make positive contributions to the child's team.

LEARN MORE ABOUT LIFE AS A SIBLING

Anyone interested in families ought to be interested in siblings and their concerns. Parents and providers can learn more about life as a sib by facilitating a Sibshop, hosting a sibling panel, or reading books by and about brothers and sisters. Guidelines for conducting a sibling panel are available from the Sibling Support Project and in the Sibshop curriculum. Visit the Sibling Support Project's website www.siblingsupport.org for a bibliography of sibling-related books.

CREATE LOCAL PROGRAMS SPECIFICALLY FOR BROTHERS AND SISTERS

If your community has a Parent-to-Parent program or a similar parent support effort, a fair question to ask is this: Why isn't there a similar effort for the siblings? Like their parents, siblings benefit from talking with others who "get it." Sibshops and other programs for preschool, school-age, teen, and adult siblings are growing in number. The Sibling Support Project, which maintains a growing database of Sibshops and other sibling programs, provides training and technical assistance on how to create local programs for siblings.

INCLUDE SIBLINGS ON ADVISORY BOARDS AND IN POLICIES REGARDING FAMILIES

Reserving board seats for siblings will give the board a unique, important perspective and reflect the agency's concern for the well-being of brothers and sisters. Developing policies based on the important roles played by siblings will help ensure that their concerns and contributions are part of the agency's commitment to families.

FUND SERVICES FOR SIBLINGS

No classmate in an inclusive classroom will have a greater impact on the social development of a child with a disability than a sibling will. They will be their siblings' lifelong role model. As noted previously, brothers and sisters will likely be in the lives of their siblings with disabilities longer than anyone else—longer than their parents and certainly longer than any service provider. For most brothers and sisters, their future and the future of their siblings with support needs are inexorably entwined. Despite this, there is little funding to support projects that will help siblings obtain the information, skills, and support they will need throughout their lives. Governmental agencies and funders interested in supporting people with disabilities and their families would be wise to invest in the family members who will take a personal interest in the well-being of people with disabilities and advocate for them when their parents no longer can. As one sister wrote: "We will become caregivers for our siblings when our parents no longer can. Anyone interested in the welfare of people with disabilities ought to be interested in us."

ABOUT THE SIBLING SUPPORT PROJECT

Founded in Seattle in 1990 by Don Meyer, the Sibling Support Project is the first national program dedicated to the lifelong and ever-changing concerns of millions of siblings of people with health, developmental, and mental health concerns. Our work spans books and publications, online communities for teen and adult siblings, and workshops and training. We are best known for helping local communities start Sibshops—lively peer support groups for school-age siblings of kids with disabilities and health concerns.

At the Sibling Support Project, we understand that disabilities and other health diagnoses affect the lives of all family members. Our goal is to expand the peer support and information opportunities available for siblings of people with support needs and to increase parents' and providers' understanding of sibling issues.

For more information about the Sibling Support Project, please visit www.sibling-support.org.

D Sample Sibshop Registration Form

Date: _____

Child's name: _____

Date of birth: _____ Age: _____ Gender: _____

School: _____ Grade: _____

Does this child receive any special services (e.g., counseling, speech therapy, special education)? _____

_____

Parent/caregiver name(s): _____

Home address: _____

_____

Telephone: _____

Name of sibling with support needs: _____

Date of birth: _____ Age: _____ Gender: _____

Nature of disability or illness: _____

_____

School: _____

What kind of related education services (e.g., speech,
occupational, or physical therapy, counseling) does this child receive? _____

_____

_____

Other siblings

Name	Date of birth	Age	Gender

(continued)

What are your reasons for enrolling your child in the Sibshop program? _____

_____

Do you have any concerns about enrolling your child in the Sibshop? _____

_____

_____

Do you have any particular topics that you would like addressed during the Sibshop?_____

_____

_____

Does your child have any food allergies or restrictions?_____

_____

_____

Is there any other information about your child that is important to know? _____

_____

Please provide any other information that you feel will make
this an enjoyable and educational experience for your child: _____

_____

I assume all risks and hazards of the conduct of the program and release from responsibility any person providing transportation to and from activities. In case of injury, I do hereby waive all claims or legal actions, financial, or otherwise against [names of cosponsoring agencies], their elected officials and employees, the organizers, sponsors, supervisors or any volunteer connected with the program. In absence of a signature, payment of fees and participation in the program shall constitute acceptance of the conditions set forth in the release. I grant full permission to use any photographs, video recordings, motion pictures, audio recordings, or any other record of this program for any purpose.

Please review statement with your agency director before using or insert agency's standard liability statement!

_____   _____
Signature of parent or guardian   Date

Please return this form and the registration fee* (a check for $[XX] made out to the [name of agency]) and mail to: [address]

*If you would like your child to be considered for a scholarship, please call [name of agency] at [phone number]. Donations to the Sibshop Scholarship fund are gratefully accepted!

E

"Dear Aunt Blabby" Letters

Since it was first introduced in the early 1980s, this activity has withstood the test of time with sibs everywhere! Aunt Blabby is a fictitious advice columnist who happens to have a stack of letters written by young siblings just waiting to be answered. Naturally, you offered to help Aunt Blabby by getting advice from the *real* experts—the siblings in your Sibshops!

You can modernize Aunt Blabby by making her a blogger. If you have a friend or colleague who enjoys acting, invite them to your next online or in-person Sibshop to play the part of Aunt Blabby (costume strongly encouraged!), who can read the questions you write. Invite the kids to ask your advice columnist/blogger their own questions and ask the group to find answers together.

The first collection of letters to Dear Aunt Blabby is from brothers and sisters of children who have developmental disabilities. The second collection, starting on page 235, is from siblings of children who have cancer or other chronic illnesses. No matter which type of sibling group you are working with, be sure to read all the letters. You will likely find letters you can easily adapt for the participants you serve.

Dear Aunt Blabby,

Sometimes, I feel like the invisible man. My brother has autism. He has a lot of needs that seem to take up all my parents' time. It seems like the only time my parents pay attention to me is when I get into trouble. How do I let them know that they have two kids instead of one?

(signed)
The Invisible Man

Dear Aunt Blabby,

Maybe you can help me with my problem. My big sister has a disability. Sometimes, my friends ask me what's the matter with her and how she got that way. Once, my teacher even asked. I never know how to explain it. Any suggestions?

(signed)
Speechless

Dear Aunt Blabby,

Boy, am I mad! For the fifth time tonight, my sister has bothered me while I'm try-ing to do my homework. She is always bugging me! Especially when my friends come over. Help!

(signed)
Fuming

Dear Aunt Blabby,

I have a problem. My brother Carlos has a disability. I hate to admit it, but some-times he embarrasses me. Don't get me wrong—in a lot of ways, Carlos is a great guy. He can really do a lot for himself, even with all of his support needs. My problem is that I get embarrassed when he acts up in church or has a temper tantrum at the shopping mall. What can I do?

(signed)
Embarrassed

Dear Aunt Blabby,

I hope you can help. My brother has a lot of problems—and I have a lot of ques-tions! My mom never really told me what happened to Josh. I feel funny asking her. Can you give me some tips on how to ask my mom about what happened to Josh?

(signed)
Need to Know

Dear Aunt Blabby,

Maybe you can help me. I really like my sister Aisha. She has a lot of support needs, but I love her a lot. My problem is that I get bored just going for walks and watching TV with her. What else can I do with her that will be fun for both of us?

(signed)
Curious

Dear Aunt Blabby,

I have a problem that maybe you can help me with. Just because my brother has a disability and I don't, my parents expect me to be a "Superkid." They expect me to get perfect grades in school. Does that seem fair to you? What can I do?

(signed)
I'm No Superkid

Dear Aunt Blabby,

I'm really worried. If I don't get an *A* in history, I won't get on the honor roll at school. My parents have so many problems with my sister. I'd really like to make them happy with my schoolwork. Do you think they will be disappointed if I don't get on the honor roll?

(signed)
Worried

Dear Aunt Blabby,

Is it okay to tease your sister? I mean, I tease my other brothers and sisters, but when I tease my "special" sister, my grandma yells at me. I'm not doing it to be mean or anything—it's just teasing. Is it okay or not?

(signed)
To Tease or Not to Tease

Dear Aunt Blabby,

I don't know what to do. My little brother Antoine has lots of problems learning. In September, Antoine started going to my school. Some kids at my school make fun of the special education kids. I even heard them call my brother names and laugh at things he does. Aunt Blabby, what should I do?

(signed)
Perplexed

Dear Aunt Blabby,

I'm not sure what I should do. I have a new friend, Oliver. We have a lot of fun together. We like the same sports and video games. My problem is that when Oliver is joking around, he will say things like "cut it out, you retard!" Ouch! I hate it when he says that because my baby sister, Jamie, has Down syndrome. How can I get him to stop using that word?

(signed)
Still Want to Be Friends

Dear Aunt Blabby,

My brother Min uses a wheelchair. When we go to the mall, people are always looking at him. I never know what to do. Sometimes, people look at him and smile. But sometimes, people just stare. Do I stare back at them or just pretend I don't see them? What can I do?

(signed)
Tired of Rude People

Dear Aunt Blabby,

My little sister is deaf. Our whole family is learning sign language. It is fun to be able to talk in a secret language! But I feel funny about using signs when I'm with my family in the mall or something. Sometimes, kids make fun of us. They will flap their hands or make weird noises. Even adults stare at us sometimes and use words that are wrong, like "deaf and dumb." Mom tells me I have to be polite to adults. How can I tell them to use the right words without sounding rude?

(signed)
Kid Teacher

Dear Aunt Blabby,

I am beginning to feel like Cinderella. My parents make me take care of my little brothers and sisters, especially my little sister who has autism. Also, I spend every Saturday helping my mom clean the house. I never get to do anything I want to do! Does that seem fair to you?

(signed)
Where's My Fairy Godmother?

Dear Aunt Blabby,

My sister is driving me nuts. Alicia is 4 years old and has Down syndrome and everybody thinks she's so cute. Wherever we go, it's "Alicia this" and "Alicia that." It's like I'm not even there! What can I do?

(signed)
Look at Me Too!

Dear Aunt Blabby,

My brother Marco has a hard time at school. My dad says he has a learning disability. School is pretty easy for me, except for last week when I really bombed a math test. Do you think that I might have a learning disability too?

(signed)
Worried

Dear Aunt Blabby,

My brother gets away with murder. He never has to do anything around the house just because he has a disability. I know he can do things. It's just that my parents won't make him.

(signed)
Ripped Off

Dear Aunt Blabby,

I feel kind of bad. Next month, I will turn 16 and my mom says that I can take driver's ed. My sister is 18 and has a disability. My mom says she won't ever be able to drive. Should I feel bad that I can do things that my sister can't?

(signed)
Confused

Dear Aunt Blabby,

Lately, I've been thinking about the future. Our family lives in Ohio, but I think it would be neat to live in California someday. When I grow up, will I have to stay in Ohio to take care of my brother who has a disability?

(signed)
California Dreamin'

Dear Aunt Blabby,

Help! No one seems to understand! When I tell my friends about my little sister Sofia, they don't understand what a neat kid she is and all the things she can do. All they see is her wheelchair and floppy arms. Am I the only one with this problem? What can I do?

(signed)
I Like My Sister!

Dear Aunt Blabby,

I wish I knew someone who has a sister with problems like Jada's. I have friends, but they don't understand what it is like when your little sister has seizures and gets sick and goes to the hospital all the time. My friends don't understand the good stuff either. I was really proud when Jada (who is 6) finally learned to go the bathroom by herself! Are there other kids who know what it's like to have a sister like Jada?

(signed)
Who Knows?

Dear Aunt Blabby,

I wish I was like my friend Ava. She has a big sister, and they do lots of things together. They borrow each other's clothes, put on plays, yell at each other, and laugh a lot too. My sister, Ellie, has lots of problems. I love her, but we're not like Ava and her sister at all. I wish we were.

(signed)
Only Sort of a Sister

Dear Aunt Blabby,

I have an older brother and sister with support needs. My parents and teachers expect me to do everything right. They call me "the lucky normal one." I know my parents have lots of problems, so I want to make them happy. But sometimes, I feel under so much pressure! Do other kids feel this way?

(signed)
Not So Lucky

Dear Aunt Blabby,

When my sister Iryna does not cooperate in school, the teachers come to me to get some help. I feel sorry that my sister is having such a hard time, but can't they deal with it? It's hard to miss my own classes and then have to catch up. How can I get the teachers to stop coming to me?

(signed)
Not My Job!

Dear Aunt Blabby,

My mother dresses my brother Alex like a nerd. I want him to look cool like a normal kid. What can I do?

(signed)
Joe Cool

Dear Aunt Blabby,

My brother has Down syndrome. When our family goes to the mall, he is very friendly with *everyone!* Even if he doesn't know someone, he will give them a hug! He's 10 years old and it's sort of embarrassing. What can I do and not hurt my brother's feelings?

(signed)
Sensitive

Dear Aunt Blabby,

I always have to babysit for my sister. She has autism and my parents say I am the only one they can trust. I want to get a job after school, but I'll feel bad if I leave them empty-handed. What should I do?

(signed)
Penniless

Dear Aunt Blabby,

My brother Mateo always wants to play with my friends and me. He can't hit the ball. He can't catch the ball. He doesn't understand the rules. My friends get frustrated. This is more than I can take!

(signed)
Caught Between

Dear Aunt Blabby,

I just started a new school. My mom said that I can invite two friends to spend the day at my house on Saturday. I'm really excited about them coming over. I'm also a little worried about my sister, Samantha. Samantha has a lot of problems, and my new friends don't know a thing about her. When should I tell them about Samantha? Before they come over? Or should I wait until they get to the house? What should I say?

(signed)
Anxious

Dear Aunt Blabby,

I got in trouble at school and almost got suspended because I punched a kid who was staring at my sister. He stared and said something to his friends, and then they all laughed and pointed at her. Okay, maybe she looks different, but she is my sister and I love her. What should I do?

(signed)
Protective

Dear Aunt Blabby,

My sister Jin has epilepsy. Last week, at my birthday party, my sister had a seizure in front of my friends. Yesterday, when my friends came over to play, my sister ran upstairs to her room, locked her door, and started to cry. How can I make her feel okay?

(signed)
The Pits

Dear Aunt Blabby,

    I have a younger brother who has autism. He is not in school yet. Sometimes, I see my school friends teasing other kids with autism at school. I feel like I should make them stop, but I want them to like me. What should I do?

(signed)
Soon It Will Be My Brother

Dear Aunt Blabby,

    My brother has Down syndrome. When we are together, people ask me questions for him. How can I get people to ask him—not me?

(signed)
He's Got Answers

Dear Aunt Blabby,

    I have a terrible secret. When my mom was pregnant with Jamie, I had this huge temper tantrum. My mom got real upset. Later that day, she went to the hospital and had Jamie. Now, Jamie has all these problems. Dear Aunt Blabby, I think Jamie's problems are all my fault!

(signed)
Guilty

Dear Aunt Blabby,

    I have this problem. Yesterday, two people I know were talking about my brother Hector and making fun of the noises he makes. They didn't see me, but I didn't stop them or stick up for my own brother! I feel bad and don't understand why I didn't stick up for him.

(signed)
Torn Up Inside

Dear Aunt Blabby,

    My sister Yareli doesn't get asked to friends' houses or birthday parties like I do. She gets mad at me or Mom when I get to do something she can't. What should I do?

(signed)
Need a Life of My Own

Dear Aunt Blabby,

    My sister always complains to me about her spina bifida. She then upsets me by saying, "Why do you think God made me different?" I really don't know what to answer.

(signed)
Feeling Guilty

Dear Aunt Blabby,

    When I was little, I used to tell my parents that I wanted my sister Mikayla to live with me when we grew up. Aunt Blabby, now I think I don't want her to always live with me. Is that okay? Where would she live? By the way, I love my sister a lot!

(signed)
Don't Know

Dear Aunt Blabby,

My brother is always getting into my room and totally trashing it. Sometimes, he breaks my stuff. My mom doesn't make him clean it up. She says he can't clean it the way it is supposed to be cleaned. Mom says she doesn't have time to do it by herself. What do I do with him? And what do I do about my room?

(signed)
Lonely Cleaner

Dear Aunt Blabby,

My older brother Andrew has epilepsy. His seizures started when he was 10. I'm going to be 10 soon. Do you think I'll have seizures like my brother?

(signed)
A Little Worried

Dear Aunt Blabby,

You would think that the only kid that mattered in our family is Jaden, my brother with Down syndrome. Whatever our family does, we do for Jaden. On our vacations, we go to these Down syndrome meetings. At dinner, it's always Down syndrome this, Down syndrome that. My parents are always at some meeting about Jaden or Down syndrome. Jaden is an okay brother, I guess, but I'm sick of everything always being for him.

(signed)
Too Much

Dear Aunt Blabby,

My summer is ruined!! I was looking forward to sleeping in every morning and having fun and goofing off. My brother Joel, who has autism, still has to go to school all summer. My mom makes me go with her when she drops him off. We have to get up at 7:00 a.m. and drive for an hour! Mom says I'm not old enough to stay by myself. There goes my time off. What can I do?

(signed)
Tired of Traveling

Dear Aunt Blabby,

I'm 11 years old and my brother is 14. My brother has lots of seizures even though he takes his medication. My parents don't want to leave him alone at home, so we never get to go anywhere like the mall, the movies, or out to dinner. Mom can't find anyone to babysit for my brother because everybody is afraid of his seizures. Why do I have to suffer and not have any fun like all my friends?

(signed)
Feeling Trapped

Dear Aunt Blabby,

My sister has something called ADHD. My mom says sugar makes her jump around. Just because she can't have sugar, we have no candy, pop, or cookies in our house. Mom says if I have it then she will want it too. That's not fair!

(signed)
Sweet Tooth

Dear Aunt Blabby,

This will sound weird, but I wish my brother had Down syndrome. Some of the kids at our Sibshop talk about how cool their sibs are even if they have Downs. My brother Ramon has autism and is a pain. All the time! It is hard to find anything positive to say about him.

(signed)
Jealous

Dear Aunt Blabby,

I have a younger brother who has a disability. We go to the same school. Whenever I want to go to a school basketball or football game with my friends, my parents make me take my brother with me. Aunt Blabby, I love my brother, but I don't think this is fair. Does that seem right to you?

(signed)
This Sister Needs Help

Dear Aunt Blabby,

My sister who has Down syndrome never gets punished like me. My mom is unfair and gives in to her moods and stubbornness too much. What can I do?

(signed)
Miss Treated

Dear Aunt Blabby,

Sometimes, I feel like I'm chained to my younger brother. He always wants to go where I go and play with my friends. My brother has cerebral palsy, uses a wheelchair, and can be a real pain. Why won't my mom let me go by myself?

(signed)
Chained

Dear Aunt Blabby,

I'm really frustrated. My sister is always kicking. I know it is part of her disability because she is really hyper. But what can I do? She just makes me so angry!!! Help!!!

(signed)
Frustrated!

Dear Aunt Blabby,

GRRR! I'm confused. My sister has many behavior problems. I love my little sister and I'd like to play with her, but I'm afraid of her because she sometimes hurts me. She bites me and punches me. My mom says I shouldn't hit her back and I should play with her. What should I do?

(signed)
Want to Play

Dear Aunt Blabby,

My brother, who has autism, sometimes hits kids when we are at the playground. These kids get mad and want to hit him back. What should I do?

(signed)
All Mixed Up

Dear Aunt Blabby,

My brother Victor has a developmental disability. Sometimes, he gets very angry and throws things. Now that he is bigger, I am afraid he might hurt me or someone else. What should I do?

(signed)
Tired of Ducking

Dear Aunt Blabby,

My sister has autism. She wakes me up all night and breaks all my toys, and I can't even have friends over because she's so mean to them. What can I do?

(signed)
What's the Limit?

Dear Aunt Blabby,

Sometimes, I can't understand my friends. They complain when their little brothers or sisters bug them. I don't see what the big deal is. They should try living with my sister Jasmine. Jasmine has autism! Then they wouldn't complain! Know what I mean?

(signed)
Life Is Not So Bad

Dear Aunt Blabby,

Most people probably wouldn't think that Caleb could teach you much—he has so many problems and can't even talk. But he has really taught me a lot about caring and love and stuff like that. Do you think that is weird?

(signed)
Learned a Lot

Dear Aunt Blabby,

Sometimes, kids look at Ariana and say, "Is that your sister?" "Who is she?" They think that because Ariana looks different that she is different on the inside. But she is just like us inside. She doesn't want to be stared at and laughed at or ignored. Am I the only one who feels this way?

(signed)
Cut It Out!

Dear Aunt Blabby,

My friends say my brother can't do very much, but you should see what he did at Special Olympics! Wow! I didn't know he could run so fast! It may sound funny to some people, but I am really proud of what my brother can do!

(signed)
One Proud Brother

Dear Aunt Blabby,

To tell the truth, my brother Wyatt is a butt most of the time, but I hate it when kids pick on him because of his disability. Sometimes, I have to defend him. Am I the only one?

(signed)
Somebody Has to Stick Up for Him!

The following Dear Aunt Blabby letters are for siblings of children who have cancer or other chronic illnesses.

Dear Aunt Blabby,

I'm 14 years old, and I have an 8-year-old sister with health problems. I'm always expected to "understand" and "know better" and "act like an adult" and "think of what your sister's been through." I'm just 14! Does that seem fair to you?

(signed)
Give Me a Break

Dear Aunt Blabby,

Kids at my school know that my sister has cancer. Most of them are pretty nice about it, except for the jerks who ask, "Is your sister going to die?" Aunt Blabby, what can I say to them?

(signed)
They're So Rude!

Dear Aunt Blabby,

It seems like everything has changed since Adalyn got leukemia. My friends won't even come to my house anymore. They say they don't want to catch her leukemia and die. What can I do?

(signed)
Home Alone

Dear Aunt Blabby,

Julian, my little brother, has a brain tumor. He needs to spend a lot of time in the hospital. When he does, I have to stay over at my aunt's house. I'm sick of staying there. None of my cousins are even my age. Any suggestions?

(signed)
I Wanna Go Home

Dear Aunt Blabby,

My brother Ren has cancer and is on these drugs. They are supposed to help him, but they made him lose most of his hair and now he's really fat. People stare at him when they see him. I know I shouldn't be embarrassed about how he looks, but I am. What can I do?

(signed)
Embarrassed

Dear Aunt Blabby,

I am sick of my sister being sick. I know she has a rare genetic disorder, and I know it is serious, but I am tired of it. We can't go on a vacation because my sister might get sick. I can't bring friends over because they might make her sick. Everything is for her. What about me?

(signed)
Sick of It!

Dear Aunt Blabby,

I know this sounds weird, but sometimes I wish I had cancer too. You should see all the stuff people give my brother! He gets video games, comic books, expensive drawing sets, you name it. Every once in a while, they'll give me and my sister a little something, but nothing like the stuff our brother gets.

(signed)
It's Not Fair

Dear Aunt Blabby,

My sister Maya has a rare genetic disease and it's really hard on all of us, especially my mom and dad. I try not to bother them with my troubles. They have enough problems with Maya. I'm glad I can write to you when I have a problem, but I'd rather talk to my parents.

(signed)
Don't Know Where to Go

Dear Aunt Blabby,

Since we learned that my brother has a very serious illness, I worry all the time. I worry that my brother might die in the middle of the night. I worry that the doctors or my parents are keeping secrets from me about Ahmad. It is getting hard to do schoolwork! Aunt Blabby, what should I do?

(signed)
Really Worried

Dear Aunt Blabby,

My sister has cancer and I think I have cancer too. A year ago, her legs hurt a lot and we took her to the hospital. That is when we found out that she has cancer. When I woke up this morning, my legs hurt. Can you catch cancer?

(signed)
Scared Stiff

F

Acknowledging Trauma Among Sibshop Participants

What is trauma? According to the Substance Abuse and Mental Health Services Administration (SAMHSA, 2014): "Trauma is a widespread, harmful and costly public health problem. It occurs as a result of violence, abuse, neglect, loss, disaster, war and other emotionally harmful experiences. Trauma has no boundaries with regard to age, gender, socioeconomic status, race, ethnicity, geography or sexual orientation."

Why acknowledge trauma in Sibshops? At Sibshops we encourage kids to talk about the good and not-so-good parts of being a sib. We recognize that no two sibling experiences are exactly alike and that some siblings struggle more than others. And we know there are siblings who have concerns for their physical and emotional safety for a variety of reasons, including challenging, even violent behaviors of their brothers or sisters who have disabilities. To be sure, not every sibling has experienced trauma. But we believe that the basic principles of trauma-informed practices reflect the values of Sibshops and can benefit all participants and facilitators alike.

What is trauma-informed practice? There is a growing movement in educational, health care, and social services programs to consider the impact of trauma and the benefits of trauma-informed practices. A program, organization, or system that embodies trauma-informed practices seeks to do the following:

- Realize the widespread impact of trauma and potential paths for recovery

- Recognize the signs and symptoms of trauma

- Respond by fully integrating knowledge about trauma into policies, procedures, and practices

- Resist re-traumatization

How can trauma-informed practices be applied to Sibshops? Here is how we suggest adapting SAMHSA's six key principles of a trauma-informed approach for Sibshops:

1. *Safety:* Ensure that children and facilitators who participate in Sibshops feel physically and psychologically safe.

2. *Trustworthiness and transparency:* The goals and activities of Sibshops are shared with transparency to build and maintain trust with participants.

3. *Peer support:* Promote connection, safety, and trust through peer support, collaboration, and sharing stories and lived experience.

4. *Collaboration and mutuality:* Facilitators and participants share power and decision making and recognize that everyone can make valuable contributions.

5. *Empowerment, voice, and choice*: Participants' experiences are validated and are given a voice in decision making and goal setting for the Sibshop.

6. *Cultural, historical, and gender issues:* We recognize cultural stereotypes and biases (e.g., based on race, ethnicity, sexual orientation, age, religion, gender identity, geography). We value our differences, and we respect the racial, ethnic, and cultural needs of participants.

ADDITIONAL RESOURCES

Books

Brown Yau, J. (2019). *The body awareness workbook for trauma: Release trauma from your body, find emotional balance, and connect with your inner wisdom.* Reveal Press.

Epstein, M. (2013). *The trauma of everyday life.* Penguin.

Harris, N. B. (2021). *The deepest well: Healing the long-term effects of childhood adversity.* Pan Macmillan.

Heller, D. P. (2019). *The power of attachment: How to create deep and lasting intimate relationships.* Sounds True.

Heller, L., & Lapierre, A. (2012). *Healing developmental trauma: How early trauma affects self-regulation, self-image, and the capacity for relationship.* North Atlantic Books.

Hübl, T. (2020). *Healing collective trauma: A process for integrating our intergenerational and cultural wounds.* Sounds True.

Levine, P. (1997). *Waking the tiger: Healing trauma.* North Atlantic Books.

Levine, P. (2008). *Healing trauma: A pioneering program for restoring the wisdom of the body.* Sounds True.

Levine, P., & Maté, G. (2010). *In an unspoken voice: How the body releases trauma and restores goodness.* North Atlantic Books.

Maté, G. (2003). *When the body says no: Exploring the stress–disease connection.* John Wiley.

Maté, G. (2010). *In the realm of hungry ghosts: Close encounters with addiction.* North Atlantic Books.

Maté, G. (2019). *Scattered minds: The origins and healing of attention deficit disorder.* Random House.

Menakem, R. (2017). *My grandmother's hands: Racialized trauma and the pathway to mending our hearts and bodies.* Central Recovery Press.

Moorjani, A. (2014). *Dying to be me: My journey from cancer, to near death, to true healing.* Hay House.

Perry, B. D. (2013). *Brief: Reflections on childhood, trauma and society.* Child Trauma. Academy Press.

Perry, B. D., & Szalavitz, M. (2011). *Born for love: Why empathy is essential—and endangered.* Harper.

Perry, B. D., & Winfrey, O. (2021). *What happened to you? Conversations on trauma, resilience, and healing.* Flatiron Books.

Porges, S. (2017). *The polyvagal theory: The transformative power of feeling safe.* Norton.

Rediger, J. (2020). *Cured: Strengthen your immune system and heal your life.* Flatiron Books.

Sarno, J. (1999). *The Mindbody prescription: Healing the body, healing the pain.* Warner Books.

Siegel, D. (2020). *The developing mind: How relationships and the brain interact to shape who we are* (3rd ed.). Guilford Press.

van der Kolk, B. (2015). *The body keeps the score: Brain, mind, and body in the healing of trauma.* Penguin.

Wolynn, M. (2017). *It didn't start with you: How inherited family trauma shapes who we are and how to end the cycle.* Penguin Books.

Videos

PBS NewsHour: Childhood Trauma
https://www.pbs.org/newshour/tag/childhood-trauma

TED Talk. Nadine Burke Harris: How Childhood Trauma Affects Health Across a Lifetime
https://youtu.be/95ovIJ3dsNk

Polyvagal Institute. Trauma and the Nervous System: A Polyvagal Perspective
https://youtu.be/uH5JQDAqA8E

Other Resources

SAMHSA's Concept of Trauma and Guidance for a Trauma-Informed Approach
https://ncsacw.samhsa.gov/userfiles/files/SAMHSA_Trauma.pdf

American Academy of Pediatrics' Trauma Toolbox for Primary Care
https://www.aap.org/en/patient-care/foster-care/supporting-children-who-have-experienced-trauma/
#traumatoolbox

American Academy of Pediatrics: *Adverse Childhood Experiences and the Lifelong Consequences of Trauma*
https://downloads.aap.org/AAP/PDF/ttb_aces_consequences.pdf

Ginwright, S. (2018, May 31). *The future of healing: Shifting from trauma informed care to healing centered engagement*
https://ginwright.medium.com/the-future-of-healing-shifting-from-trauma-informed-care-to-healing-
centered-engagement-634f557ce69c

References

Abramovitch, R., Stanhope, L., Pepler, D., & Carter, C. (1987). The influence of Down's syndrome on sibling interaction. *Journal of Child Psychology and Psychiatry, 28*(6), 865–879.

Angell, M. E., Meadan, H., & Stoner, J. B. (2012). Experiences of siblings of individuals with autism spectrum disorders. *Autism Research and Treatment, 2012,* 949586. https://doi.org/10.1155/2012/949586

Antonovsky, A. (1993). The implications of salutogenesis: An outsider's view. In A. P. Turnbull, J. M. Patterson, S. K. Behr, D. L. Murphy, J. G. Marquis, & M. J. Blue-Banning (Eds.), *Cognitive coping, families, and disability* (pp. 111–122). Paul H. Brookes Publishing Co.

Arnold, C. K., Heller, T., & Kramer, J. (2012). Support needs of siblings of people with developmental disabilities. *Intellectual and Developmental Disabilities, 50*(5), 373–382. doi:10.1352/1934-9556-50.5.373.

Bank, S. P., & Kahn, M. D. (1982). *The sibling bond.* Basic Books.

Barak-Levy, Y., Goldstein, E., & Weinstock, M. (2010). Adjustment characteristics of healthy siblings of children with autism. *Journal of Family Studies, 16*(2), 155–164. doi:10.5172/jfs.16.2.155.

Barr, J., McLeod, S., & Daniel, G. (2008). Siblings of children with speech impairment: Cavalry on the hill. *Language, Speech, and Hearing Services in Schools, 39,* 21–32.

Bendor, S. J. (1990). Anxiety and isolation in siblings of pediatric cancer patients: The need for prevention. *Social Work in Health Care, 14,* 17–35.

Binkard, B., Goldberg, M., & Goldberg, R. E. (Eds.). (1987). *Brothers and sisters talk with PACER.* PACER Center.

Black, S. E., Breining, S., Figlio, D. N., Guryan, J., Karbownik, K., Nielsen, H. S., Roth, J., & Simonsen, M. (2017, January). *Sibling spillovers.* National Bureau of Economic Research, Working Paper 23062. http://222.nber.org/papersw23062

Braddock, D., Hemp, R., Rizzolo, M. C., Coulter, D., Haffer, L., & Thompson, M. (2005). *The state of the states in developmental disabilities.* Coleman Institute for Cognitive Disabilities, University of Colorado.

Bradford, R. (1997). *Children, families and chronic disease: Psychological models and methods of care.* Routledge.

Burke, M., Arnold, C., & Owen, A. (2018). Identifying the correlates and barriers of future planning among parents of individuals with intellectual and developmental disabilities. *Intellectual and Developmental Disabilities, 56,* 90–100.

Burke, M. M., Taylor, J. L., Urbano, R., & Hodapp, R. M. (2012). Predictors of future caregiving by adult siblings of individuals with intellectual and developmental disabilities. *American Journal on Intellectual and Developmental Disabilities, 117,* 33–47. https://doi.org/10.1352/1944-7558-117.1.33

Burslem, A. (1991). Never a dull moment! *Mencap News: The Journal of the Society for Mentally Handicapped Children and Adults, 19*(11), 12–13.

Cairns, N., Clark, G., Smith, S., & Lansky, S. (1979). Malignancy. *Journal of Pediatrics, 95*(3), 484–487.

Callahan, C. R. (1990). *Since Owen.* The Johns Hopkins University Press.

Canary, H. E. (2008). Negotiating dis/ability in families: Constructions and contradictions. *Journal of Applied Communication Research, 36,* 437–458. https://doi.org/10.1080/00909880802101771

Cleveland, D. W., & Miller, N. (1977). Attitudes and life commitments of older siblings of mentally retarded adults: An exploratory study. *Mental Retardation, 15*(3), 38–41.

Cobb, M. (1991). A senior essay. *Outlook, the Newsletter of the Down Syndrome Association of Charlotte, NC, 5*(6), 3.

Coleman, S. V. (1990). The sibling of the retarded child: Self-concept, deficit compensation motivation, and perceived parental behavior [Doctoral dissertation, California School of Professional Psychology, San Diego]. *Dissertations Abstracts International, 51*(10-B), 5023 (University Microfilms No. 01147421-AAD9I-07868).

Collins, K. (Producer), & Emmerling, D. P. (Director). (1991). *The rest of the family* [Video]. Epilepsy Foundation of America.

Corsano, P., Musetti, A., Guidotti, L., & Capelli, F. (2017). Typically developing adolescents' experience of growing up with a brother with an autism spectrum disorder. *Journal of Intellectual & Developmental Disabilities, 42*(2), 151–161.

Costa, T. M., & da Silva Pereira, P. (2019). The child with autism spectrum disorder: The perceptions of siblings. *Support for Learning, 34*(2), 193–210.

Cramer, S., Erzkus, A., Mayweather, K., Pope, K., Roeder, J., & Tone, T. (1997, September, October). Connecting with siblings. *TEACHING Exceptional Children, 30,* 46–51.

Cuskelly, M., Chant, D., & Hayes, A. (1998). Behaviour problems in the siblings of children with Down syndrome: Associations with family responsibilities and parental stress. *International Journal of Disability, Development and Education, 45,* 195–311.

D'Arcy, F., Flynn, J., McCarthy, Y., O'Connor, C., & Tierney, E. (2005). Sibshops: An evaluation of an interagency model. *Journal of Intellectual Disabilities, 9,* 43–57. https://doi.org/10.1177/1744629505049729

de Vinck, C. (1985, April 10). Power of the powerless. *The Wall Street Journal,* 28.

de Vinck, C. (2002). *Power of the powerless: A brother's legacy of love.* Zondervan Publishing House.

Deavin, A., Greasley, P., & Dixon, C. (2018). Children's perspectives on living with a sibling with a chronic illness. *Pediatrics, 142.* https://doi.org/10.1542/peds.2017-4151

Dickens, R. (1991). *Notes for siblings/adult children.* (Available from National Alliance for the Mentally Ill, 2101 Wilson Blvd. Suite 302, Arlington, VA 22201).

Diener, M. L., Anderson, L., Wright, C. A., & Dunn, M. L. (2015). Sibling relationships of children with autism spectrum disorder in the context of everyday life and a strength-based program. *Journal of Child and Family Studies, 24,* 1060–1072. https://doi.org/10.1007/s10826-014-9916-6

Disability Data Digest (2018). A collection of infographics presented by MediSked and The Arc of the United States. August 2018. http://www.inarf.org

Doherty, J. (1992). A sibling remembers. *Candlelighters Childhood Cancer Foundation Newsletter, 16*(2), 4–6.

Drotar, D., & Crawford, P. (1985). Psychological adaptation of siblings of chronically ill children: Research and practice implications. *Developmental and Behavioral Pediatrics, 6,* 355–362.

Dudish, M. P. (1991). My sister Ellen…, my daughter Tara. *Sibling Information Network Newsletter, 7*(3), 1–3.

Duvall, E. M. (1962). *Family development.* J.B. Lippincott.

Dyson, L. L. (1989). Adjustment of siblings of handicapped children: A comparison. *Journal of Pediatric Psychology, 14*(2), 215–229.

Dyson, L. L. (1996). The experiences of families of children with learning disabilities: Parental stress, family functioning, and sibling self-concept. *Journal of Learning Disabilities, 29,* 280–286.

Dyson, L. L., & Fewell, R. (1989). The self-concept of siblings of handicapped children: A comparison. *Journal of Early Intervention, 13*(3), 230–238.

Eisenberg, L., Baker, B. L., & Blacher, J. (1998). Siblings of children with mental retardation living at home or in residential placement. *Journal of Child Psychology and Psychiatry, 39,* 355–363.

Ellis, A. (1992). *Siblings: The "forgotten child" in childhood cancer* [Unpublished manuscript].

Faber, A., & Mazlish, E. (2012a). *How to talk so kids will listen and listen so kids will talk.* Scribner.

Faber, A., & Mazlish, E. (2012b). *Siblings without rivalry: How to help your children live together so you can live too.* Norton.

Farber, B. (1960). Family organization and crisis: Maintenance of integration in families with a severely mentally retarded child. *Monographs of the Society for Research in Child Development, 25*(1, Serial No. 75).

Faux, S. A. (1993). Siblings of children with chronic physical and cognitive disabilities. *Journal of Pediatric Nursing, 8,* 305–317.

Featherstone, H. (1980). *A difference in the family: Life with a disabled child.* Basic Books.

Ferraioli, S. J., & Harris, S. L. (2009). The impact of autism on siblings. *Social Work in Mental Health, 8,* 41–53.

Ferrari, M. (1984). Chronic illness: Psychosocial effects on siblings. 1: Chronically ill boys. *Journal of Child Psychology and Psychiatry, 25,* 459–476.

Fink, L. (1984, November 6). Looking at the role played by siblings of the retarded. *Newsday,* 6–9.

Fish, T. (Producer). (1993). *The next step* [Video]. (Available from Publications Office, Nisonger Center UAP, 434 McCampbell Hall, The Ohio State University, 1581 Dodd Drive, Columbus, OH, 43210.)

Fish, T., & Fitzgerald, G. M. (1980, November). *A transdisciplinary approach to working with adolescent siblings of the mentally retarded: A group experience.* Paper presented to Social Work with Groups Symposium, Arlington, TX. (Available from T. Fish, The Nisonger Center, The Ohio State University, 1580 Canon Drive, Columbus, OH, 43210.)

Flugelman, A. (Ed.). (1976). *The new games book.* Doubleday.

Flugelman, A. (Ed.). (1981). *More new games!* Doubleday.

Fowle, C. (1973). The effect of a severely mentally retarded child on his family. *American Journal of Mental Deficiency, 73,* 468–473.

Fujiura, G. T. (1998). Demography of family households. *American Journal on Mental Retardation, 103,* 225–235.

Gath, A. (1974). Sibling reactions to mental handicap: A comparison of the brothers and sisters of mongol children. *Journal of Child Psychology and Psychiatry, 15,* 187–198.

Gerdel, P. (1986). Who are these researchers and why are they saying such terrible things about me? In M. Hanson & A. Turnbull (Eds.), *Research in family involvement practices monographs, No. 3: The family support network series.* University of Idaho.

Gettings, S., Franco, F., & Santosh, P. J. (2015). Facilitating support groups for siblings of children with neuro-developmental disorders using audio-conferencing: A longitudinal study. *Child and Adolescent Psychiatry and Mental Health, 9,* 1–15.

Giallo, R., & Gavidia-Payne, S. (2006). Child, parent and family factors as predictors of adjustment for siblings of children with a disability. *Journal of Intellectual Disability Research, 50,* 937–948.

Glasberg, B. A. (2000). The development of siblings' under standing of autism spectrum disorders. *Journal of Autism and Developmental Disorders, 30,* 143–156.

Gorelick, J. (1996, July 8–13). A *strong sibling network: Forgotten children no more.* Presentation to the 10th World Congress of the International Association for the Scientific Studies of Intellectual Disabilities, Helsinki, Finland.

Gorjy, R. S., Fielding, A., & Falkmer, M. (2017). "It's better than it used to be": Perspectives of adolescent siblings of children with an autism spectrum condition. *Child & Family Social Work,* 1–9. https://doi.org/10.1111/cfs.12371

Gregson, B. (1982). *The incredible indoor games book.* Fearon Teacher Aids.

Gregson, B. (1984). *The outrageous outdoor games book.* Fearon Teacher Aids.

Grossman, F. (1972). *Brothers and sisters of retarded children: An exploratory study.* Syracuse University Press.

Gruszka, M. A. (1988). *Family functioning and sibling adjustment in families with a handicapped child* [Unpublished doctoral dissertation]. University of Rhode Island.

Hall, S. A., & Rossetti, Z. (2017). The roles of adult siblings in the lives of people with severe intellectual and developmental disabilities. *Journal of Applied Research in Intellectual Disabilities, 31,* 423–434.

Hamama, R., Ronen, T., & Feigin, R. (2000). Self-control, anxiety, and loneliness in siblings of children with cancer. *Social Work in Health Care, 31,* 63–83.

Hannah, M. E., & Midlarsky, E. (1999). Competence and adjustment of siblings of children with mental retardation. *American Journal on Mental Retardation, 104,* 22–37.

Harkleroad, D. (1992). Growing up with Raymond. *Parents and Friends Together for People with Deaf-Blindness News, 1*(5), 5.

Harland, P., & Cuskelly, M. (2000). The responsibilities of adult siblings of adults with dual sensory impairments. *International Journal of Disability, Development, and Education, 47*(3), 295–307.

Harvey, D. H. P., & Greenway, A. P. (1984). The self-concept of physically handicapped children and their non-handicapped siblings: An empirical investigation. *Journal of Child Psychology and Psychiatry, 25,* 273–284.

Hastings, R. P. (2007). Longitudinal relationships between sibling behavioral adjustment and behavior problems of children with developmental disabilities. *Journal of Autism and Developmental Disorders, 37,* 1485–1492.

Hastings, R. P. (2014). *Children and adolescents who are the siblings of children with intellectual disabilities or autism: Research evidence.* University of Warwick. www.sibs.org.uk

Hastings, R. P., & Petalas, M. A. (2014). Self-reported behaviour problems and sibling relationship quality by siblings of children with autism spectrum disorder. *Child Care Health and Development, 40*(6), 833–839. doi:10.1111/cch.12131.

Hayden, N. K., McCaffrey, M., Fraser-Lim, C., & Hastings, R. P. (2019). Supporting siblings of children with a special educational need or disability: An evaluation of Sibs Talk, a one-to-one intervention delivered by staff in mainstream schools. *Support for Learning, 34,* 404–420. Published by John Wiley & Sons on behalf of National Association for Special Educational Needs. https://doi.org/10.1111/1467-9604.12275

Heller, T., & Arnold, C. K. (2010). Siblings of adults with developmental disabilities: Psychosocial outcomes, relationships, and future planning. *Journal of Policy and Practice in Intellectual Disabilities, 7,* 16–25.

Heller, T., & Kramer, J. (2009). Involvement of adult siblings of persons with developmental disabilities in future planning. *Journal of Intellectual and Developmental Disabilities, 47,* 208–219.

Helsel, E., Helsel, B., Helsel, B., & Helsel, M. (1978). The Helsels' story of Robin. In A. P. Turnbull & H. R. Turnbull (Eds.), *Parents speak out: Views from the other side of the two-way mirror* (pp. 99–114). Charles E. Merrill.

Hodapp, R. M., Sanderson, K. A., Meskis, S. A., & Casale, E. G. (2017). Adult siblings of persons with intellectual disabilities: Past, present, and future. *International Review of Research in Developmental Disabilities, 53,* 163–202.

Hodapp, R. M., Urbano, R. C., & Burke, M. M. (2010). Adult female and male siblings of persons with disabilities: Findings from a national survey. *Intellectual and Developmental Disabilities, 48,* 52–62.

Hoskinson, J. E. (2011). *How does having a sibling with autism spectrum conditions impact on adolescents' psychosocial adjustment?* [Doctoral clinical psychology thesis, University of Leeds]. https://etheses.whiterose.ac.uk/2029/

Iles, P. (1979). Children with cancer: Healthy siblings' perceptions during the illness experience. *Cancer Nursing, 2,* 371–377.

Institute on Community Integration/University of Minnesota. *Community living and employment.* https://ici.umn.edu/program-areas/community-living-and-employment

Itzkowitz, J. (1990). Siblings' perceptions of their needs for programs, services, and support: A national study. *Sibling Information Network Newsletter, 7*(1), 1–4.

"Jennifer." (1990). Mailbag: A column for siblings to speak out. *Sibpage: A Newsletter for and by Brothers and Sisters of Children with Special Needs, 2*(4), 2.

Johnson, A. B. (2005). *Sibshops: A follow-up of participants of a sibling support program* [Unpublished master's thesis]. University of Washington, Seattle.

Johnson, A. B., & Sandall, S. (2005). *Sibshops: A follow-up of participants of a sibling support program*. University of Washington.

Jones, E. A., Fiani, T., Stewart, J., Neil, N., McHugh, S., & Feinup, D. M. (2020). Randomized controlled trial of a sibling support group: Mental health outcomes for siblings of children with autism. *Autism, 6*, 1468–1481.

Jones, E. A., Fiani, T., Stewart, J., Neil, N., Sheikh, R., & Feinup, D. M. (2019). Sibling mental health when one sibling has autism. *Journal of Child and Family Studies, 28*, 1272–1283. https://doi.org/10/1007/s10826-019-01374-z

Kao, B., Romero-Bosch, L., Plante, W., & Lobato, D. (2012). The experiences of Latino siblings of children with developmental disabilities. *Child Care Health and Development, 38*, 545–552. doi:10.1111/j.1365-2214.2011.01266.x.

Kazak, A. E., & Clarke, M. W. (1986). Stress in families with myelomeningocele. *Developmental Medicine and Child Neurology, 28*, 220–228.

Killilea, M. (1952). *Karen*. Buccaneer Books.

Koch-Hattem, A. (1986). Siblings' experience of pediatric cancer: Interviews with children. *Health and Social Work, 10*, 107–117.

Konstam, V., Drainoni, M., Mitchell, G., Houser, R., Reddington, D., & Eaton, D. (1993). Career choices and values of siblings of individuals with developmental disabilities. *The School Counselor, 40*, 287–292.

Koocher, G. P., & O'Malley, J. E. (1981). *The Damocles syndrome: Psychological consequences of surviving childhood cancer*. McGraw-Hill.

Kowal, A., Kramer, L., Krull, J. L., & Crick, N. R. (2002). Children's perceptions of the fairness of parental preferential treatment and their socioemotional well being. *Journal of Family Psychology, 16*, 297–306.

Kramer, J., Hall, A., & Heller, T. (2013). Reciprocity and social capital in sibling relationships of people with disabilities. *Intellectual and Developmental Disabilities, 51*, 482–495.

Krauss, M., Seltzer, M., Gordon, R., & Friedman, D. (1996). Binding ties: The role of adult siblings of persons with mental retardation. *Mental Retardation, 34*(2), 83–92.

Larson, S. A., Eschenbacher, H. J., Anderson, L. L., Taylor, B., Pettingell, S., Hewitt, A., ... Bourne, M. L. (2017). *In-home and residential long-term supports and services for persons with intellectual or developmental disabilities: Status and trends through 2015*. Minneapolis, MN: University of Minnesota, Research and Training Center on Community Living, Institute on Community Integration.

Leder, J. M. (1991). *Brothers and sisters: How they shape our lives*. St. Martin's Press.

Lee, C. E., Burke, M. M., & Arnold, K. (2020). Sibling participation in service planning meetings for their brothers and sisters with intellectual and developmental disabilities in the United States. *Journal of Policy and Practice in Intellectual Disabilities, 18*, 104–112.

Liska, V. D. (1996, July 8–13). *The siblings: A lifelong journal of care*. Presentation to the 10th World Congress of the International Association for the Scientific Studies of Intellectual Disabilities, Helsinki, Finland.

Lobato, D. J. (1990). *Brothers, sisters, and special needs: Information and activities for helping young siblings of children with chronic illnesses and developmental disabilities*. Paul H. Brookes Publishing Co.

Lobato, D., Barbour, L., Hall, L. J., & Miller, C. T. (1987). Psychosocial characteristics of preschool siblings of handicapped and nonhandicapped children. *Journal of Abnormal Child Psychology, 15*, 329–338.

Luijkx, J., van der Putten, A. A. J., & Vlaskamp, C. (2016). "I love my sister, but sometimes I don't": A qualitative study into the experiences of siblings of a child with profound intellectual and multiple disabilities. *Journal of Intellectual and Developmental Disability, 41*, 279–288. https://doi.org/10.3109/13668250.2016.1224333

Mailick, M., Osmond, S., Osmond, G., & Esbensen, A. (2009). Siblings of individuals with an autism spectrum disorder: Sibling relationships and wellbeing in adolescence and adulthood. *Autism, 13*, 59–80.

Malcolm, C., Gibson, F., Adams, S., Anderson, G., & Forbat, L. (2014). A relational understanding of sibling experiences of children with rare life-limiting conditions: Findings from a qualitative study. *Journal of Child Health Care, 18*, 230–240.

Marquis, S., Hayes, M. V., & McGrail, K. (2019). Factors that may affect the health of siblings of children who have an intellectual/developmental disability. *Journal of Policy and Practice in Intellectual Disabilities, 16*, 273–286.

Martins, M. (2007). *Siblings of individuals with autism: Perceptions of the sibling experience, psychological functioning, and the developmental tasks of young adulthood* [Unpublished doctoral dissertation]. Rutgers University.

Mascha, K., & Boucher, J. (2006). Preliminary investigation of a qualitative method of examining siblings' experiences of living with a child with ASD. *British Journal of Developmental Disabilities, 52*, 19–28. https://doi.org/10.1179/096979506799103659

McConachie, H. (1982). Fathers of mentally handicapped children. In N. Beal & J. McGuire (Eds.), *Fathers: Psychological perspectives* (pp. 144–173). Junction.

McCullough, M. E. (1981). Parent and sibling definitions of situations regarding transgenerational shift in the care of a handicapped child [Doctoral dissertation, University of Minnesota]. *Dissertation Abstracts International, 42*(1-B), 161 (University Microfilms No. 8115012).

McHale, S. M., Sloan, J. L., & Simeonsson, R. J. (1986). Sibling relationships of children with autistic, mentally retarded, and nonhandicapped brothers and sisters. *Journal of Autism and Developmental Disorders, 16,* 399–413.

McHale, S. M., Updegraff, K. A., Jackson-Newsom, J., Tucker, C. J., & Crouter, A. C. (2000). When does parents' differential treatment have negative implications for siblings? *Social Development, 9,* 149–172.

McKeever, P. (1983). Siblings of chronically ill children: A literature review with implications for research and practice. *American Journal of Orthopsychiatry, 53*(2), 209–218.

Meyer, D. J. (1986). Fathers of handicapped children. In R. Fewell & P. Vadasy (Eds.), *Families of handicapped children* (pp. 35–73). PRO-ED.

Meyer, D. J. (Ed.). (2005). *The sibling slam book: What it's really like to have a brother or sister with special needs.* Woodbine House.

Meyer, D. J., Breshears, C., & Martin, P. (2016). *How to let young siblings know that you care.* https://siblingsupport. org/wp-content/uploads/2021/09/How-To-Let-Young-Siblings-Know-You-Care-2021.pdf

Meyer, D. J., & Erickson, E. L. (1992). *Survey of Seattle area adult siblings of people with disabilities* [Unpublished raw data].

Meyer, D. J., & Erickson, E. L. (1993, Winter). *The National Association of Sibling Programs Newsletter, 6.*

Meyer, D. J., & Vadasy, P. F. (1996). *Living with a brother or sister with special needs: A book for sibs.* University of Washington Press.

Meyer, D. J., Vadasy, P. F., Fewell, R. R., & Schell, G. (1985). *The Fathers program: How to organize a program for fathers and their handicapped children.* University of Washington Press.

Meyer, K. A., Ingersoll, B., & Hambrick, D. Z. (2011). Factors influencing adjustment in siblings of children with autism spectrum disorders. *Research in Autism Spectrum Disorders, 5,* 1413–1420.

Miller, S. G. (1974). An exploratory study of sibling relationships in families with retarded children [Doctoral dissertation, Columbia University]. *Dissertation Abstracts International, 35*(6-B), 2994–2995 (University Microfilms No. 74-26m 606).

Morrow, J. (1992). Terry Cunningham: A brother who sticks up for his siblings. *Parents and Friends Together for People with Deaf-Blindness News, 1*(5), 2.

Moyson, T., & Roeyers, H. (2012). "The overall quality of my life as a sibling is all right, but of course, it could always be better." Quality of life of siblings of children with intellectual disability: The siblings' perspectives. *Journal of Intellectual Disability Research, 56,* 87–101.

Murphy, A. T. (1979). Members of the family: Sisters and brothers of handicapped children. *Volta Review, 81*(5), 352–362.

Murphy, A. T. (1981). *Special children, special parents.* Prentice-Hall.

Murray, G., & Jampolsky, G. G. (Eds.). (1982). *Straight from the siblings: Another look at the rainbow.* Celestial Arts.

Neece, C. L., Blacher, J., & Baker, B. L. (2010). Impact on siblings of children with intellectual disability: The role of child behavior problems. *American Journal on Intellectual and Developmental Disabilities, 115,* 291–306.

Nester, J. (1989, March). Adult sibling panel notes. *Down Syndrome Association of New Jersey, Inc.* [Newsletter], p. 4.

"1988 award winning summer programs." (1989, March). *Exceptional Parent, 19,* 16–26.

Opperman, S., & Alant, E. (2003). The coping responses of the adolescent siblings of children with severe disabilities. *Disability and Rehabilitation, 25,* 441–454. https://doi.org/10.1080/0963828031000069735

Orm, S., Haukeland, Y., Vatne, T., Silverman, W., & Fjermestad, K. (2021). Prosocial behavior is a relative strength in siblings of children with physical disabilities or autism spectrum disorder. *Journal of Developmental and Physical Disabilities.* https://doi.org/10.1007/s10882-021-09816-7

Orsmond, G. I., & Seltzer, M. M. (2000). Brothers and sisters of adults with mental retardation: The gendered nature of the sibling relationship. *American Journal of Mental Retardation, 105,* 486–508.

Parfit, J. (1975). Siblings of handicapped children. *Special Education: Forward Trends, 2*(1), 19–21.

Pavlopoulou, G., & Dimitriou, D. (2020). In their own words, in their own photos: Adolescent females' siblinghood experiences, needs and perspectives growing up with a preverbal autistic brother or sister. *Research in Developmental Disabilities, 97,* 1–14.

Petalas, M., Hastings, R. P., Nash, S., Dowey, A., & Reilly, D. (2009). "I like that he always shows who he is": The perceptions and experiences of siblings with a brother with autism spectrum disorder. *International Journal of Disability Development and Education, 56,* 381–399.

Petalas, M. A., Hastings, R. P., Nash, S., Reilly, D., & Dowey, A. (2012). The perceptions and experiences of adolescent siblings who have a brother with autism spectrum disorder. *Journal of Intellectual and Developmental Disability, 37,* 303–314.

Piers, E. (1984). *The Piers Harris Children's Self-Concept Scale* (Rev. ed.). Western Psychological Services.

Pit-Ten Cate, I., & Loots, G. M. P. (2000). Experiences of siblings of children with physical disabilities: An empirical investigation. *Disability and Rehabilitation, 22*(9), 399–408.

Podeanu-Czehotsky, I. (1975). Is it only the child's guilt? Some aspects of family life of cerebral palsied children. *Rehabilitation Literature, 36,* 308–311.

Powell, T. H., & Gallagher, P. A. (1993). *Brothers and sisters: A special part of exceptional families* (2nd ed.). Paul H. Brookes Publishing Co.

Pruchno, R. A., Patrick, J. H., & Burant, C. J. (1996). Aging mothers and their children with chronic disabilities: Perception of sibling involvement and effects on well-being. *Family Relations, 45,* 318–326.

Remsberg, B. (1989). *What it means to have a handicapped brother or sister* [Unpublished manuscript].

Rinehart, J. (1992, May). My sister's hand. *Children's Health Issues, 1*(1), 10–11.

Salena, K., Tobon, J., & Boyle, H. (2018). Longitudinal civic-mindedness in siblings of Ontario children with chronic illness. *McMaster University Medical Journal, 15,* 21–30.

Schild, S. (1976). Counseling with parents of retarded children living at home. In F. J. Turner (Ed.), *Differential diagnosis and treatment in social work* (2nd ed., pp. 476–482). Free Press.

Schorr-Ribera, H. (1992). Caring for siblings during diagnosis and treatment. *Candlelighters Childhood Cancer Foundation Newsletter, 16*(2), 1–3.

Seligman, M. (1979). *Strategies for helping parents of exceptional children.* Free Press.

Seligman, M. (1983). Sources of psychological disturbance among siblings of handicapped children. *Personnel and Guidance Journal, 67,* 529–531.

Seligman, M. (1991). Siblings of disabled brothers and sisters. In M. Seligman (Ed.), *The family with a handicapped child* (2nd ed., pp. 181–198). Allyn & Bacon.

Seltzer, G. B., Begun, A., Seltzer, M., & Krauss, M. W. (1991). Adults with mental retardation and their aging mothers: Impact on siblings. *Family Relations, 40*(3), 3310–3317.

Seltzer, M. M., Greenberg, J. S., Krauss, M. W., Gordon, R. M., & Judge, K. (1997). Siblings of adults with mental retardation or mental illness: Effects on lifestyle and psychological well-being. *Family Relations, 46*(4), 395–405.

Seltzer, M. M., & Krauss, M. W. (2002). *Adolescents and adults with autism: Reflections from adult siblings who have a brother or sister with an autism spectrum disorder.* http:// www.uic.edu/orgs/rrtcamr/autism report3.htm

Shanley, S. (1991). My brother Peter. *Sibling Information Network Newsletter, 7*(4), 1–2.

Shivers, C. M. (2019). Self-reported guilt among adult siblings of people with intellectual and developmental disabilities. *American Journal of Intellectual and Developmental Disabilities, 124,* 470–477.

Simeonsson, R. J., & McHale, S. M. (1981). Review: Research on handicapped children: Sibling relationships. *Child: Care, Health and Development, 7,* 153–171.

Skrtic, T., Summers, J. A., Brotherson, M. J., & Turnbull, A. (1983). Severely handicapped children and their brothers and sisters. In J. Blacher (Ed.), *Severely handicapped young children and their families: Research in review* (pp. 215–246). Academic Press.

Sloper, P., & White, D. (1996). Risk factors in the adjustment of siblings of children with cancer. *Journal of Child Psychology and Psychiatry, 37,* 597–607.

Smith, L. O., & Elder, J. H. (2010). Siblings and family environments of persons with autism spectrum disorder: A review of the literature. *Journal of Child and Adolescent Psychiatric Nursing, 23*(3), 189–195. https://doi.org/10.1111/j.1744-6171.2010.00240.x

Smith, T., & Perry, A. (2005). A sibling support group for brothers and sisters of children with autism. *Journal on Developmental Disabilities, 11,* 77–88.

Sourkes, B. M. (1980). Siblings of the pediatric cancer patient. In J. Kellerman (Ed.), *Psychological aspects of childhood cancer* (pp. 47–69). Charles C. Thomas.

Sourkes, B. (1990). Siblings count too. *Candlelighters Childhood Cancer Foundation Newsletter, 12*(3), 2, 6.

Sourkes, B. M. (1995). *Armfuls of time: The psychological experiences of the child with a life-threatening illness.* University of Pittsburgh Press.

Spinetta, J. (1981). The sibling of the child with cancer. In J. Spinetta & P. Deasy-Spinetta (Eds.), *Living with childhood cancer* (pp. 133–142). C.V. Mosby.

Stoneman, Z. (2005). Siblings of children with disabilities: Research themes. *Mental Retardation, 43,* 339–350.

Stoneman, Z., & Brody, G. H. (1993). Sibling relations in the family context. In Z. Stoneman & P. W. Berman (Eds.), *The effects of mental retardation, disability, and illness on sibling relationships* (pp. 3–30). Paul H. Brookes Publishing Co.

Stoneman, Z., Brody, G. H., Davis, C. H., & Crapps, J. M. (1987). Mentally retarded children and their older same-sex siblings: Naturalistic in-home observations. *American Journal on Mental Retardation, 92,* 290–298.

Stoneman, Z., Brody, G. H., Davis, C. H., & Crapps, J. M. (1988). Child care responsibilities, peer relations, and sibling conflict: Older siblings of mentally retarded children. *American Journal on Mental Retardation, 93,* 174–183.

Stoneman, Z., Brody, G. H., Davis, C. H., & Crapps, J. M. (1989). Role relations between mentally retarded children and their older siblings: Observations in three in- home contexts. *Research in Developmental Disabilities, 10,* 61–76.

Stoneman, Z., Brody, G. H., Davis, C. H., Crapps, J. M., & Malone, D. M. (1991). Ascribed role relations between children with mental retardation and their younger siblings. *American Journal on Mental Retardation, 95*, 527–536.

Substance Abuse and Mental Health Services Administration (SAMHSA). (2019). *Trauma and violence.* https://www.samhsa.gov/trauma-violence

Summers, A. (2004, Winter). Siblings. *Connections: A Newsletter for Fathers and Families of Children with Special Needs, 8*(2), 7–8.

Thibodeau, S. M. (1988). Sibling response to chronic illness: The role of the clinical nurse specialist. *Issues in Comprehensive Pediatric Nursing, 11*, 17–28.

Torrey, E. F. (1992, July). Sibling issues. *Siblings of people with mental illness.* Conference sponsored by Washington Alliance for the Mentally Ill, Seattle.

Tritt, S., & Esses, L. (1988). Psychosocial adaptation of siblings of children with chronic medical illnesses. *American Journal of Orthopsychiatry, 58*(2), 211–220.

Tsao, L-L., Davenport, R., & Schmiege, C. (2011). Supporting siblings of children with autism spectrum disorders. *Early Childhood Education Journal, 40*(1), 47–54. https://doi.org/10.1007/s10643-011-0488-3

Tsao, L. L., & Odom, S. L. (2006). Sibling-mediated social interaction intervention for young children with autism. *Topics in Early Childhood Special Education, 25*, 106–123.

Tudor, M. E., & Lerner, M. C. (2015). Intervention and support for siblings of youth with developmental disabilities: A systematic review. *Clinical Child and Family Psychological Reviews, 18*, 1–23.

Turnbull, A. P., & Turnbull, H. R. (1993). Participatory research on cognitive coping: From concepts to research planning. In A. R. Turnbull, J. M. Patterson, S. K. Behr, D. L. Murphy, J. G. Marquis, & M. J. Blue-Banning (Eds.), *Cognitive coping, families, and disability* (pp. 1–14). Paul H. Brookes Publishing Co.

Usdane, S., & Melmed, R. (1988). *Facilitator's manual. Siblings exchange program.* Phoenix Children's Hospital.

Vermaes, I. P. R., van Susante, A. M. J., & van Bakel, H. J. A. (2012). Psychological functioning of siblings in families of children with chronic health conditions: A meta-analysis. *Journal of Pediatric Psychology, 37*, 166–184.

Watson, J. (1991). The Queen. *Down Syndrome News, 15*(8), 108.

Watson, L., Hanna, P., & Jones, C. J. (2021). A systematic review of the experience of being a sibling of a child with an autism spectrum disorder. *Clinical Child Psychology and Psychiatry, 26*(3). https://doi.org/10.1177/13591045211007921

Westra, M. (1992). An open letter to my parents. *Sibling Information Network Newsletter, 8*(1), 4.

Wikler, L. (1981). Chronic stresses of families of mentally retarded children. *Family Relations, 30*, 281–288.

Williams, P. D. (1997). Siblings and pediatric chronic illness: A review of the literature. *International Journal of Nursing Studies, 34*, 312–323.

Williams, P. D., Piamjariyakul, U., Graff, J. C., Stanton, A., Guthrie, A. C., Hafeman, C., & Williams, A. R. (2010). Developmental disabilities: Effects on well siblings. *Issues in Comprehensive Pediatric Nursing, 33*, 39–55. https://doi.org/10.3109/01460860903486515

Williams, P. D., Williams, A. R., Graff, J. C., Hanson, S., Stanton, A., Hafeman, C., Liebergen, A., Leuenberg, K., Setter, R. K., Ridder, L., Curry, H., Barnard, M., & Sanders, S. (2002). Interrelationships among variables affecting well siblings and mothers in families of children with a chronic illness or disability. *Journal of Behavioral Medicine, 25*, 411–424.

Ylven, R., Bjorck-Akesson, E., & Grandlund, M. (2006, December). Functioning in families with children with a disability. *Journal of Policy and Practice in Intellectual Disabilities, 3*(4), 253–270.

Zatlow, G. (1981, Winter). A sister's lament. *Our Home Newsletter and Annual Report, 5*, 1–2.

Zatlow, G. (1992, Fall). *Just a sister* (pp. 13–16). Momentum.

Index

Page numbers followed by *f* indicate figures; those followed by *t* indicate tables.